T0342110

ENTROPY ECONOMICS

ENTROPY ECONOMICS

The Living Basis of Value and Production

James K. Galbraith and Jing Chen

The University of Chicago Press   *Chicago and London*

The University of Chicago Press, Chicago 60637
The University of Chicago Press, Ltd., London
Published 2025

34 33 32 31 30 29 28 27 26 25   1 2 3 4 5

ISBN-13: 978-0-226-82719-3 (cloth)
ISBN-13: 978-0-226-83784-0 (e-book)
DOI: https://doi.org/10.7208/chicago/9780226837840.001.0001

Library of Congress Cataloging-in-Publication Data

Names: Galbraith, James K., author. | Chen, Jing, 1966– author.
Title: Entropy economics : the living basis of value and production /
    James K. Galbraith, Jing Chen.
Description: Chicago ; London : The University of Chicago Press, 2025. |
    Includes bibliographical references and index.
Identifiers: LCCN 2024023285 | ISBN 9780226827193 (cloth) |
    ISBN 9780226837840 (ebook)
Subjects: LCSH: Economics. | Value. | Production (Economic theory) |
    Entropy. | Life (Biology)—Economic aspects.
Classification: LCC HB171 .G13 2025 | DDC 330.1—dc23/eng/20240612
LC record available at https://lccn.loc.gov/2024023285

For Nico and Tahvy

And I may add that the sign of a crank or half-baked speculator in the social sciences is his search for something in the social system that corresponds to the physicist's notion of "entropy."

PAUL A. SAMUELSON, 1972

It is only because miners sweat their guts out that superior persons can remain superior. . . . All of us really owe the comparative decency of our lives to poor drudges underground, blackened to the eyes, with their throats full of coal dust, driving their shovels forward with arms and belly muscles of steel.

GEORGE ORWELL, 1937

Contents

Preface

AN ECONOMIC THEORY COMPATIBLE WITH LIFE PROCESSES AND PHYSICAL LAWS

In this book, we present an economic theory that is consistent with life processes and physical laws. We do this because it is necessary, for a simple reason: the economic theory that underlies modern "mainstream" economics and practically all textbook teaching in economics is *not* consistent with life processes and physical laws. And this, we believe, is a problem.

Human beings are living organisms. All human activities are consistent with physical laws: they use resources; they operate under the power of physical forces, such as gravity and electromagnetism; their life spans are finite. It is natural, then, to build an economic theory on the foundations of biology and physics. In this book, we undertake this task for two foundational elements of economics: the theories of value and production.

In this preface, we discuss two issues. First, why is a biophysical approach resisted in modern mainstream economics, even though its main elements were very familiar to economists of an earlier era? Second, how can a biophysical approach guide us toward simple mathematical expressions that describe value and production and are highly consistent with reality?

Modern mainstream economics is a theory of balance, or equilibrium. The basic terms of reference are the concepts of *supply and demand*, which interact in a market and come to rest at certain prices and quantities. There are a thousand different ways in which this process may be disturbed by "imperfections" and "shocks." But at the heart of the matter lie the concepts of *balance* and *equilibrium*—the immanent order toward which a market system is supposed to tend. This immanent order is sometimes called a *steady state*. This is a very comforting idea, compatible with such notions as the "end of history" and the triumph of market capitalism over competing social systems.

In real life, there is no such thing. In real life, time moves from the past, through the present, to the future, in an unceasing process of change. The changes take many forms, including birth, growth, decline, death, and the rise and fall of societies and civilizations. All of them occur under the influence of physical and biological laws, including especially the second law of thermodynamics and the laws of biological evolution. In our view, economics should adhere to the same broad principles. It should not rest on the illusion of an underlying steady state.

In modern mainstream economics, there are two separate and distinct institutions or arenas for action. One is the market; the other is the government. These two arenas have separate functions: the market allocates resources according to the preferences of households and business firms; the government enforces contracts and property rights and provides security and protection. Apart from that, government economic activity is described as "intervention" in the market, which is sometimes justified, but often not.

In real life, there are no markets (of any consequence) without governments to regulate them. Regulation creates the conditions under which complex economic activities can occur, and it sets the terms and limits of economic competition. Regulation has the same function in economics that it does in every mechanical and biological system: it keeps (or tries to keep) the flow of resources within the capacity of the system to handle it safely and sustainably. When regulation fails, markets crumble—or to use the apt metaphor, they "melt down."

From physics, *entropy* flow is the fundamental driving force of the universe. Entropy exerts its influence on all physical systems, including living systems. Human societies are living systems, whose economic activities are inseparable from all other aspects of their existence. It is therefore natural that economic analysis should take account of entropy. Yet, for the most part, it does not. Indeed, the most powerful authority in twentieth-century economics, Paul Samuelson, rebuked any such association in scathing terms:

> And I may add that the sign of a crank or half-baked speculator in the social sciences is his search for something in the social system that corresponds to the physicist's notion of "entropy." (Samuelson 1972, 450)

We will not return the favor and accuse the late Professor Samuelson, a personal and family friend to one of us, of having been a crank. He was not. But the vehemence of this statement reveals that the law of entropy posed a threat to the foundations of his worldview. That is because equilibrium and entropy stand in contradiction to each other; you can have one or the other, but not both. And while entropy is a universal law of nature, equilibrium is nothing more than a figment of economic models and the imagination of their creators.

The theories of value and production are the foundations of economic theory. Both should be consistent with life processes and physical laws. In the following chapters, we present such theories, and we integrate them into the structure of markets, market power, and regulation, within which all real-life economies function.

Given the universality of the entropy law, it is natural to suspect that entropy somehow forms the basis of economic value. And indeed, this thought is not entirely new; an entropy theory of value is a scarcity theory, very familiar in the history of economic thought. *Scarcity*, for any good or service, is, in part, a matter of availability relative to market size. It is also, in part, a function of number of producers or service providers. This too is very familiar in the history of economic thought. In practice, the most important method to enhance valuation is to reduce the number of providers, creating *monopoly* or *oligopoly*.

Governments enjoy many forms of monopoly, including over legalized violence, judicial punishments, and taxation. Governments grant monopolies, through patents, intellectual property rights, regulation, and industry standards. Businesses seek monopoly through technological innovation and market dominance, sometime legal and sometimes not. Unions seek monopolies in bargaining—also called *countervailing power*—to help workers enjoy some of the fruits of their employers' monopoly power.[1] The phenomenon extends beyond economics; monotheistic religions hold monopolies on reaching heaven, giving them power to prescribe codes of conduct.

Once acquired, monopoly power is naturally guarded. The ruling class in a society generally adopts the policy of "divide and rule." From their point of view, monopoly power is something *not* to be shared. The ruling class therefore often divides the ruled, by race, ethnicity, religion, culture, and other criteria, and encourages small groups to define themselves as distinctive and separate from their fellow citizens. Similarly, businesses often prefer to stratify their employees by credentials and occupational categories and to negotiate with them (if at all) one-on-one rather than face an organized union. This division lowers the value of voters in a democracy and the power of workers in a contract dispute, making them easier to rule. Monopoly is for the powerful; competition is for the weak.

If a subgroup grows too large or too strong, so that it threatens the monopoly position of the ruling class, one solution is to split it up into smaller entities, at war with each other. Another solution is to suppress the upstart group altogether. This pattern plays out often on the world stage, and at every scale in the organization of human affairs, from the family to the nation-state. A realistic theory of value should take account of how value is created and maintained through the exercise of monopoly power.

For most goods, therefore, economic valuation depends both on the abundance or rarity of the product (in relation to the market) *and* on the number of suppliers with the ability to produce and access to the market. However, the role of monopoly is modified, in most societies, by social decisions—regulations—that govern economic conduct, including the prices of most types of human labor and also the rate of interest. Monopoly power at the level of the business or oligarch is rarely absolute; it would not be tolerable if it were. Or to put the matter in evolutionary terms, societies that do not limit monopoly power are generally unstable and do not last very long.

A key regulatory function is control of inequality; inequality is necessary, but it is dangerous if becomes too great. Economic inequality motivates activity: economic agents compare themselves with others and strive to improve their position—to make more money, to grow their wealth. Without this incentive, human societies would be much harder to organize and sustain. But too much inequality is like an overheated engine or a person with high blood pressure. It is a sign of discontent, of trouble ahead, and a warning of potential breakdown.

Mathematically, the entropy theory of value is very simple. It is given by a logarithm function, in which the argument is a measure of market scarcity and the base is given by the number of suppliers. Some may call this superficial. But such a simple theory can describe the value of monopoly and oligopoly, among the most important phenomena in the economic and social world. It can also help us understand the integration of markets and regulation that is an indispensable feature of all organized economic life. These are qualities the prevailing mainstream theory does not have.

Value applies to goods and services that are produced. Economic activities are mostly about the production of goods and services. Consumption may be the ultimate goal of economic activity, but without production there is nothing to consume. For production to occur, economic decision-makers, such as business firms and governments, must make the decisions to produce. A production theory should explain those decisions. Our production theory takes up this question.

Conventional economics, such as you find in textbooks, usually doesn't start with production. It usually starts with exchange, with trade. The goods to be exchanged already exist. Where did they come from? Who created them? Why and how? This is usually left to a later chapter. And when production makes an appearance, the theory describing it usually looks a lot like the exchange theory. The difference is that instead of a consumer choosing between eggs and butter, the theory now describes a firm choosing various combinations of labor and capital.

In mainstream economics, production theory is built around the concept of a production function. In these functions, and the theory that underlies them, there is no *decision* to produce. The decision is assumed; production always occurs to the maximum feasible extent; resources (including labor) are not left unemployed. At both the micro- and the macroeconomic levels, the production function is a parable of cooperation between capital and labor in the production of goods and services. It also provides the basis of a theory of wages and profits, relating each to the contribution they make to total output. Production functions work to rationalize and to justify market processes and market distributions. They associate the high incomes of some people with their productivity, which is very comforting to those people.

For us, production comes before exchange. Production is the concentration of resources into finished products. Exchange is the diffusion of those products to those who use them up. For production, regulation is generally essential, though it is often unpopular with those experiencing it. For exchange, regulation is somewhat less essential—though it is often desired to ensure that the process of exchange is fair to all parties. Production therefore happens in organizations; exchange generally happens in markets. A production theory is a theory of the role of organization in economic life.

A production theory based on biophysical principles bears a close resemblance to the production issues faced by actual businesses (and other economic decision-makers, including households and government planners) in the real world. The theory is a compact analytical model of the major factors, including fixed cost, variable cost, duration of production, discount rate, expected return, uncertainty, and, of course, the final output of goods or services. It spells out with precision the relationships between these factors. And so it provides a realistic understanding of economic (as well as social and biological) phenomena, which the neoclassical production theory does not. Indeed, we argue that economic systems should be understood as extensions of our understanding of life processes and the physical realities that underpin them.

A key fact is that all activity—physical, biological, economic—requires access to and the use of resources. But we observe that, despite the obvious importance of physical resources, mainstream economic theories often pay little attention to them. Indeed, standard measures of economic activity, the national income accounting which underpins our concept of gross domestic product (GDP), treats all market-based activities as equivalent in dollar terms. According to that accounting, industries such as mining, energy production, and agriculture are just a small part of economic activity—practically negligible, in relation to the scale of the whole economy.

Why is that? Perhaps it has something to do with the way people who design theories like to look at the world—and at their own place in the world.

Long ago, George Orwell asked a similar question about coal and physical work. In his 1937 book, *The Road to Wigan Pier,* he concluded,

> Practically everything we do, from eating an ice to crossing the Atlantic, and from baking a loaf to writing a novel, involves the use of coal, directly or indirectly. . . . But most of the time, of course, we should prefer to forget that they were doing it. It is so with all types of manual work; it keeps us alive, and we are oblivious of its existence.
>
> It is only because miners sweat their guts out that superior persons can remain superior. . . . All of us really owe the comparative decency

of our lives to poor drudges underground, blackened to the eyes, with their throats full of coal dust, driving their shovels forward with arms and belly muscles of steel. (Orwell 1937, 31)

If we acknowledge the essential role of (let's say) coal (or oil, or gas, or water power) in our life, we can no longer ignore the harsh life of essential workers, the coal miners and farmers and other frontline workers who bring basic resources and food to our homes. But if we recognize them for the essential role that they play and improve their working conditions and pay, many of the rest of us will no longer afford as many of the luxuries of modern life that we now enjoy. It was convenient for superior persons to ignore the essential role of coal in the past, and it remains convenient to ignore the role of many other essential workers today.

Our theory of value explains the very small weight of natural resources in our measures of economic activity—they are ubiquitous and essential, but they are abundant and cheap. More accurately, they have been abundant and cheap until now. But this has not always been the case, and several centuries of resource abundance may be coming to an end soon. What then? Conventional mainstream theories are not worried; they assume that new resources can be substituted for the old ones, that technologies will adjust and life will continue as it has. At the very worst, in mainstream theory, the producers of key resources will become wealthier, and others will be less wealthy, as part of the ordinary process of market adjustment.

A biophysical theory of production undermines this optimistic view. It shows how complex societies, such as our own, become more fragile and more vulnerable to increases in the cost of resources—and therefore more prone to disruption, crisis, and even collapse. Signs of trouble emerge in the asset markets, where prices fall. They emerge in production systems, which become unprofitable and cease operations. And they emerge in the biological system, as fertility rates crash and, ultimately, population declines. These are familiar facts in economic, social, and civilizational history. But when they happen in our own time, the economists all say, "No one could have predicted it!"

A key function of mainstream economic theory is to make trouble unforeseeable—a "shock" whose occurrence need not detract from the underlying theory. In this way, mainstream economics provides a protective shield, a cushion of illusion, within which people are encouraged to go about their daily lives. It has been aided as well by the spectacular failures of millennial and revolutionary ideologies, which promise that an existing, flawed system can be replaced with a new and better one that will endure. That experiment is sometimes tried, and it doesn't work out. In the real world, history and human societies are revolutionary; they change with conditions, and there is no final destination or predetermined end state. For many people, this is a very uncomfortable thought. Illusions are useful. Properly built and carefully maintained, they are a shared story that makes for tribal unity, social consensus, and common purpose. Most countries have them; sometimes they are affectionately described as the national myth. Mainstream economics plays this role on a larger stage; it aims to forge a kind of universal consensus in favor of certain institutions (markets) and against others (big government, central planning, regulation). To criticize the illusion is, therefore, to threaten the social consensus. It is to suggest that another way might be possible. To propose a different theory, as we now prepare to do, is to suggest that the existing theories are dangerous—and that another way is necessary.

In earlier parts of human history, approved social theories were mostly based on the favor of gods, conveyed by religions. Religious leaders, a priesthood, would defend their favored theories fiercely against heretics, among whom the most dangerous were the exponents of what we now term science. Later, when science took the high ground of power and prestige, many social theories began to call themselves scientific, such as the political ideology of scientific socialism that developed in the nineteenth century and became the basis for communism in the twentieth. Later still, social theories became "social sciences." But this does not mean the purpose of social sciences is to seek truth or to dispel illusions.

Very much like religions, social sciences protect and defend their core beliefs against critics and dissidents. This brand of fashionable conformity—orthodoxy, or even "conventional wisdom," an enduring phrase introduced by John Kenneth Galbraith in 1958—functions to limit access to resources, power, and prestige within a field and to cast out those who explore alternatives. In economics, this takes the acute professional forms of highly restricted access to publication in major journals, tenured positions in the influential universities, and thus to representation in the media that communicate economic ideas to the larger public.

For this reason, and in an age of professionalized social conformity, ideas that are politically and socially correct will tend to dominate. This is optimal for those who profit from the prevailing climate. But—as a biophysical principle—maintaining a state of untruth (or even half-truth) is costly. If misconceptions become too obvious, people will resist them. When that happens, the work of defending the orthodoxy, however implausibly, becomes onerous. Anyone who has ever taught introductory mainstream economics—or ever taken such a class—has seen this phenomenon in miniature, as instructors try to condition students to the peculiar way economists are supposed to think.

If the burden of enforcing a false vision on a society grows too great, the public will tend, at best, to tune out—even to rebel. This is a potent danger to the survival of society itself. To take an easy example from the "other side" of the world, the fall of the Soviet Union can be attributed, in part, to the fact that no one could any longer believe in the promises of the Communist Party. This is a lesson that should be applied generally—including to our own social system.

A social and economic theory consistent with the laws of nature and of life processes—that is, consistent with physics and biology—is much easier to state and to defend. That is because it is consistent with underlying truth, which is universal. Scarcity and monopoly power form the basis of economic value under all systems. Regulation is essential to all biological, mechanical, and economic processes. Consistency and simplicity give one an edge in understanding the world—the parts where others live and the parts we inhabit ourselves. We do not claim absolute truth for every statement we make. We do claim that they have strong advantages over the complicated, implausible mess that is mainstream economics.

For this reason, in our view, seemingly esoteric matters of economic theory can take on a larger importance. We must choose between accepting a viewpoint that is socially convenient but unreal and useless, or attempting to rethink premises and to draw realistic—if sometimes harsh—conclusions. The first course is much easier, for most people, but in the long run, much more dangerous. And there is always the risk, since societies do compete in the world, that if our own does not embrace reality, some other society, with more courage and determination and clearer minds, may beat us to it.

We are not the first to recognize the need to rebuild economics on a physical and biological foundation. We are not the only ones working on this problem at the present time. Energy, environmental, and ecological problems have attracted others to the cause of biophysical analysis. And there is important work going on, which shows the power of the entropy law to describe the distribution of incomes. One of us has spent many years exploiting the power of entropy-based measurements to capture the evolution of economic inequalities, in the United States and around the world. Our contribution in this book is to underpin this work, and complement it, with simple statements of basic theory, with respect to value and to production.

This book is organized into four major parts. The first part, comprising chapters 1 and 2, deals with some key concepts in economic thought: the choice between equilibrium and disequilibrium (or nonequilibrium) and the role of government in relation to the market. We try to establish the necessity of thinking in terms of economics without equilibrium, and therefore the equal necessity of governments and regulations for the very existence of markets. Chapters 3 and 4 take up the theory of value, reviewing past and mainstream thinking on this topic and advancing our proposal, which is an entropy theory of value captured in a simple way by the logarithm function, which permits us to combine physical scarcity with market power in a compact expression. The third part, chapters 5 through 7, takes up the theory of production, in a way that permits us to take account of resources, fixed investments, expected profitability, and uncertainty—all critical elements in actual economic production that, somehow, are abstracted away from mainstream equilibrium models. In chapter 8, the book closes with reflections on the implications of our theory for certain major concerns: resources, climate, demography, and the future of our species.

◉ 1 ◉

Economics without Equilibrium

Theories and terminologies are invented by humans to describe our world. In turn, they greatly influence our thinking.

General equilibrium forms the foundation of the established economic theories. Although the foundation was laid down long ago, and many departures and variations on the theme exist—so much so that the underlying structure is sometimes obscured—the concept of a *general equilibrium* is still the underpinning of most mainstream economic thought. It is rooted in that most basic of textbook diagrams, supply and demand, which depicts two curves that cross at a point designated *equilibrium*. General equilibrium is just an elaborate extension of this idea, with influence over many aspects of economic thought.

In formal theories, the general equilibrium may be stable or unstable. There may be one or more equilibrium states. An equilibrium may, or may not, correspond to full employment, depending on assumptions about conditions in the macroeconomy or the labor market. There are many variations on the theme. What they share is the idea of a state of balance; an economy in general equilibrium will reproduce itself over time because the economy consists of a collection of interdependent markets, and in each one, there is a balance between the forces of supply and those of demand.

There is a kinship between this idea and the notion that wealthy countries in the world economy are the developed countries. *Developed* means, roughly, having reached a desired final state, which can in principle be maintained over time—an equilibrium. Poor countries are certainly not in the desired equilibrium state. Under the influence of notions of general equilibrium, we therefore assume that poor countries are moving toward the state of balance that we associate with wealth—and that will be reached, eventually, through the free functioning of markets. Hence poor countries are called *developing* countries.

Since wealthy countries are called *developed* countries, it is hard for most mainstream economists to imagine, let alone predict, that wealthy countries will fall into deep recessions, let alone depressions or systemic collapse. Their prosperity is normal. Their stability is expected. Their economic growth, now and in the future, may be assumed. When deep recessions or crises do occur in wealthy countries, economists attribute these to "shocks" and imagine that the economies will return, sooner or later, to the growth path of the equilibrium state.

In the United States, the quintessential developed country, recent years have been called the age of a "Great Moderation." This notion is closely associated with the idea that free-market policies produce a stable growth trajectory. This illusion is why, in great part, the US and related societies were unprepared for the 2008 financial crisis and the 2020 COVID-19 pandemic.

Since poor countries are called developing countries, their conditions are expected to improve over time. Overall, global conditions will improve indefinitely, with only occasional temporary setbacks. When improvements don't occur, it must be due to institutional deficiencies that distort market functions, such as corruption or "crony capitalism." Equilibrium theory is not compatible with ideas of dependency or exploitation, still less with the idea that free markets may not be in the best interest of poor countries.

Intuitively, we recognize that there is no equilibrium in real life. People are born; people die. Companies are founded; companies fail. In a broader perspective, countries rise and fall; species emerge; species go extinct. Life is a competition, but competition doesn't ensure equilibrium. There are winners and losers in competition. Everyone knows these things—and yet, year after year, students in economics are introduced to the mystique of equilibrium.

Today, the nonequilibrium theory of living systems has been widely accepted in biology and other scientific studies. However, in social sciences, nonequilibrium theories are only discussed sporadically, and mainstream theories remain centered on equilibrium models. Modestly dissenting discussions often advocate for augmentation, rather

than outright rejection, of the equilibrium theory. The following statement, from two scholars whose work aims to bridge physics and economics, offers a recent example.

> On one hand, we worry that physicists often misunderstand the equi-
> librium framework in economics and fail to appreciate the very good
> reasons for its emergence. On the other hand, the majority of econo-
> mists have become so conditioned to explain everything in terms of
> equilibrium that they do not appreciate that there are many circum-
> stances in which this is unlikely to be appropriate. We hope that phys-
> icists will begin to incorporate equilibrium into their models when
> appropriate, and that economists will become more aware of analogies
> from other fields and begin to explore the possibilities of alternatives
> to the standard equilibrium framework.
>
> Our own belief is that one must choose modeling methods based
> on the context of the problem. In situations where the cognitive task
> to be solved is relatively simple, where there is good information avail-
> able for model formation, and where the estimation problems are
> tractable, rational expectations equilibrium is likely to provide a good
> explanation. Some examples where this is true include option pricing,
> hedging, or the pricing of mortgage-backed securities. (Farmer and
> Geanakoplos 2009, 34)

What is a *rational expectations equilibrium*? It is yet another variation
on the equilibrium theme, which attempts to account for the fact that
economic decisions are taken at a moment in time, when the future
lies ahead, and is (to a degree) uncertain. Rational expectations theory
holds that economic decision-makers have a good predictive model,
which they use, and therefore do not make systematic errors. The errors that they do make, which are unavoidable, are random and fall
around the actual outcome according to a normal distribution. Thus,
economic agents make the best possible use of available information.

By the end of 2008, the idea that mortgage-backed securities could
be priced using a rational expectations equilibrium method did not
appear very credible to most observers. But there is a deeper problem
with this framing of the issue. It is that the concepts of equilibrium
and nonequilibrium have very different meanings in physics and in
economics. In economic theory, the free-market, perfectly competitive
equilibrium is the optimal state. In thermodynamics, a system reaches

equilibrium at the maximum entropy state, which is death. In economic theory, nonequilibrium (and imperfect-market equilibrium) is away from the optimal state. In thermodynamics, a system is alive only when the system is in a nonequilibrium state. The standard economic theory is not compatible with the physical theory of life. Mixing them together merely generates complexity and confusion.

Nonequilibrium theory, meanwhile, describes physical reality well. But these same nonequilibrium theories typically fail in satisfying some important emotional needs. There is a natural longing for the good life that accompanies our understanding of the world and its natural laws. Typically, in human history, successful religious and political theories have met this demand, whether in Christianity's promise of a good life in heaven or Marxism's promise of a good life in the future, under communism. In essence, these theories promised a great product without having to deliver it. Furthermore, by separating heaven and earth, religions can provide realistic and practical advice on our current life—do x here, you'll get y there. This is the key to long-term success for any religion or ideology. Similarly, the pursuit of revolution—just out of reach in most cases—provided a formula for personal conduct and for the success of Marxism as a mass movement.

But a nonequilibrium theory tells us that life with material abundance is difficult to attain—and if it is attained, then it's difficult to maintain for a long period of time. In contrast, the general equilibrium theory, as an adaptive product from an age of affluence, promises not only better life in the distant future but also a great life right now (for developed countries) and just ahead (for the developing world). It says that many of us already live in the best of all available worlds and that we can continue to live in such a world so long as we do as little as possible to disturb it. This is the attraction of general equilibrium theory and of similar standard theories in social sciences, despite their inconsistency with reality and basic scientific principles. Although it may be hard to see how they can continue to hold up against the battering rams of unpleasant reality, their survival to date is testimony, in part, to built-in defenses and to the rigidities of academic institutions and intellectual hierarchies.

The famed Chicago economist Milton Friedman understood that the equilibrium theories he espoused were not, in a certain sense, realistic. He argued, therefore, that an equilibrium theory should be tested only by its predictions and not by the realism of its descriptions:

> In so far as a theory can be said to have "assumptions" at all, and in so far as their "realism" can be judged independently of the validity of predictions, the relation between the significance of a theory and the "realism" of its "assumptions" is almost the opposite of that suggested by the view under criticism. Truly important and significant hypotheses will be found to have "assumptions" that are wildly inaccurate descriptive representations of reality, and in general, the more significant the theory, the more unrealistic the assumptions (in this sense). (Friedman 1953, 16)

Unfortunately, it's not merely that neoclassical equilibrium theory has unrealistic assumptions. It is also the case that the predictive power of such theory is very poor.

A simple matter of language can tell us that the predictions of the equilibrium theory generally go wrong. We observe that many phenomena that are not consistent with theories are labeled as *imperfect*, or similar terms: imperfect competition, imperfect or asymmetric information, incomplete contracts, inefficient property rights, market failure, government failure, externality, and many others. Against these phenomena, neoclassical equilibrium theory emphasizes the concept of *perfection*. This concept and its close relatives—*completeness, efficiency, rationality*—bear some further discussion.

The concept of perfection is very popular in the literatures of mainstream economics and finance. There are perfect markets, complete contracts, rational behavior, complete information, perfectly competitive markets, efficient markets. When people point out that these concepts don't relate to reality very well, economists often argue that similar concepts are used in natural science. In science, there are frictionless worlds, ideal gases, and rational numbers.

But in physics—which at one time produced a robust literature on the concept of a frictionless world, with a corresponding mathematical theory—researchers didn't stop there. After exhausting the frictionless model, physicists went on to develop mathematical theories that model movements *with* friction. Today, they can calculate the trajectories of moving objects through mediums of various frictions. These models are fluid and realistic. In physics, frictionless is not "better" than friction; it is merely the earlier and easier version of a developing theory.

In mathematics, too, there are *rational* numbers and *irrational* numbers. Initially, there must have been strong emotions attached to these terms. But over time, rational numbers and irrational numbers acquired very technical and precise definitions. The emotional or normative implications went away. Irrational numbers are in no way inferior to rational numbers.

In economics, the emotional or normative implications never went away. Economic systems are supposed to aspire to perfection; a perfect market is supposed to be better than an imperfect market; rational is better than irrational; complete is better than incomplete; symmetry is better than asymmetry. For example, a perfect market is one where many companies are competing in the same line of business. In such a market, the profit margin is very low. But if centuries of observing markets has taught us anything, it's that rational economic actors do not appreciate low profit margins, and if they do nothing about them, they'll often fail. Similar fictions exist in other assumptions. Agents with rational expectations, economic theory holds, do not make systematic mistakes. Power in markets with asymmetric information is distributed in a manner that is intrinsically unfair—even though all information, in all markets, is to a degree asymmetric.

When we refer to the concept of perfect market, we suggest that we already know what the best society looks like. Our only task is to reduce the amount of "imperfection" over time. There is no more need for fundamental change in society. There is no more need for fundamental change in economic theory. There is simply a struggle to reduce or eliminate imperfections.

In the standard economic theory, monopoly or near-monopoly markets are highly "imperfect." In real economies, the highly profitable and dominant companies are the ones that achieve monopoly or near monopoly. This means that all companies are striving to make the market less "perfect." Economic actors and economic theory operate here in direct contradiction. A prediction of behavior based on a theory of perfect competition and perfect markets is unlikely to reflect actual economic behavior. In fact, there is little to no correspondence.

Incomplete information, theory holds, is an "imperfection." If you were to publish the password of your bank account, that would make the information shared between you and counterparties in your financial "market" more "complete." But you don't publish your password, and for good reason. A move toward complete information would not only be "irrational," it would lead to economic failure and bankruptcy in short order. So why does economics call incomplete information an imperfection? Because the theory is about a certain type of model and not about the real world. A theory predicting better performance with more complete information is unlikely to give an accurate prediction of this obvious consequence in real life.

When problems like this arise, it is often the theory (and not the world) that needs to change. The concept of the perfect (or imperfect) market and related notions work to obscure that reality.

Neoclassical economics was founded around 1870 by William Stanley Jevons, Leon Walras, and others. They were economists with good knowledge of the scientific currents of their own day, and they believed that economics should be built on a sound physical foundation. The dominant physics in the time of Jevons and Walras was Newtonian mechanics, with its famous laws of motion. It was therefore natural for them to adapt mechanics to economics. And it remains the case, to this day, that Newtonian mechanics is the underpinning of textbook economics. The result is that model economies bear an uncanny resemblance to astronomical objects interacting in space and following such laws as the principle of least action.

Yet theories derived from rational mechanics often do not offer good explanations of economic behavior. Gradually, therefore, the explicit identification of economics with physics faded, or was repudiated, while casual analogies between physics and economics endured—just enough to give an impression. Optimization theory, which holds the central position in neoclassical economics, provides a good example. Paul Samuelson's 1970 Nobel Memorial Lecture was titled "Maximum Principles in Analytical Economics." The following quote is representative:

> There is really nothing more pathetic than to have an economist or a retired engineer try to force analogies between the concepts of physics and the concepts of economics. How many dreary papers have I had to referee in which the author is looking for something that corresponds to entropy or to one or another form of energy. (Samuelson 1970, 7)

In the very next paragraph, however, Samuelson found an analogy himself: "Pressure and volume, and for that matter absolute temperature and entropy, have to each other the same conjugate or dualistic relation that the wage rate has to labor or the land rent has to acres of land" (Samuelson 1970, 7).

Philip Mirowski observed, "The key to the comprehension of Samuelson's meteoric rise in the economics profession was his knack for evoking all the outward trapping and ornament of science without ever coming to grips with the actual content or implications of physical theory for his neoclassical economics" (Mirowski 1989, 383).

In the rest of this chapter, we first examine the nature of equilibrium systems in economics more closely. We then explore some alternatives that are popular on the edges of mainstream thought because they depart from the simplest versions of equilibrium theory, but not in a deep or fundamental way. These developments include theories of chaos and complexity. We then turn to our preferred model, which is of a nonequilibrium system adhering to biophysical principles and natural laws.

EQUILIBRIUM IN LINEAR, NONRECURSIVE SYSTEMS

A linear system is the simplest arrangement of multiple equations for representing an economy or any other phenomenon. A nonrecursive system is one in which the output of a previous period is not fed back into the system to generate a result for the period ahead. Linear, nonrecursive systems are a standard tool of equilibrium economics.

As we have already seen, the Arrow-Debreu model is the standard general equilibrium model for linear, nonrecursive systems. It has had a profound impact on the whole of economic theory. What are the conditions in the Arrow-Debreu paper that ensure the existence of an equilibrium? This is the first question that drives us to examine the Arrow-Debreu model more carefully.

Roy Weintraub summarized the implications of the Arrow-Debreu model as follows:

> Each year, new economics Ph.D. students learn the proof of the existence of a competitive equilibrium as if a rite of passage. From the

utility-maximizing behavior of consumers and the profit-maximizing behavior of firms, neophyte economists soon can demonstrate that under certain conditions there exists a competitive market-clearing general equilibrium price vector. . . . Indeed, economists with even scant knowledge of the history of economics can identify Kenneth Arrow and Gerard Debreu's 1954 *Econometrica* paper as having provided the proof that settled the issue.

That paper, "On the Existence of an Equilibrium for a Competitive Economy," appeared to bring closure to an argument that was (at least) two centuries old. (Weintraub 2002, 184)

Most economists believe the Arrow-Debreu paper did "bring closure to an argument that was (at least) two centuries old." But few economists read the paper carefully. Even the referee of the paper and the editors who accepted the paper for publication did not read the paper carefully. They didn't understand the paper. The paper was accepted based on the reputation of the authors and the great implications of the model. Weintraub made a detailed description of the whole process and concluded:

How did it come to pass that a particular paper, in a journal at that time read by very few economists, came to be accepted as having established a foundational truth about market economics? These are not questions economists typically ask. 'The theorem proves that . . .' is enough information to persuade economists that the knowledge associated with the theorem is secure knowledge. Professional economists are confident about the result and the implications of the equilibrium proof, and no one needs to attend to the means of its construction: the validity of the equilibrium proof is incontrovertible. (Weintraub 2002, 20)

Is the theoretical foundation as solid as most people assume?

Let us examine the proof in the Arrow-Debreu 1954 paper carefully. First, they set the scene:

We suppose there are a finite number of distinct commodities (including all kinds of services). Each commodity may be bought or sold for delivery at one of a finite number of distinct locations and one of a finite number of future time points. For the present purposes, the same commodity at two different locations or two different points of time will be regarded as two different commodities. (Arrow and Debreu 1954, 266)

Then they made several assumptions about the model. The key assumption, which ensures the existence of equilibrium, is about the initial possessions of each individual. Arrow and Debreu wrote as follows:

> The second half of [assumption] IV.a. asserts in effect that every individual could consume out of his initial stock in some feasible way and still have a positive amount of each commodity available for trading in the market. This assumption is clearly unrealistic. However, the necessity of this assumption or some parallel one for the validity of the existence theorem points up an important principle; to have equilibrium, it is necessary that each individual possess some asset or be capable of supplying some labor service which commands a positive price at equilibrium. In IV.a, this is guaranteed by insisting that an individual be capable of *supplying something of each commodity*. (Arrow and Debreu 1954, 270, emphasis added)

Arrow and Debreu acknowledged that "this assumption is clearly unrealistic." Then, they asserted that "to have equilibrium, it is necessary that each individual possess some asset or be capable of supplying some labor service which commands a positive price at equilibrium." But the assumption they actually made does not say that each person merely "possess[es] some asset." The assumption holds that each "individual be capable of supplying something of each commodity" to the market. What does this statement mean?

Let us recall that the Arrow-Debreu model is not about market transactions restricted to a single moment in time. It is about market transactions through all time. That is, each "commodity" in an Arrow-Debreu model has a time subscript, identifying it with the moment when it may be brought to market for purchase or sale. As they write, "The same commodity at two different locations or two different points of time will be regarded as two different commodities" (1954, 266).

Therefore, the statement quoted means that, at the very beginning, every individual is assumed to possess all the food she will consume in her life, all the houses, vehicles, and computers she will own, including all the models and fancy gadgets that will appear in the future, and all the gasoline and all the electricity she will need for all time.

Under this assumption, no individual in an Arrow-Debreu economy *is obliged* to produce anything or trade with anybody to satisfy all her current and future needs. Moreover, she must have something "of each commodity" available, potentially to trade with every other individual in the market—even though those individuals also are fully supplied with everything they need or ever will need. Trade and exchange—the heart of economics in the Arrow-Debreu model—occurs, it appears, only for fun.

(No, we are not making this up. You can read and reread the quotations from Arrow and Debreu. They really said this.)

In effect, the Arrow-Debreu model indicates that equilibrium only occurs in a system in which no one needs to do anything. Production and consumption play no role in the existence of an equilibrium. The existence of an equilibrium has nothing to do with market competition or profit maximization. It is present from the beginning.

In real life, we may possess land to grow food for consumption. We may possess iron ore, coal, and furnaces to produce iron. We may possess petroleum and a refinery to refine petroleum into propane, gasoline, and diesel. But in the Arrow-Debreu model, as they wrote it down, everyone possesses all the final consumption goods in their initial stock, not only for now but for all time. Of course, this is absurd. That this highly unrealistic assumption was deemed necessary by Arrow and Debreu to ensure equilibrium indicates that there is no equilibrium in real life. Various interpretations of Arrow-Debreu have attempted to soften this conclusion, such as the claim that "contingent insurance" contracts would be sufficient. But these are not offered up in the original Arrow-Debreu statement, as quoted here.

The Cambridge economist Nicholas Kaldor makes a similar observation about equilibrium theory:

> Returning to prevailing theory, as far as I understand it, the axioms of equilibrium theory were originally chosen in order to secure the desired result, in other words, the assumptions required for proving the existence of a unique and possibly stable general equilibrium. But its authors were motivated by the belief that they were only laying the foundations of an explanation of how a market economy works, an initial stage of the analysis which is in the nature of "scaffolding": it has to be erected before the permanent building can be built but will

be removed step by step as the permanent building nears completion. However, since Walras first wrote down his system of equations over 100 years ago, progress has definitely been backwards not forwards in the sense that the present set of axioms are far more restrictive than those of the original Walrasian model. The ship is no nearer to the shore, but considerably farther off, though in a logical, mathematical sense, the present system of derived tautologies is enormously superior to Walras's original effort. (Kaldor 1985, 13)

"A system of derived tautologies" is indeed exactly what the Arrow-Debreu framework amounts to. Given the assumptions, the conclusions follow. The assumptions, however, bear no relationship to actual economies. That they have become the foundation stone of economic teaching and the development of economic theory is . . . well, it's a calamity. Something should be done. The question is, what?

As others have observed (Saith 2022, 43–56), critics of Arrow-Debreu have long argued the nonviability of general equilibrium. In a pungent comment, quoted by Saith, Terry Barker makes the point as follows:

It will also be seen that the supply-demand curves used extensively to describe the determination of prices do not appear in [Barker's] book [*Space-Time Economics*]. The reason is that the well-known chart of intersecting curves completely misrepresents the fundamental features of economic behavior. The curves are not usually dated, they show an equilibrium outcome, they are continuous, they are certain. In economic life all actions take place in time, all markets are more or less in disequilibrium, indivisibilities and discontinuities are pervasive in production, distribution and consumption (and essential to the explanation of economic behavior) and uncertainty rules . . . The curves are pure speculation invented for their mathematical properties. (Saith 2022, n55, 662)

Mainstream economics has reacted, in effect conceding the case, by building variations of, elaborations on, and departures from general equilibrium theory. A great deal of work within mainstream economics has gone into such variations as agent-based modeling and "dynamic stochastic general equilibrium" (DSGE) models, the latter of which amount to false advertising, as they rely on a "representative agent" and have nothing to do with markets nor with general equilibrium. The question then becomes, Have these refinements overcome the basic difficulty, which is that of theory disconnected from reality?

If a model is broadly consistent with reality, then refinements of the model will be more consistent with reality. However, in the general equilibrium model and its successors, further refinement of the mathematical models requires increasingly unrealistic assumptions. We cannot cover every case, but we take up several examples in the next two sections.

QUASI EQUILIBRIUM IN CHAOTIC, NONLINEAR SYSTEMS

Linear, nonrecursive models, such as the Arrow-Debreu model, are clearly unrealistic; they cannot accurately describe the behavior of economic systems. Because of this, effort has been devoted to the application of nonlinear and recursive models, most of which were developed in natural science, to understand economics. These models use simple equations to generate patterns or classes of outcomes, such as bifurcations, multiple equilibria, and deterministic chaos.

Chaos theory is an important and interesting development in nonlinear mathematics, showing that simple recursive equations, in which the output from one round is fed back into the equation to generate a new round of calculated results, can produce spectacularly unstable patterns. Chaos theory is closely associated with fractal geometry, which captures some important properties of nature, including "self-similarity at different scales." Multifractal generators have, in turn, been shown to capture many of the behavioral properties of financial asset prices (Mandelbrot 1999). They help us understand the relative frequency of extreme events in financial markets.

However, chaos theory has an affinity with equilibrium theories. That is, the equations are deterministic, in the sense that given a particular starting point, the next step is fully specified, and given a particular structure of the equations, the general picture of the "outcome space" is known. Although the specific outcomes of a nonlinear dynamic system are unpredictable—the only way to find out is to run the equations—there are nevertheless values or regions that confine and define the outcomes. These are called *attractors* and *strange attractors* in the theory. They function somewhat like equilibria, giving definition to a disorderly world. Chaos theory is useful in disposing of misleading concepts such as "efficient markets theory," but it does not entirely escape the mental framework set out by the concept of equilibrium. And it is not entirely compatible with some basic principles of physics and biology.

From chaos theory, for example, there comes the *butterfly effect*. In economics, this is an idea about how small disturbances—for instance, in the stock market—can lead to large-scale panics and financial crises, even to the collapse of the financial system. The butterfly effect is drawn by analogy to weather forecasting. It is said, for instance, that when a butterfly flips its wings in Brazil, it could generate a hurricane in the United States. Is it true? Definitely not! The air movement generated by the butterfly is quickly dissipated, not amplified. It disturbs the surrounding air for a few millimeters, not for thousands of miles. This is a basic property of thermodynamic systems. This is also why weather can be forecast with reasonable accuracy.

If there is no butterfly effect in real weather, how was the theory of the butterfly effect developed? In earlier days, researchers could not solve the thermodynamic equations that represent weather phenomena. Edward Lorenz, a meteorologist, modified the original thermodynamic equations, which are partial differential equations, into simpler ordinary differential equations. For these simplified equations, small changes in initial conditions—"sensitive dependence on initial conditions"—could lead to big changes in the results (Lorenz 1963). This idea was used to explain the difficulty of weather forecasting. But with better mathematical methods and computing power, meteorologists can now forecast weather—with the original equations—at much higher accuracy than was true back in the 1960s or before.

Meteorologists have never used the wings of a butterfly in Brazil to explain a thunderstorm in Miami. However, the term *butterfly effect* has become very popular in social theories. It is often invoked to explain catastrophic events, especially financial crises. One of us used it to describe the Asian financial crisis, which broke over Thailand in 1997 and spread to `Indonesia, Korea, and elsewhere. However, the reference was in jest; the butterfly we named, in Washington, was Alan Greenspan. Greenspan, then chair of the US Federal Reserve Board, had precipitated the crisis by raising interest rates, an action with global impact. Also consistent with our skeptical view, Xue, He, and Shao (2012) find that there was no "butterfly" contagion from US real-estate markets to conditions in Asia in the Great Financial Crisis.

The use of *butterfly effect* to describe the 2008 financial crisis is not innocuous, for it suggests an unpredictable phenomenon beyond human control. In fact, the financial crisis was the consequence of many policies and activities operating over many years. Early on, leg-islation set up prefunded pension systems and tax-sheltered savings plans. These forced or encouraged employers and employees to place large amounts of money into funds, which were then directed by fund managers—what is sometimes called *money-manager capitalism*. This in turn created a huge demand for financial securities and so generated great wealth for the financial industry. This provoked a further set of institutional changes, called *deregulation*, dating in the United States from the early 1980s, which greatly weakened the real economy and strengthened the financial economy. Finance became the dominant career choice of the social elite.

In 1998, when Long Term Capital Management (LTCM), a hedge fund, was going to default on its contracts—potentially endangering the big banks that had lent their funds to LTCM—the Federal Reserve Bank of New York organized a rescue (Lowenstein 2000). The rescue kept the New York banks from having a crisis. But the Federal Reserve's help encouraged financial institutions to engage in ever-more-leveraged positions. Then, in the first decade of the twenty-first century, large-scale financial frauds were generally decriminalized, with regulators and investigators assigned to other duties, notably counterterrorism, so that financial insiders could defraud the public with impunity. The purpose of these and other activities is not to generate a finan-cial crisis—the job was not done by subversive mathematicians from Russia. It is to transfer wealth from society to the financial elites and to download the risk from the best informed to the least informed. It is to create an entire class of activities that the whole society must bear as a fixed cost, come what may.

Through this period, the Federal Reserve kept the basic interest rate (which it controls) low for a long time, to encourage borrowing and support the accumulation of debts, which are also managed by the financial sector. It did this while relaxing, rather than stiffening,

regulations on how debt could be created and used. Banks then originated many innovative (and largely fraudulent) mortgages, such as
adjustable-rate and subprime mortgages, which generate high incomes
for themselves but are destined to default when the mortgage rates
adjust to market levels, often after two or three years. Next, the market
of mortgage-backed securities transferred credit risk from informed
insiders to uninformed outsiders. The credit rating agencies certified
low-quality mortgage bonds with their highest rating, comparable to
US government debt, to increase their value and marketability. And
when large-scale defaults occurred or were going to occur, regulatory
authorities stepped in to bail out the banking system. In 2006, one
year before Lehman Brothers failed, Lehman generated the highest
recorded profit in its history (Chadha 2016).

None of this was unpredictable. It had nothing to do with any kind
of butterfly. If it was not seen or predicted by mainstream economists,
the reasons lie in a willful unwillingness to examine the institutional
details—the flood of policies that supported economic financializa-
tion. But the coordinated effort to make high profits for the financial
elites increases the leverage of the financial system. This makes the
economy and society very unstable.

It takes many coordinated efforts to increase the leverage of a financial system to high levels. The theory of chaos and butterfly effects
became popular in part because it helps to cover up the results of
these efforts by attributing their catastrophic consequences to random events. (The metaphor of "black swans" is another example, as
discussed in Galbraith [2014].) "Nobody could have seen this coming"
was a common refrain at the time, meaning that anyone who did see
it coming was, by construction, a crank, whose views should be disre-
garded. Similarly, neoclassical economic theory becomes popular in
social theory not because it helps uncover truth, but because it helps
to cover up some of the most basic truths about modern economic life,
of which perhaps the most basic is, *there is no equilibrium.*

Now let us return to the modeling issue. The atmosphere, as a system, involves many particles. It is a thermodynamic system. Thermodynamic equations are partial differential equations. In earlier days,
people could not solve these equations. As we have seen with the butterfly effect, researchers simplified the partial differential equations
into ordinary differential equations, which exhibit chaos. But when

we can already solve the original equations, should we still cling to the results obtained from watered-down systems? We shouldn't, and we shouldn't translate those misleading concepts into ideologically convenient parables for economics.

DREAMS OF SELF-ORGANIZATION: THE SANTA FE SCHOOL

The concept of self-organization is a popular further variation on equilibrium theories. It gives rise to the concept of complexity as a phenomenon generated by the interaction of individuals in free markets. It is also misleading. It doesn't distinguish between structures of non-living systems and living systems. Living systems survive and prosper not because they self-organize. Rather, they survive and prosper only when they can organize in ways that generate positive returns. Living systems are subject to the constraints of thermodynamics and must organize themselves *in such a way* as to overcome those constraints for a certain time. Mechanical systems and economic systems are no different in this critical respect.

Self-organization is a particular theme of the Santa Fe school of mainstream economists and natural scientists. The essence of the Santa Fe doctrine is that certain simple properties of some physical systems can be married to mainstream, general equilibrium economics. The output of the model is a complex structure—for example, a pattern generated on a computer screen by *cellular automata*, a kind of rules-based interacting element in a computer program. A physical counterpart may be the growth of mineral crystals—sometimes large and very beautiful—which is the consequence of the chemical properties of the underlying mineral and particular environmental conditions. These processes are at the heart of the Santa Fe conception of free markets. They have attracted the interest of a group of researchers who seek to model the development of structure from free association and to characterize the results in statistical terms.

The Santa Fe school attempts to depart from the simplest conception of equilibrium in economics, but it does not go very far. There is an underlying observation: complex structures exist, which would not arise under the assumptions of a perfectly competitive market. The questions then become, How did they arise? What properties do they exhibit? The Santa Fe approach attempts to answer these questions in the most parsimonious way. Models of complex interaction and arrangement achieve this goal, at least on the surface. As a critique of simpler forms of equilibrium theory, the Santa Fe method has enjoyed a certain degree of success.

But living organisms do not grow from the interaction of freely associating, self-organizing atoms, molecules, or cells. Living organisms grow according to plans. They first make an appropriate choice of fixed investment—they choose materials they can work with, and then they assemble those materials according to blueprints that have been well tested over time. These blueprints are encoded in genes. Once an organism exists, it takes advantage of a source of energy to meet the needs of variable cost, while regulating the use of that energy so that it doesn't immediately wreck the system that has been built. Maintaining the balance between structures and inputs is the task of living. When it breaks down, life ends. The plans and blueprints may be just a bit improved compared with past practice, by mutations or design, but past plans and past practices are always the foundation of future action.

Human societies follow the same principle. They develop, over time, a system of laws, regulations, and institutions, which transcend the life spans of any individual in the social system. The purpose of these laws, regulations, and institutions—we may think of them as "habits"—is to guide the conduct of future members of the society down certain paths and to steer them away from others. More "developed" societies are typically characterized by a very thorough set of such rules. The rules may be onerous for some people, since hierarchy exists, and the welfare of some may depend on the repression of others. But in the most successful societies, they are not onerous for most people, because they have been worked out to generate positive returns for society taken as a whole. Thus, in the successful cases, compliance with established habits is experienced as a combination of freedom and security.

Social and economic habits—laws, regulations, institutions—can become dysfunctional over time, especially if conditions change so that the returns from one set of habits cease to be positive for large parts of the society. This generally happens in one of two ways. One is that the enforcement of rules becomes overly strict—a dictatorship or (in the currently fashionable expression) authoritarianism—generating rebellion. The other is that the rules become too lax or their enforcement starts to fail. This is called anarchy.

Note that the standards that apply in one society may not be those preferred by members of a different society. A society that is regarded as "authoritarian" by outsiders may not feel that way to many of its own members, and so it does not provoke a rebellious or unstable attitude. A society that regards itself as law-abiding (for the most part) may appear dangerously anarchic and unsafe to outsiders. In some countries, extreme poverty provokes a feeling of horror; in others, it is accepted as the way of things. Most ordinary citizens do not generally compare themselves with some other country of which they know little, but with their own history and experience; what usually matters for them is whether conditions are getting better or getting worse. Only a small fraction generally has the opportunity or the motivation to change from one society to another via migration—and when they do so, they usually must start at the bottom of the society they enter.

From this, we draw an obvious inference. Just like successful organisms, successful societies can be quite diverse. Each is guided by its own system of habits (laws, regulations, institutions) developed over time, sometimes hundreds or thousands of years. There is no single best formula, such as free markets or "dictatorship of the proletariat." There is no single standard, as members of a society formed by a given set of traditions will look at other societies through a lens that the members of that society do not share. And although boundaries between one society and another can be crossed, blurred, or even erased, such boundaries generally exist. A society, after all, is defined by the difference between what it is and what it is not.

What is true for the organization of cells inside a living organism, and true for the grouping of living persons into societies, is also true at every intermediate level of social organization. Government agencies, business firms, nonprofit organizations—all are constructed through the development of enduring rules and habits, intended to outlast any individual. All are generically similar in that they obey the same broad principles and laws. If they are not so constructed, chances are that they will not survive very long. But all are also distinctive and different. They embody variations that are permitted within the framework of those principles and laws—and sometimes variations that stretch the boundaries of existing principles and laws.

All of this is quite at odds with the idea that one can understand social organization in general, in a meaningful way, by modeling the interaction of autonomous entities in a model with a single set of rules. Complexity is an improvement over the search for a unique stable equilibrium. But compared with an analysis rooted in plans, rules, investments, and resources, the work of the complexity school appears very close to the framework of general equilibrium.

In the next several sections, we take up some of the essential properties of living systems, which include boundaries, organization, and inequalities.

BOUNDARY AS A PRECONDITION OF ORGANIZATION

In standard economic theory, a free market is the most efficient system. There are no alternative systems worth preserving, hence there is no fixed case for boundaries between systems. This is equally true of the chaos and complexity approaches; both are occupied with attempting to model the behavior of a single system, without considering the possibility of outside influences except as "shocks" to that system. It is easy to see the appeal of *Free Trade* as an artifact of this belief structure, likewise the case for "open borders." The famous Stolper-Samuelson factor price equalization theorem is also about a world in which borders and boundaries do not really matter, because capital can cross freely even if labor cannot.

Of course, outsiders do exist, both with respect to exchanges in local markets and with respect to social systems taken as a whole. Mainstream economics attempts to account for them by introducing the concept of externalities. An *externality* is defined as some effect of a transaction on those who are not direct parties to the transaction. This is treated as a special case of the theory—an important special case, but nevertheless something outside the main line of the argument. The core of the free-market theory is aimed at transactions between two (or more) parties operating in perfect isolation from all others. It is a theory of particles in a void. Where there is no void, things are complicated by introducing the concept of externalities.

However, as we have noted, all living organisms have boundaries; all cells have membranes. All organisms have skins or shells or other boundaries that separate them from the environment. They have boundaries because they necessarily exist in environments with other living things. They have neighbors. They must separate themselves from their neighbors, to protect themselves, to compete, and to coexist. In most cases, larger organisms have thicker and less permeable skins, although many examples of relatively small organisms with hard shells, scales, and other protections also exist. Boundaries are essential to life.

Similarly, all organizations have boundaries, and the larger and more successful organizations have thicker boundaries that are harder to cross. Prestigious organizations are more exclusive. Top universities generally have higher rejection rates. Big corporations have more complex recruitment routines. Wealthy countries generally have stringent visa requirements for entry and even more stringent ones for acquiring the political rights of a citizen. At the US-Mexico border, entry into Mexico from the United States is virtually unrestricted. But entry into the US from Mexico is heavily scrutinized. The European Union has (largely) abolished internal border checks. But it tries to impose strict controls on entry into the EU from Africa or the Middle East.

Markets also have boundaries. The New York Stock Exchange (NYSE) is a stock market. But not every company can get listed on the NYSE. There is a stringent requirement for listing. If certain conditions are not maintained, a listed company may be delisted. The failed cryptocurrency exchange FTX operated from the Bahamas, because in theory (though not in practice), some of its activities could not cross the boundary of the United States. Similarly, your local supermarket has standards; there are goods it will buy and goods it will not buy. If you want to purchase low-quality goods, it is often necessary to buy them from small operators or in poorer countries where high standards—or tough boundaries—do not apply.

From the entropy law, a system tends to dissipate its resources. A boundary is an essential way to retain those resources. This is the fundamental reason why boundaries are a precondition for organization. This is also why more prestigious organizations, which control more resources, have tighter boundaries.

BOUNDARIES AND INEQUALITIES IN
NATURE AND SOCIETY

Boundaries and inequalities are two parts of the same story, and both parts are necessary for life and for human societies.

A dam is a boundary. The water level inside a dam is higher than that outside the dam. The difference of water levels drives the movement of generators to produce electricity. The air pressure inside an engine is higher than that outside the engine. The difference of air pressure propels the movement of the engine. The biggest source of energy on the Earth is from the Sun. The temperature on the Sun is much higher than the temperature on the Earth. The difference in temperature drives much of the atmosphere's movement, ocean currents, rainfall, and photosynthesis on the Earth. Without inequality, the world is a dead place.

From thermodynamic theory, the efficiency of an engine is determined by the difference of temperature inside and outside the engine. The higher the temperature differential, the more efficient an engine becomes. This is a general principle. The efficiency of a dam in generating electricity is determined by the height of the dam. The higher the dam, the more electricity can be generated. The efficiency of transmitting electricity over long distances is determined by the voltage differential. The higher the voltage differential, the less energy loss during transmission.

Because of the need to maintain differentials, systems generally have barriers to separate inside from outside. Engines have combustion chambers. Dams are constructed to separate water above from water below. Cells have membranes, where concentration of many materials and the electric potentials are different inside and outside. A system maintaining a higher differential needs to withstand greater pressure.

At the same time, systems with higher differentials are more costly to build. An engine that can withstand higher temperature and pressure is more expensive. So are higher dams and high-voltage transmission systems. Systems with higher differentials, when they fail, can cause greater damage. A high-pressure engine causes greater damage when it explodes. A higher dam causes greater flooding when it collapses. A nuclear power plant, which uses high-density nuclear energy as fuel, can cause great environmental damage when accidents occur. Inequalities are necessary, but they are dangerous.

There is a strong parallel in human societies. Human societies everywhere are unequal. In businesses, there are supervisors and subordinates. In academics, in the military, and in government, there are different ranks. Among different countries, there are rich countries and poor countries. Enormous efforts go into building and maintaining these inequalities; the gradient of ranks and hierarchies within a group is what makes that group organized, dynamic, and motivated. At the same time, excessive inequality is dangerous—it can cause a human society to explode.

In human societies, boundaries exist to create and preserve social inequalities. This is obvious, since as organizations or societies come to control more resources, they increase their exclusivity and the difficulty of getting in. Education (from the beginning of time) has two elements. One is the imparting of a specific skill: for instance, in a medieval village, weaving or carpentry or blacksmithing. The other is the acquisition of the right to practice that skill—admission to membership in the guild. This dual practice continues to the present day, in ever more complex forms. Law and medical schools train lawyers and doctors. Bar associations and hospitals admit (or exclude) graduates of those schools to practice. A major purpose of professional education is social advancement—and this is a relative process, requiring and enforcing inequalities.

Greater inequality often means greater profits. Companies can raise prices when they have a competitive edge, for instance a superior technology or clever marketing. Universities that are more exclusive can charge higher tuition. In a wealthy and democratic society, it is often difficult to maintain a high level of inequality. The elites will therefore move production to authoritarian countries where inequality is high and profit margins are high. They can take advantage of lax environmental standards, low taxes, lucrative profit-sharing agreements, and cheap labor. That is why elites in Western countries often support governments in authoritarian countries and suppress democratic movements in these countries, even though they are willing to accept a certain amount of taxation, environmental and labor standards, and democratic processes at home. Moving inequality across recognized boundaries makes it less of a political risk.

In short, inequality is everywhere. Why then do many people, especially among the richest and the most powerful, claim to fight for equality? Partly, they worry about their own safety in an excessively unequal system. But also they realize that most people are at the lower end of the society. Today the richest person has more than a hundred billion dollars in assets (Forbes 2022). But many families, even in the United States, have less than a few thousands in net assets (Perry 2021). Thus, almost all public statements, whose main listeners have very few assets, promote and celebrate equality, solidarity, and similar values. Those who promote equality gain the moral high ground. Those with high morals gain social status. Equality breeds inequality.

Indeed, almost everything we do personally or in small groups strives to increase or maintain inequality, even though we often avoid that word. We try to stand out or to be outstanding. We want to excel, to be distinguished. Many people who become prominent fighting against inequality send their children to "top" universities. We produce patents to create monopoly. We hope our books, protected by copyright, will sell. Our gods, our political systems, and our moral standards are superior. We profess equality as a moral goal but subvert it every day. If equality is equilibrium, we work against it. This is the way of the entropic world.

NO EQUILIBRIUM IN ECONOMICS

Why abandon equilibrium? Our answer in a nutshell is: because it doesn't exist. Because no economy in the world has ever been in equilibrium and none ever will be. Because to recognize these facts changes in fundamental ways how we view the world. It forces us to focus our attention on boundaries, inequality, instability, precarity, and change. It forces us to recognize that "development" has a cost, which is fragility and the possibility of collapse. It forces us to confront the many hypocrisies in our conventional theories and the way they shape conventional thinking. It forces us to think about the world as it is.

From a nonequilibrium theory, wealthy countries are not in equilibrium. In fact, they are further away from any equilibrium (or sustainable) state than poor countries, because they must consume more resources, consistently and without interruption, to sustain themselves.

This is consistent with empirical observation. When resources are abundant, wealthy countries, which have developed technologies and institutional structures to utilize large amounts of resources, especially energy resources, are more powerful than poor countries. Wealthy countries, whose high-fixed-cost structures require a stable environment, devote more resources to maintain stability.

As a result, wealthy countries are more stable than poor countries most of the time—but not always. Wealthy countries, due to their higher fixed costs, may suffer more than poor countries when they fail to develop effective responses to specific instabilities. (In the common expression: the bigger they are, the harder they fall.) Poor countries have less technology to utilize large amounts of energy and other resources. They are less powerful than the wealthy countries. But simpler technologies also require fewer resources to maintain them. Poor countries can endure resource scarcity and unpredicted uncertainty better than wealthy countries. Poverty—it is sad to say—is indefinitely sustainable at low cost, whereas affluence requires unending maintenance and good luck.

What is true of countries is also true of firms and households. Large businesses and rich households are more stable, most of the time—but not always. They develop fixed obligations, such as large factories, global supply chains, big mortgages, college tuition, and on and on. A war, a trade disruption, a market crash, a recession—these things can hit hard. Small businesses and poor people can be destroyed, but they are also more easily brought back.

Biologists have pondered similar questions about the concept of equilibrium. In 1932, Walter Cannon wrote as follows:

> The constant conditions which are maintained in the body might be termed equilibria. That word, however, has come to have fairly exact meaning as applied to relatively simple physic-chemical states, in closed systems, where known forces are balanced. The coordinated physiological processes which maintain most of the steady states in the organism are so complex and so peculiar to living beings—involving, as they may, the brain and nerves, the heart, lungs, kidney and spleen, all working cooperatively—that I have suggested a special designation for these states, homeostasis. The word does not imply something set and immobile, a stagnation. It means a condition—a condition which may vary, but which is relatively constant." (Cannon 1932, 25)

Cannon considered and rejected the term *equilibrium* in describing steady states in the internal environment of human bodies. He was aware his thoughts "would be suggestive for other kinds of organizations—even social and industrial." Indeed, biologists since the time of Darwin have recognized that nonequilibrium theories provide better descriptions of living systems than equilibrium theories. "In the old system, each species was imagined to have been created according to some ideal type. Variation was just so much noise superimposed on the ideal type. After Darwin, the variation itself was seen as real and important, while the notion of an ideal type was recognized as a useless abstraction" (Trivers 1985, 22).

Life systems are nonequilibrium thermodynamic systems. The current dominant economic theory is a general equilibrium theory—even though social systems are a special case of living systems. When a theory about a special case is inconsistent with a general foundation, either the general foundation or the special theory is wrong. So far, economists have not challenged the validity of the nonequilibrium thermodynamic theory of life systems. That is because we cannot extend the principles of mainstream economics to these systems. Doing so would expose the similarity of their theories to, say, the pre-Darwinian doctrine of "intelligent design." However, we will show that an analytical theory of economics *can* be directly derived from the basic physical and biological principles of thermodynamic life systems. In this way, we hope to establish social sciences as an integral part of physical and biological sciences.

CONCLUDING REMARKS

Milton Friedman tried to reconcile the maximization principle with evolutionary theory:

> Confidence in the maximization-of-return hypothesis is justified by evidence of a very different character. . . . Unless the behavior of businessmen in some way or other approximated behavior consistent with the maximization of returns, it seems unlikely that they would remain in business for long. Let the apparent immediate determinant of business behavior be anything at all—habitual reaction, random chance, or whatnot. Whenever this determinant

happens to lead to behavior consistent with rational and maximization of returns, the business will prosper and acquire resources with which to expand; whenever it does not, the business will tend to lose resources and can be kept in existence only with addition of resources from outside. The process of "natural selection" thus helps to validate the hypothesis—or rather, given natural selection, acceptance of the hypothesis can be based largely on the judgment that it summarized appropriately the conditions for survival. (Friedman 1953, 22)

In these remarks, Friedman—like Samuelson in the remarks we quote above—evoked the language of another discipline; in this case, evolutionary biology. But his description is inaccurate. Rationality and maximization of returns are not the criteria of success in life systems. For life to prosper, it is only necessary to generate a positive return. When a system posts positive returns, it will expand, however imperfect or irrational you might think it is, and whether it pursues maximizing behavior or not. When a system posts negative returns, it will shrink, however perfect or rational it may be, and even though it may be achieving the maximum feasible rate of return. A system may post positive returns under one set of conditions and then negative returns under another—as when a country that depends on natural gas faces a disruption in the supply of gas. Under both conditions, behavior is rational, and returns may be maximized. This does not prevent severe difficulties and even the risk of collapse.

By conflating maximization with natural selection, Friedman committed an act of sophistry that would be transparent to most children. Parents almost universally teach their children to show restraint, to have patience, to wait their turn, not to grab. That is because they understand very well that maximization at each moment of time—Friedman's statement of good economic behavior—is not compatible with survival and success over the long run. Luckily for human societies, practically all businesses and working people understand this principle as well and adhere to it. Reputation, honesty, respect, good customer relations, and repeat business are the foundations of long-term success in business. Businesses and workers who take Friedman's advice are usually regarded as undesirable—even as crooks.[1] And yet, Friedman's statement has managed to dominate the teaching of economics for decades. Why is that?

When we discuss rival theories—theories not our own—we have no problem recognizing that they are propaganda, that they are used to cover up truth instead of uncover truth. We readily acknowledge Marxist economic theory as once taught in communist countries as propaganda. But students in Western countries are taught to regard neoclassical economic theory as a representation of social truth. That is because neoclassical economic theory, with its dreams of equilibrium, is the propaganda of our own system.

Researchers and theorists are part of a social system. In the social system to which they belong, researchers strive for gains in social and professional standing, along with income, and for this, they must show allegiance to the dominant creed. In mainstream economics, for many decades, Friedman and Samuelson defined that creed, and the differences between them spanned the range of acceptable economic thought. For this reason, the obvious flaws in their arguments largely passed without criticism, especially from their followers. Only a few economist-dissidents spoke out, and they paid a professional price.

In communist countries, scholars pretended to be dogmatic Marxists even though they largely were not. In our capitalist societies, scholars profess to believe in the neoclassical, neoliberal, free-market, and general equilibrium doctrines. Whether they really believe in these doctrines is hard to say, and it is also irrelevant; if they do not pretend to believe, they mostly will not survive as scholars. There were battalions of commissars under communism to root out dissidents, just as the Inquisition rooted out heretics or the Puritans burned witches. Similarly, the citadel of mainstream economics is well protected against its critics, who consider themselves lucky if they can stay afloat professionally in second-tier academic institutions.

Truth is secondary, therefore, to professional survival—as we should expect. Scientific research, like law or politics, is a way to make a living. Scientists and economists, like lawyers or politicians, are human beings. Like all other animals, we seek a positive return on our investments—in this case, in education and academic striving. This is largely served by conformity—or professed conformity—with an accepted creed. We seek truth only when truth happens to be aligned with our professional goals. In mainstream academic economics, this happens relatively rarely.

Are there any researchers striving for truth as their ultimate and sole objective? Yes, there are a few who are irrational enough to seek truth without profit. There are a few for whom profit doesn't matter, because they have independent means or exceptionally thick skins. There are a few who arrive at truth late in life, perhaps from a guilty conscience.[2] But most of the time, those few who strive for truth are sidelined, if, as it often does, the search for truth runs against the dominant theory. Those who seek truth against professional status and personal profit in science will be crushed, mercilessly, by others without the same ethical scruples. They are also despised by the public for being losers. In most cases, the pursuit of truth for its own sake does not pay.

⊙ 2 ⊙

No Economy without Government

In the mainstream economic theory, the purpose of regulation—what economists often describe as *government intervention* in the market—is to "make the market work." Regulation plays a secondary role with respect to markets. In real life, there is no life without regulation. In real economies, there is no market without regulation and therefore no economy without government. Indeed, the difference between an "advanced" and a simple society is, at heart, a matter of the complexity, good design, and effectiveness of regulations. This is a fundamental difference between a biophysical and a "self-regulating" equilibrium theory; the former accounts for origins and adjustments; the latter does not.

Regulatory patterns observed from other organisms provide valuable lessons to human societies. In this chapter, we offer observations on the relationship between regulation and markets, between regulations and financial institutions, and on other policy issues. As a general observation, we argue that the mainstream economic theory of markets corresponds most closely to the physics of inanimate particles and the biology of the simplest organisms. For the study of advanced or complex social systems, this is inadequate, just as those simple theories do not describe the operation of complex living creatures.[1]

Although all organisms and organizations regulate their activities, the levels of regulations differ. Small simple organisms or organizations generally regulate less than large complex organisms or organizations.

Many small organisms obtain oxygen by diffusion through their body surfaces, without having any special respiratory organs and without circulating blood. Larger and more complex animals often have specialized surfaces for gas exchange and also a blood system to transport oxygen more rapidly than diffusion alone can provide. (Schmidt-Nielsen 1997, 16)

The above discussion shows that simple organisms can utilize a market for gas exchange, whereas complex and large animals need more-regulated systems. The theory of pure market exchange is an idealization of simple organisms and organizations. Large markets, such as a chain of supermarkets or the New York Stock Exchange, are always governed by complex regulations.

When certain materials are abundant, organisms and organizations often adopt a simple diffusion—or free-market—approach. For example, the absorption of oxygen in humans occurs inside the lungs through a simple diffusion process. This method works because oxygen density from the atmosphere is higher than the oxygen density inside the human body. When biological organisms need to move particles against the concentration gradient, active transport is required. An example of active transport is the sodium-potassium pump of the nerve cells. The pump transports the potassium ion from the exterior to the interior of the cell and the sodium ion in the opposite direction, against the concentration gradient. The purpose of this active transport is to maintain a gradient differential along the membranes of the nerve cells so that signals can transmit rapidly. Since active transport is a nonspontaneous process, energy must be supplied from the external sources and active regulation is required.

There are parallels in human societies. When merchandise diffuses from high-concentration places to low-concentration places, markets are often the best means. For example, many people will gather at grocery stores or supermarkets, where merchandise is of high concentration, and bring them to individual homes, where the merchandise concentration is low. People go to supermarkets expecting that what they buy will have passed through many levels of standard-setting and regulatory control. Getting quality products into the supermarkets is a concentrating process that requires a high level of regulation, whereas getting them from the supermarket to the home does not. People get on airplanes only if they believe that the airline industry, including air traffic control and flight safety, is carefully and effectively regulated.

Getting them from the airport back to their houses is much more lightly regulated. When developing new products that are previously nonexistent and hence of low concentration, regulations are often required and adopted. Resources are allocated to scientific research and development efforts through regulatory guidelines and company and public policies instead of through markets.

REGULATION AS A PRECONDITION OF COMPLEX SYSTEMS

Mainstream economic theory fosters a belief that the unregulated free market produces optimal results—and equilibria—most of the time. But what is optimal, and for whom? To understand this argument, we may consider optimality in lawn management. If lawns are left to free-market competition, weeds, such as dandelions, quickly dominate the lawns. For dandelions, free-market competition is indeed optimal. But most people prefer to regulate lawns with weed killers and lawnmowers to remove as many weeds as possible. This shows that the concept of *optimality* means different things to different parties. A result favored by one group of people—or plants in this example—is not necessarily favored by other groups. Regulation is, inevitably, a matter of choice and distribution.

In the mainstream economic theory, regulation is warranted only when the market is "imperfect." Yet all organisms and organizations regulate their internal environments. In general, "higher" animals, such as human beings, regulate their internal environment more than "lower" animals, such as jellyfish. Most people think human beings are more perfect than jellyfish. (The jellyfish may not agree, but they have not been consulted.) Similarly, in social organizations, "higher" professions—those with greater social status, more income, and job security, such as physicians—are more regulated than "lower" professions, such as cashiers, cooks, and waitstaff. People in "lower" professions may take just as much pride in their work, they may be more honest and reliable, but nevertheless it is the "higher" professions that dominate resource distribution in social systems. There is much effort, and great investment in education and training, to move from lower to higher professions. This is despite—or more accurately, because of—the higher level of regulation in the higher professions.

One important function of regulation is to maintain systems in desirable conditions. For example, as we have seen many times, the body temperature of warm-blooded animals is tightly regulated within a narrow range to keep their bodies functioning effectively. This regulation is highly energy intensive. The body temperature of cold-blooded animals is not continuously regulated with internal energy resources. This saves them energy expenditure, but at the same time, their bodies are not always at their most desirable temperature. Cold-blooded animals often bask under the Sun to increase their body temperature. When possible, many cold-blooded animals keep their body temperature at similar levels to that of warm-blooded animals (Gisolfi and Mora 2000). This shows that both warm-blooded and cold-blooded animals prefer similar internal environments. Warm-blooded animals regulate their internal environments more precisely, with higher resource expenditure. Cold-blooded animals regulate their internal environments less precisely, with lower resource expenditure.

Many organisms and organizations also regulate their external environments. As the most dominant species, human beings' regulatory efforts are most visible. We cut through mountains to build roads. We clear fields to erect houses. We apply chemicals to kill weeds. We burn the forests to graze cattle and plant grains. Human agricultural activities probably have the greatest regulatory effects on the landscape. Forests are replaced by fast-growing grasses, such as wheat, rice, and corn, to satisfy the high metabolic needs of human beings. It is likely that the spread of grasses in general has been regulated by mammals. Grasses first appeared on the Earth about sixty million years ago, around the time that dinosaurs went extinct (Kellogg 2001). The extinction of dinosaurs provided mammals with wide-open ecological niches, and mammals multiplied rapidly.

Mammals, as warm-blooded animals, have much higher metabolic rates than cold-blooded animals. They need more energy than the dinosaurs did. Fast-growing grasses can provide more energy than trees. Hence the spread of grasses will benefit mammals. Since mammals are more active than reptiles, they disturb the landscape more, which makes the environment more hospitable to fast-growing grasses than to slow-growing trees. In the past sixty million years, grasses have spread very fast and now cover approximately 20 to 40 percent of the Earth's land surface (Nunez 2022). If this speculation is correct, then mammals have played an active role in regulating the environment to benefit the spread of grasses, which in turn benefits the spread of mammals. But not all species benefit from the rise of mammals, including the most notorious among them, the human beings. The period of rising human domination is also one of the great periods of mass extinction in evolutionary history.

In human society, organizations often apply regulatory tools to improve their competitive edge. Large companies in an industry often propose regulations that are costly to implement, so as to drive out smaller competitors. Advanced states often develop and enforce tough patent laws to create monopolies, whereas technologically less advanced states prefer a freer flow of knowledge and easy acquisition of new technologies. Regulations are an important tool in market competition; indeed, one cannot separate regulation from market competition. For this reason, the very notion of "externalities" is suspect, as it focuses attention (and therefore regulation) on the effects of market relations on nonparticipants. But regulation is equally, or even more, a tool to shape the relationship between participants in the same general market.

The importance of regulation can be understood by studying the effect when part of an organism escapes regulation and turns into a free market. In medicine, this phenomenon is called *cancer*. "All cancer cells share one single, common feature: they have lost their ability to regulate DNA synthesis and cell division" (Clark 2008, 163).

> A cancerous tumor, for example, is born when one batch of cells no longer cooperates with others. By dividing endlessly, or by failing to die properly, these cells can destroy the necessary balance that makes a living individual person. Cancers break the rules that allow cells to cooperate with one another. Like bullies who break down highly cooperative societies, cancers behave in their own best interest until they kill their larger community, the human body. (Shubin 2008, 119)

Cells need to break several regulatory barriers to become free. Cancer tissues have to induce blood vessels to grow new branches into them so they can obtain resources for further growth (Clark 2008). By all accounts, cancer systems are highly innovative.

Although regulations are indispensable to organisms and organizations, the effects of regulatory systems can be very subtle. For example, immune systems will attack and destroy foreign objects. But some viruses evolve to integrate into host cells tightly or resemble a host's own tissues. When a host's immune systems attack these viruses, either immune systems have to work less vigorously or the systems will cause damage to the host's own tissues and organs (Clark 2008). Similarly, in human societies, activities that only benefit a small group of people are often more successful when they are integrated into activities that are essential to most people. Galbraith (2008), in *The Predator State*, describes a dominant form of politics in the United States as the effort by elite groups to function as predators (or parasites) on large public programs, such as Medicare, Medicaid, Social Security, and national defense. As they increase the costs of these programs—for example, by failing to control the price of pharmaceutical products or that of a weapons system—they weaken the programs as a whole.

Insights from biology are often mentioned in economic literature. However, it is often thought that the ideas from biology cannot be applied literally to human societies because there are supposed to be some fundamental differences between human beings and other biological organisms. We turn now to some of these arguments.

One major argument is that human activities are purpose-driven, whereas biological evolution is generated by random mutation. This argument confuses activities at different levels. Many animal behaviors are purpose-driven, and human biological evolutions are largely determined by genetic mutations as well (Jablonka and Lamb 2006; Cochran and Harpending 2008). Furthermore, research in biology has provided strong evidence to support the old idea that biological evolution is not entirely random. In a recent review article on evolutionary theory, Rando and Verstrepen state:

> According to classical evolutionary theory, phenotypic variation originates from random mutations that are independent of selective pressure. However, recent findings suggest that organisms have evolved mechanisms to influence the timing and genomic location of heritable variability. . . . Both Darwin and Lamarck, two of the founders of evolutionary theory, predicted evolution itself may favor the development of self-guiding mechanisms, maximizing variability where and when it

is most likely to yield positive changes while minimizing phenotypic variability when and where it is not needed. It is increasingly difficult to argue that their general idea of nonrandom evolution was entirely wrong. (Rando and Verstrepen 2007, 666)

A system that is more resourceful or wealthy has a stronger incentive to regulate the entry of new members to share its wealth. All organisms have skins or membranes that are selectively permeable. Through membranes, organisms absorb and retain resources and discharge wastes. Membranes of organisms also prevent the entry of foreign entities, such as bacteria and viruses, that would share their resources. In general, the more resourceful organizations or organisms are more exclusive and more tightly regulated than those that are less resourceful. As noted above, if we stand at the US-Mexico border crossing at San Diego, we will notice that there is virtually no control on the Mexican side. The US side, however, carefully checks the identity of travelers to limit entry only to selected people. Europe and Japan follow similar policies, whereas poor countries generally welcome visitors and immigrants from wealthier countries.

Wealthy countries not only regulate the flows at their borders more than poor countries; they also regulate their internal working environments more. High-paying jobs often require lengthy and costly training. But discount rates for individual persons are high (Ainslie 1992). If left to individual decisions, a substantial portion of people will leave school early. To ensure a uniformly high-standard working force, most wealthy countries regulate their education systems to require a minimum number of years of mandatory education. This mandatory educational system is a constant source of strain between children and their parents and their educators.

Many poor countries follow the example of wealthy countries to expand their education systems. Very often, the number of graduates greatly exceeds the number of job openings. This generates a potential source of instability and revolution, or the phenomenon of "brain drain," as the well-educated citizens of poor countries move to wealthier countries. Wealthy countries tend to encourage this phenomenon, since it gives them a ready-made source of qualified professionals, saving the cost of maintaining their own educational systems. Graduate schools in rich countries—especially the United States—are a well-known way for the US to acquire capable young people from other countries, who have already passed through all the earlier stages of education. Indeed, in recent decades the potential flow of qualified young people from somewhat poorer societies—notably in Asia—has been so large as to reduce the demand for and erode the quality of technical education within the United States.

Large firms and small firms often have different regulatory structures. Large firms have more strict policies in hiring employees than small firms. Once hired, new employees in large firms often go through lengthy training, whereas new employees in small firms go to work immediately. Although large firms are more regulated internally, they often prefer a less-regulated external environment. Small firms often prefer a more-regulated and protected business environment, because otherwise they will not survive in competition with larger firms. For example, small firms often lobby governments to hire local contractors in government projects, to avoid competition from large outside firms. The same argument applies to countries. Wealthy countries prefer free trade most of the time because free trade increases the market for their products. Poor countries often support infant-industry protections and import-substitution policies so their new industries can be shielded from competition from more established competitors (Stiglitz 2002).

Protection of new industries has often been criticized on the grounds that once government provides support to a new industry, it is difficult to decide when this industry should become independent. Similarly, and in line with biophysical arguments, it is difficult for parents to decide when their children should become independent. But parents would not expose infants to "market competition" immediately after they are born. The fact that we cannot time the optimal moment to let infants (or adolescents, as they eventually become) reach independence does not mean that infants should be abandoned while they are still infants. For the same reason, the difficulties involved in deciding when to end a protective policy does not discredit infant-industry policy itself.

In mainstream economic theories, it is sometimes argued that regulation exists to help overcome inefficiencies, and so more efficiency will reduce the need for regulation. Achieving efficiency is then left to the autonomous processes of technical change and the workings of the free market. In general, more-efficient systems require more, instead of less, regulation. For example, cars are more efficient in transporting people than bicycles, and car traffic is more regulated than bicycle traffic. High-voltage systems are more efficient in transmitting electricity than low-voltage systems, and the regulations on high-voltage systems are tougher. Nuclear power plants produce enormous amounts of electricity but require the eternal vigilance of cooling systems, maintenance crews, and radiation monitors. This relationship between efficiency and regulation is practically universal—and quite the opposite of the claim sometimes made by advocates of "free-market" theory. For this reason, the cult of "deregulation"—a key feature of mainstream economic policy since the 1970s—often leads toward disasters.

Although many economists preach the theory of unregulated free markets, the profession of economists itself, as well as other academic disciplines, is highly regulated by the tenure and promotion system. Only those contract lecturers who are not in the tenure system are subject to the perils of the free market. They get much lower pay than those inside the regulated tenure system and must worry constantly about their jobs. This shows again that privileged groups are highly regulated and are maintained by regulation, whereas in a freely competing market, most face both precarity and very low incomes.

FINANCIAL REGULATION AS A KEY CASE

Regulation and deregulation of financial institutions is a case of special importance, since banks, money, and credit lie at the core of capitalism. Finance is special also for another reason: it is about money and nothing else. In medicine, there is an objective standard of success: Did the patient recover, or not? In engineering, similarly: Did the bridge hold up? Did the spacecraft fly and land as projected? These matters are intertwined with business and moneymaking, but they are linked to matters that are measured by other yardsticks. In finance, the only yardstick is money itself, and for this reason, effective regulation is especially important. That is because financial systems run on trust, and trust depends on confidence in the quality of regulations.

In most business transactions, such as in retail, service and payment occur simultaneously. At the checkout counter of a grocery store, customers pay cash (or run a debit card) and get groceries. In the latter case, the bank debits their deposit balance immediately, and that is the beginning and the end of the transaction. So long as the seller can check to see that the payment is approved, there is no need for any outside party to play a role.

But in other business transactions, and especially in financial services, there is often a time gap between payment and service. In insurance, one pays premiums regularly but gets service only when insured-for incidents occur. With pension funds, one often starts paying while in one's twenties, although benefits begin four decades later. Because of the large time gap, uncertainty is high, and the level of trust is low. To reduce uncertainty and build up trust, regulations, guarantees, and secondary insurance by governments—which are more stable and long-lasting than individual businesses—are required to protect individuals and companies involved in long-term transactions. Conversely, in a highly regulated financial system, trust in the financial system is high and people are willing to invest their money in such systems.

With the increase of wealth under asset management (retirement accounts, pensions, endowments), the profit potential of financial services increases as well. However, in a highly regulated financial system, much of the short-term profit potential cannot be realized—it is the purpose of regulations to protect weaker players from exploitation. Therefore, for many years, the US financial system was considered overregulated by many financial practitioners. At the same time, many foreign assets flowed into the US financial system because of the safety of a highly regulated system, and this became a major source of the power of the US dollar, and of the United States itself, in the world economy.

The tremendous wealth managed by the US financial system generated great political pressure to deregulate the sector. Deregulation became a major theme in economics research, which focused on the costs of regulation, as against the efficiencies of an unregulated financial market. "Big Bang" deregulation was proposed, and, in some countries, it was put into effect. This placed competitive pressure on other countries to follow suit.

When the US financial system finally was deregulated, beginning in the late 1970s and cumulating in the 1990s and the subsequent decade, the trust that was accumulated over many years of the regulation was still intact. But transactions allowed in a deregulated environment that would have been prohibited by regulations were greatly increased. This led to much higher incomes for financial operators and higher profits for financial institutions, which seemed to confirm that a deregulated financial system is superior to a highly regulated one. The illusion lasted until the crisis hit in the fall of 2007 and spring of 2008. By then, it was too late.

Sadly, the time horizons for a healthy financial system and for a healthy income for financiers are very different. Financial contracts often last many years. A mortgage contract may last thirty years (although most thirty-year mortgages don't last that long). Bonuses to individual employees in finance, however, are distributed every year. When mortgages are securitized, the value of a thirty-year contract is reflected in a single transaction. There is a corresponding need to prop up the market value of the mortgage in the short run so that annual bonuses for the bankers involved will be high. This happened in the middle of the first decade of the twenty-first century.

Inevitably, these overvalued mortgages would be devalued at some point. Although there are still nominally "independent" third parties, such as government regulators and the rating agencies, by around 2005 they had become wholly complicit in this game and shared the incentives of the financial industry. As a result, expert voices were highly uniform as well, and only so-called nonexperts with no appreciable stake in the system—plus a few experienced past regulators with principles intact—could see accurately what was about to happen. But of course, by definition, a nonexpert is an outsider who lacks influence over regulatory and deregulatory decisions. Outsiders and "nonexperts" have the Cassandra problem: they may be right, but they will not be believed.

The differential of time horizons between individuals and institutions is also reflected inside each financial institution. At first, many of the trades that salespeople started, or traders proposed, were rejected by risk managers. From the point of view of salespeople and traders, the restrictions imposed by the risk managers greatly reduced the profit for the bank and for themselves. But from the bank's point of view, allowing unsound trades to be executed jeopardized the long-term prospects of the bank. There is a constant tension between the sales force on one side and the risk managers on the other.

In a financial institution where credit and market risk regulations are rigorously enforced, the actual risk is small. To keep warning against risk looks like crying wolf when there is no wolf. In the end, the principle of risk management was traded away for short-term profit, and those who insisted on speaking out were muffled or sent packing. When the wolf arrived, there was no one there to give a warning. The fact that these are well-known metaphors, familiar to children for hundreds of years, shows that human societies are built on biophysical principles. It takes a great deal of hard instruction in mainstream general equilibrium economics to create a caste of specialists who can pretend to be unaware of the dangers of deregulation.

The 2008 financial crisis is often described as the result of deregulation of the financial system. The reality is more subtle and even more dangerous. If finance were truly "deregulated," the financial system as we know it would no longer exist at all, since the institutions would have failed in 2008 if not before. What we have is a move toward a predatory form of regulation (Galbraith 2008) in which the regulators bring the power of the state to the support of the financial sector while failing to protect the public, as regulations were once designed to do. This was accomplished by inserting doctrines of free-market valuation into the regulatory structures. In this way, finance itself came to control the terms of its own regulation.

Thus, while regulations were still present, the regulation of the financial institutions moved toward a market-based measurement from an accounting-based measurement of the value of assets held by regulated institutions. That is, regulators came to accept the valuations of the market. This allowed financial institutions to operate at higher leverage, which enhances the reported profits of financial institutions. But it also subjected financial institutions to more serious risks in a downturn (Chen 2003).

An important development in the financial industry in the past several decades is the gradual reintegration of commercial banking and investment banking. This put risky trading activities under the same protective umbrella that used to cover unsophisticated individual depositors only. This extension of regulatory privilege, enabling sophisticated financial institutions to engage in highly leveraged activities, "guaranteed record profits in the early years . . . It also makes it inevitable that there's going to be a disaster down the road" (Black 2009).[2]

The original intention of government guarantees was to protect the safety of ordinary bank deposits. But in 1999, with the repeal of the Glass-Steagall law in the United States, government guarantees were extended from commercial loans to trading activities; banks engaged in risky trading and securitization could effectively rely on the federal deposit insurance system and on the discount window of the Federal Reserve. Because of the extension of government guarantees, these banks enjoyed large credit lines in speculative trading activities, which enabled them to make large profits with little effort. In effect, governments became the largest enablers and protectors of speculation. As a result, financial institutions became free to seek activities with the highest upside potential, which are often the same activities with the highest downside potential. Therefore, going a step beyond Minsky (2008), government support destabilized, instead of stabilizing, the financial markets and the whole society. The risk of financial meltdowns was transferred in an ultimate sense to the state itself, to be borne, finally, by society at large.

In finance, diversification and liquidity are generally regarded as positive. However:

> Consider the chemical industry of forty years ago, back when such pollutants as PCBs were dumped into the air and water with little or no regulation. For years, the mantra of the industry was "the solution to pollution is dilution." Mixing toxins with vast quantities of air and water was supposed to neutralize them. Many decades later, with our plagues of hermaphrodite frogs, poisoned ground water, and mysterious cancers, the mistake in that logic is plain. Modern bankers, however, have carried this mistake into the world of finance. (Janszen 2008, 43)

Modern bankers bundle illiquid mortgages (and other debts) into liquid mortgage-backed securities (and collateralized loan obligations) and distribute these securities to diverse investors. With diversification and liquidity, risks are diluted. As a result, society accumulates large amounts of risk without feeling particularly alarmed. A major cause of the 2008 financial crisis was the widespread distribution of toxic assets such as securities backed by low-quality mortgages. If government or government-linked agencies were to stop guaranteeing mortgages, this would reduce the liquidity of mortgage-backed securities. Financial institutions would then have to hold most of their mortgages to term, bearing the risks themselves. There would be less incentive to generate toxic assets—though there would also be fewer mortgages. This is similar to the chemical industry. If companies are required to clean up the pollutants they generate, there is much less incentive to make otherwise profitable products. Right now, it is up to individuals to become "financially literate." However, in the first years of the twenty-first century, "the shareholders themselves—the millions of lumpen pseudo-investors who own mutual funds . . . had neither the time, the money, nor the training to be real capitalists; they were merely chumps for Wall Street" (Bonner and Wiggin 2006, 214). The only institution capable of preventing disaster was the government—and the government deliberately chose not to do the job.

Is it possible to have a financial system that is reasonably stable and effective in the service of larger social objectives? Of course. But it requires a simplified structure and effective regulation of each element of the system, which (in turn) means that financial systems must be effectively confined within the jurisdiction of an independent regulator. If the sector is going to be a fixed cost—or public utility—then it is essential to keep the size of that cost down to the minimum necessary for smooth operations. In the Great Depression, the United States established such a system and operated it with considerable success for about forty years. There were no financial crises or bank failures in that interval. Similarly, in Europe after the Second World War, national financial systems were closely tailored to the needs of reconstruction, industry, housing, and public welfare. But with the recovery, these needs became less pressing, the financial institutions themselves reasserted their power, and financial markets developed across national boundaries and therefore escaped effective regulation. The cost escalated. An era of booms, busts, and crises has followed, with no end in sight. When finance goes international, the essential by-product of effective regulation—trust—disappears from view.

INTEREST RATES ARE A REGULATORY DEVICE

Interest rates are a powerful regulatory device. When recessions occur, the market response of banks would be to increase interest rates to compensate for the increase in default risk. Higher interest rates would push the economy into deeper recession. Central banks, which are regulatory bodies, then lower interest rates to reverse the slowdown of economic activity.

After the burst of the internet bubble in the year 2000, regulatory bodies lowered interest rates to generate new bubbles to offset the bursting of the old bubbles. In the aftermath, housing prices and commodity prices rose sharply. High commodity prices (which were very good for resource-producing countries) eventually slowed down overall economic activity in the United States. This caused the reversal of housing prices, which in turn exposed the large-scale weakness of subprime and even prime mortgages. The housing bubble and commodity bubble proved to be even bigger than the internet bubble. The inevitable burst brought the North American economy to its worst recession since the Great Depression. And then the cycle started up again with a new round of very low interest rates, which continued through the COVID-19 pandemic. This period became known, to some analysts, as the "everything bubble" (Curran and Anstey 2021).

Conventional economic theory obscures the regulatory power of central banks over interest rates. The classical theory of interest rates was (and is) called the theory of loanable funds. The idea is rooted in supply and demand, with the supply of savings balanced against the demand for investment, and the price of funds that resulted being the prevailing rate of interest. The supply of savings is, essentially, a scarce resource, and the demand for investment reflects the expected profit, or utility, from mobilizing this resource and converting savings into construction or the purchases of equipment or inventories. This theory is still to be found in many textbooks and in the thinking of many mainstream economists. But there is no actual market in which savings and investment are determined by a pricing mechanism. The classical theory operates in an institutional never-never land, in which banks and the central bank have no reason to exist.

John Maynard Keynes offered what is, essentially, a utility theory of the interest rate, which he called liquidity preference. Keynes situated the determination of the interest rate in the desire of those who hold financial assets to keep a certain portion of their holdings in the most liquid form—ready money—so they can protect themselves against uncertainties and take advantage of opportunities that may arise in financial and other markets as economic conditions change. The interest rate associated with a bond of a given maturity, in that case, is the reward necessary to induce a potential investor to relin-quish liquidity and make her holdings available—it is the measure of the degree of liquidity preference. Keynes's theory had big advantages over the loanable-funds theory, for two reasons. It describes an ac-tual market—the money market—and not a hypothetical abstraction represented only by supply and demand curves. And it accounts in a clear-cut way for the normal pattern of interest rates, which are usually higher for long-dated financial instruments with comparable degrees of risk. This is known as the *term structure*.

In the modern world, however, neither loanable funds nor liquid-ity preference is necessary, or especially useful, to determine the *base* interest rate in the monetary system, which is the short-term rate on the most secure assets, namely reserves held by the banking system at the central bank, or (almost equivalently) the short-term bills issued by the Treasury. That rate is simply set, by fiat, by the central bank. It is an administered price, and it takes exactly the value that central bank-ers decide. Since the central bank in the United States—the Federal Reserve—now pays interest on reserves (and has done since 2009, just after the financial crisis), this rate is essentially a channel for passing income from the government to the banks, just as the civil-service wage structure is a channel for passing income to civil servants. When a central bank raises this rate, as the Federal Reserve did in 2022 and 2023, it is directly raising the return to financial capital and the income of the banks. No scarcity or utility is involved.

This base interest rate is primarily a regulatory and distributional tool. The tool is used, first and foremost, to affect the incomes and profits of the banking sector, the distribution of income between the financial sector and the rest of the economy, and the level of activity in sectors that rely on credit to function, including especially investment and construction. It also is used to influence the value of a nation's cur-rency in relation to those of other countries, since short-term interest rates have a strong influence on the disposition of funds around the world. Looking at the interest rate in this way greatly simplifies and demystifies the conduct of monetary policy, which the conventional theory very conveniently obscures.

Many economists, otherwise devoted to free markets, advocate for the manipulation of interest rates to "stimulate growth" or to "control inflation." They do so because the power to set interest rates is very great and very concentrated in just a few hands—often enough, the hands of professional economists. It is a power that is cheap to use. However, control of interest rates is a very crude form of regulation. It does not help to ensure that new loans are taken out for purposes that generate wide social benefits over the long run. It does not help to protect against sharp practices or fraud. It does not reduce the risk that there will be a financial crisis later on. To do those things requires regulatory measures that are much more complex and costly, which necessarily limit the growth rate that, on the surface, cutting interest rates can achieve. Likewise, to control inflation by raising the interest rate is much easier than to fix all the conflicts and resource problems that lie behind inflation, and it imposes costs that fall, through recession and unemployment, on weak and vulnerable people who have little political clout. That free-market economists favor manipulation of interest rates and oppose more complex but potentially effective financial regulation tells us, among other things, that those economists have short time horizons. The same can be said about many people who work in the financial sector.

REGULATION AND INEQUALITY

We have discussed inequality as an artifact of boundaries and a necessary feature of all life systems. However, though inequality is necessary, it must also be kept under control. Safety and resilience require that the inequality that is permitted not become too extreme. Thus, the degree of inequality is properly an important element of regulatory concern.

For the designers of a mechanical or, say, electrical system, the choice of the level of inequality depends on the trade-off between efficiency and maintenance costs. In North America, electric voltage in residential areas is 110 V, whereas in most other parts of the world, it is 220 V. To carry the same amount of electric energy in a 110 V system requires much thicker wire than in a 220 V system. However, when accidents occur, 110 V causes less shock than 220 V. In a system with abundant natural resources, such as North America, we often choose options that are safer but less resource efficient. In systems with scarce natural resources, we often choose more resource-efficient but riskier options.

There is a parallel in social systems. In a social system that controls more resources, the internal inequality is often low. Low inequality may be less efficient, but it is much safer. For this reason, dominant parties of a society do not necessarily hope to increase inequality all the time. Rich societies can afford to be relatively egalitarian, and in fact wealthy countries are systematically more equal than poor countries (Galbraith 2016). Rich countries can use abundant resources as "energy slaves"—so that humans can live in relative equality and with the security and quality of life that equality makes possible. Indeed, rich countries have elaborate wage structures that are determined by social and political decisions, not in markets (Galbraith 1998). This is the basis of the social element in a theory of value, which we will discuss later. Rich societies purchase internal resilience and safety through institutions that limit and mitigate inequalities—not through the stasis of equilibrium, but with a tolerated gradient of resource distribution, within which people move up and down all the time.

In a social system that controls fewer resources, the internal inequality is often high. In such a system, efficiency is very high for the elites, the designers of the system. They can afford many servants, retainers, and cheap factory hands. Their living standards are higher—often much higher—than those of wealthy people in richer countries. The living standards of the poor are lower—much lower—than those of poor people in richer countries. The protections of social valuation do not apply. However, such systems also have a higher probability of experiencing revolts, rebellions, and revolution. Elites in poor societies usually live behind high walls and employ security guards—sometimes even private armies. This is rarely necessary in New York or London.

Measures to limit inequalities within a national community are necessary to preserve the concept of a national community—of a common social system to which all members (qualified persons, or citizens) have a plausible degree of access. These pressures take the form of taxes—limiting accumulations—and of social insurance, public education, and other common benefits paid from a common fund, as well as the wage structure. Highly unequal institutions are called upon to make a show of supporting this goal. Prestigious universities and big corporations are pressured to maintain affirmative-action programs and forbidden to discriminate by race or gender. Thus, the boundaries of subnational entities are infringed, or restricted, to help preserve the substance, or at least the impression, of a larger national equality. Without that, a society will tend to disintegrate into an openly predatory system dominated by oligarchs and favoring some ethnic or racial groups over others, as well as men over women. Oligarchs—if they are wise—often prefer to operate in the shadows, so that the extent to which they enjoy exclusive wealth, privileges, and power is not widely visible to lesser members of the same community.

It requires higher fixed cost to maintain a more equal society. With higher fixed investment, there is the possibility of stability and endurance. Fixed investments such as railroads and highways and parks and libraries are shared by the whole society; they reduce inequality, but they are costly to maintain. When the British Empire was expanding rapidly in the nineteenth century, it built many public works and abolished slavery, an extreme form of inequality. By adopting a less unequal social system internally, Britain was able to maintain and expand a huge empire with relatively little cost and huge profit. Victorian Britain issued bonds, called consols, that were to be paid in perpetuity and never redeemed (they were, eventually, bought back and retired). The British Empire expected to last forever. Similarly, great egalitarian movements in the United States, such as the New Deal and Great Society, combined public investments in energy, transportation, public administration, and education with comprehensive social insurance. These were programs designed to create a society that would last, and dominate the world economy, for a long time.

The inequality of a system thus depends in part on how long the dominant parties expect the system to last. For an unequal system to last, the level of inequality cannot be too extreme. This applies both in nature and in human societies. When we go fishing, we hope to have some inequality over fish. But not too much. For this reason, we use a line to hook fish—this gives the fish a sporting chance. A fishing net would be more efficient. However, if everyone were allowed to use fishing nets to an unlimited degree in rivers, lakes, and oceans, the fish population would decline rapidly. When the dominant parties expect the system to end soon, the inequality of the social system tends to increase so that dominant parties can extract more profits while the system lasts. It may be that when a society is governed largely by older people, the tolerance for inequality goes up as time horizons shorten. When Ronald Reagan became president of the United States in 1981, he was both the most inegalitarian modern president and the oldest president in the United States to that date. There have been other elderly presidents since.

CONCLUDING REMARKS

Economic activities are like biological and mechanical activities in two critical respects. First, as argued in chapter 1, they are necessarily nonequilibrium processes, prone to instability and breakdown as they become larger and more powerful. Second, they require regulation, and therefore government, to exist in the first place and to function after they are created. Effective regulation permits them to grow and succeed, even on a large scale, and even in complex and opaque, long-lasting activities such as credit, debt, and pension systems. Effective and trustworthy regulation is equally important to win acceptance for complex technologies and networks, and for medical interventions such as vaccination, as the COVID-19 pandemic showed. But regulation is inherently controversial, and it inherently fosters its own opposition. The more successful it is, the more it contains the seeds of its own erosion and eventual demise. This is another demonstration of nonequilibrium in the real world.

Theories of Value in Economics

Value theory forms the foundation of economic theory. Foundations are vital, but they are not generally inspected very often. Most of the time, value theory is of little concern to (mainstream) economists, because they generally suppose it to be completely resolved. But schools in economics are distinguished by different ideas about value, and major shifts in economic thinking have begun with the emergence of a new understanding. For example, John Stuart Mill (1871) understood value to be based on labor and asserted that he had left nothing in the laws of value for any future economist to clear up. This was just as William Stanley Jevons and others were developing a marginal utility theory of value, which became the core of neoclassical economics.

According to Leon Walras (1873), the founder of general equilibrium theory, there are three main theories of value: labor theory, utility theory, and scarcity theory. Walras argued that value is a function of scarcity. He said that it is too broad to define utility as value, since many things with high utility, such as oxygen, have little or no economic value. Likewise, it is too narrow to define labor as value, for many things that take little labor have high value. To take a modern example, although oil produced in Alberta takes much more labor than oil produced in Saudi Arabia, Alberta oil is not more expensive than Saudi oil. In classical political economy, additional concepts such as rent were invoked to explain this phenomenon. This made the labor theory of value less general and the overall theory more complex.

If economics is the study of the allocation of scarce resources to their best uses, as declared by Lionel Robbins (1935), then a scarcity theory of value is better aligned with the goal of economics than the marginal utility theory. Yet Walras's scarcity theory of value did not become the standard theory in economics. Instead, the marginal utility theory proposed by Jevons and others became the standard. Utility places the consumer, rather than the producer, at the core of economic reasoning, and it makes the market, rather than the business firm, the key institution.

In this chapter, we discuss the three classical schools of value theory: labor, utility, scarcity. At the end we take up a question: Which of these theories underpins our system of national income accounts? The perhaps surprising answer is that none of them do, in a fully consistent way, raising some important questions about the meaning and appropriate uses of those accounts. Along the way, we will begin to make our case for a scarcity theory of value tied to basic life principles, limited by government and regulation, yet realistic enough to account for many observed phenomena in actual economies. We call this an *entropy theory of value*. In the next chapter, we present such a theory.

LABOR: RICARDO, MARX, SRAFFA, PASINETTI

Adam Smith, writing in the mid-eighteenth century and publishing in the famous year of 1776, was aware that the "wealth of nations" consisted, as he put it, of "the necessaries and conveniences" produced each year by the laboring people of the nation. This was, if not an entirely new idea, a powerful departure from the notion that wealth was an accumulation of treasures—say the royal hoards stored in customs houses or the Tower of London, earned by trading surpluses or by pillage. Wealth, to Smith, consisted in the capacity to produce—a capacity that must be renewed, season after season, to give the whole population the chance of a decent and contented life, and to give their collective form, the nation, a place of power and prominence in the world.

But if one looks for a clear-cut theory of value in Smith's *Wealth of Nations*, it's not so easy to find. His chapter on wages reads like an encyclopedia of specific types of work and rationalizations about how different occupations are paid. Miners, he said, must be paid well because their work is dangerous; professors and priests can be paid poorly because they are compensated, in part, by prestige. Long apprenticeships exist to maintain the monopoly power of master artisans. And on and on. There are many different types of labor, for Smith, and they are not directly comparable, so he deployed his keen powers of observation to explain the value—so to speak—of each one.

David Ricardo followed Smith by about thirty eventful years. Ricardo, a stockbroker, had (unlike Smith) a mathematical or at least arithmetic bent; his work is full of numerical examples and illustrations, perhaps mostly fanciful rather than drawn from observation. But Ricardo was much more deeply ensconced in the emerging industrial age than Smith was. To him, labor was a far simpler thing, having much less to do with the specific skills, tools, and social standing of the laboring person. For Ricardo, the prototype of the worker was the factory hand: a person who works in a facility owned by someone else, at a rhythm controlled by foremen and clocks, with tools provided by someone else, for stipulated hours and at a stipulated rate of pay. Ricardo could more easily envision the labor-hour as the foundation of value in the eventual product.

Something else had happened between Smith and Ricardo, and that was the French Revolution and the introduction in 1799 of the metric system. Although there had been in England policies to standardize weights and measures before that (and England has not, to this day, adopted the metric system!), the French revolutionaries were ambitious. For them, the meter—a metal stick preserved under stable atmospheric conditions in a Paris vault—was an *invariable* measure—supposedly one-ten-millionth of the distance from the equator to the pole. With the metric system, much of economic, mechanical, construction, and scientific life could be standardized. Standardization assisted the coordination of production and trade on the national and even international levels.

It was in this spirit that Ricardo proposed a fixed unit of pure labor—unadorned by any specific training, skill, or prestige—as the invariable standard of economic value. Different types of labor, if their existence need be conceded, could be accommodated in this scheme as multiples of the basic unit; John Maynard Keynes would later refer to these as "efficiency units" of labor. Different levels of productive efficiency using different technologies could likewise be accommodated by stretching the notion of *rent*, which Ricardo explained was due to differences in the productive power of different parcels of land. Given an efficient process using basic labor, Ricardo argued that the value of the final output—cotton textiles or forged iron, say—would be proportional to its cost in terms of labor hours. As technology improved, the quantity and quality of a product might get better. But its value would decline since less labor would be involved in the production of any one unit. This was the essence of the labor theory of value.

Ricardo did not feel a need to explain what, in his system, workers would be paid. For that, he had the work of his friend and epistolary sparring partner, Thomas Robert Malthus. Malthus in 1798 had published a famous book, *An Essay on the Principle of Population*, which resolved the matter so far as Ricardo was concerned. Workers' pay would tend, inevitably, to the minimum, that would support their subsistence and the reproduction of the labor force. Any more than that would lead to loose moral behavior, which would lead to population growth, which would create more mouths to feed from a given food supply and drive the "real wage" back to the subsistence level. Efforts to raise the living standards for workers, or to alleviate the miseries of the poor, were inevitably futile. This was a very convenient view for those who were not workers—for the handful who controlled economic profits and land rents.

Karl Marx picked up the threads of Ricardo's analysis, which over the intervening half century had become the established doctrine of what was then mainstream political economy. Marx despised the harsh fatalism and crude "biodeterminism" of Malthus and Ricardo. He sought instead an explanation for low wages in the internal dynamics of the capitalist competition. In *Capital* (1867), he zeroed in on the critical anomaly. If labor produced value, and the capitalist did not, why then did the workers enjoy such a small share of the value of their output? This was indeed a question fraught with revolutionary potential. To analyze it, Marx gives us the concept of the labor-time socially necessary to keep the laborer on the job. How many hours of work per day does it take to produce the means of subsistence—the "socially necessary labor time"—allotted to the workers themselves? In his chapter on "The Working Day," Marx demonstrates how this number can be driven down, in relation to the total number of hours that the worker must work to be paid at all.

Suppose that a worker must work three hours to produce the value-equivalent of his own means of subsistence. If the working day is ten hours, Marx reasoned, then the value of seven hours is *surplus value*—appropriated by the owner of the shop, factory, or other business. The ratio, $7/3$, is the ratio of surplus value (s/v)—and the goal of the capitalist is to increase this ratio as much as possible. If, for example, the working day can be extended to twelve hours, the ratio becomes $9/3$. If women and children can be hired for less—say, just two hours' worth of labor in their subsistence—it becomes $10/2$. If a new technology doubles the productivity of the system, it becomes $11/1$, and so on. Conversely, movements against child labor, for an eight-hour working day, and for weekends—all can be seen as aimed at reducing the ratio of surplus value and bringing the degree of exploitation under control. All of these were major objectives of the early trade-union movements, and in some cases the struggles continue to this day.

Marx's theory of surplus value fed the revolutionary spirit in the workers' organizations of the industrial era. For this reason, it made the labor theory of value into a problem for the dominant classes. A theory of exploitation, class conflict, the immiseration of the proletariat, and of eventual communist revolution was not, after all, comfortable material for scholarly discussions or the education of the well-bred young. So once Malthus and his smug complacencies had been challenged by Marx, it was hard for political reasons to stick with a labor theory of value.

But there were other difficulties as well. What was the relationship, in the labor theory, of value to price? How did machinery figure into the relationship? In a world of pure labor, with no machines, we could work out a system where (in principle) I trade the fruits of my hours of production for yours. In the Garden of Eden, where labor consists of picking apples (and other fruits), this is a reasonable basis for exchange. But after the Fall, it isn't. All labor requires tools, and tools are the product of prior labor, which bleed their value into the current products over time. But how do we make this past, "dead" labor comparable to the work now going on? And who is entitled to own the contribution of that past labor?

This is called the transformation problem, and while Marx wrestled with it in the later volumes of *Capital*, it was (so many have said) beyond his powers to give a fully satisfactory solution. And so, in addition to the political issues, there was a "scientific" or at least mathematical justification for abandoning the labor theory of value.

To be fair, the labor theory was never entirely abandoned. In 1960, an Italian economist at Cambridge, Piero Sraffa, published a small book called *Production of Commodities by Means of Commodities*, of which drafts had been circulating since the late 1920s. Sraffa's work specified the precise meaning of an "invariant standard" of labor content, involving a construct called the standard commodity, a hybrid unit of output that forms the basis of the consumption basket of the working class. Building on the insights and arguments of Sraffa, a school of Cambridge economists led by Luigi Pasinetti (1981) came to argue that prices of produced consumer goods (as distinct from prestige objects and real estate) are, indeed, determined by labor costs and not by the interplay of supply and demand. But by the time Sraffa and Pasinetti made their case, the mainstream had long abandoned the labor value theory in favor of a theory based on utility. In this vision, the consumer takes over from the producer as the source of economic value.

UTILITY: JEVONS, MARSHALL, AND MORE ON ARROW-DEBREU

Jevons (1871) presented an elegant argument for the marginal utility theory in an economy of two persons. At equilibrium, he argued, marginal utilities are equalized; each person gets the same level of satisfaction from the ownership of the last unit of each good. This equalized marginal utility translates into the exchange value between two goods. Further, at the allocation or level of exchange where marginal utilities are equalized, total utility reaches a maximum. This is a very appealing property. Further, Jevons was able to derive a beautiful mathematical expression for the marginal utility theory of value. He observed, "The Laws of Exchange are found to resemble the Laws of Equilibrium of a lever as determined by the principle of virtual velocities" (Jevons 1871, vii). The simplicity of this metaphor was very appealing.

Jevons's derivation impressed many later economists. However, Jevons's derivation cannot be satisfactorily extended to an economy with many people. In a two-person economy, prices can be established by bargaining. Each person therefore withholds agreement until they are satisfied that total utility cannot be improved; this is the point at which prices are such that marginal utilities are equalized across both persons and all goods. But in larger economies, such as in a supermarket, customers don't bargain individually, and they don't all buy at the same time. The prices are fixed by the stores; the customer has no direct bargaining power with the store or with other customers. The best she can do is to allocate her own budget and purchases optimally for her, given the prices set by the store. If the store responds eventually, say by cutting prices on unsold inventory or raising them after a rush, that happens after some customers have made their purchases, or declined to purchase, and gone home. There are few refunds or second chances.

To deal with this situation, a new term, *Pareto optimality*, was created to replace simple optimality. Pareto optimality does not require total utility to be at a maximum, but only that it be impossible to make one person better off without making some other person worse off. It is a very conservative criterion, since it disapproves of all efforts to redistribute income or wealth, even if doing so would increase the total utility of the population.

Alfred Marshall, author of the first "modern" textbook on principles of economics, is broadly credited with introducing the framework of supply and demand as the formal foundation of a theory of exchange. Marshall's theory is a utility or marginal utility theory. In each market, consumers spend up to the point where the utility of an extra unit purchased is just offset, for the marginal consumer, by the price. In each market, sellers (producers) offer their wares up to the point where the price just offsets the disutility, or effort (and expense) of bringing that extra unit to market. The result of adding up the preferences of consumers is a downward-sloping demand curve—so that as prices fall, more is demanded—and an upward-sloping supply curve. The point of balance, or intersection of supply and demand, gives the price and quantity (for each commodity) that can be produced without leaving unsold products or unsatisfied customers.

Marshall's theory had a powerful appeal—the appeal of equilibrium. Which it retains, because for most students of economics even now, supply and demand are the foundations of what they absorb from a class in economics. The theory embeds the idea that a given set of goods and services sell at a given price, in a given quantity, which can be reproduced over time. The theory also covered the case of wages and employment, suggesting that there need be no involuntary unemployment if workers are willing to cut their pay to make themselves more attractive. This added an additional element of appeal to employers, placing the burden and blame for unemployment on the stubbornness of the workers. Marshall's theory was, however, relatively unsophisticated from a mathematical standpoint, and so it was not the last word; already in the 1920s Sraffa, a rigorous logician, argued that it should be abandoned. Formalization and rigor would come only after the Second World War.

The marginal utility theory of value was formalized by Kenneth Arrow and Gerard Debreu (1954) and systematically represented by Debreu's famous book *Theory of Value: An Axiomatic Analysis of Economic Equilibrium* (Debreu 1959). Arrow and Debreu set out to define the conditions under which perfect competition and rational behavior would yield a competitive general equilibrium in a model economy. Their work signaled the triumph of formal mathematics as the dominant language of economic theory and of the model of perfect competition as the starting point for high-level economic theorizing.

The Arrow-Debreu model is a static model by design. All possible production modes and all commodities are available at the outset. A maximization process from producers and consumers leads to a choice of technique and to an equilibrium point. This gives a formal justification of the equilibrium theory. Arrow and Debreu specify the conditions under which a perfectly competitive equilibrium will occur, and (as for Marshall) this is the central appeal of their theory.

Not everyone was overwhelmed. In a review of Debreu's *Theory of Value*, Martin Shubik wrote:

> It represents a tidying up of old work and problems which will not necessarily provide a stepping-stone for new work . . . I suggest that further development of economic theory will rest heavily upon the utilization and exploration of assumptions radically different from those employed in this work . . . Economics is not mathematics. Rigour is a necessary but not a sufficient condition for a valuable contribution to economic theory. (Shubik 1961)

As an economic theory, the Arrow-Debreu model has little relevance to reality, as we and many others have observed (Shubik 1961; Weintraub 2002; Düppe 2012; Shiozawa 2016; Móczár 2020). Arrow and Debreu were very aware of that. Many years after the Arrow-Debreu model became established as the foundation of economic theory, Debreu (1991) offered a lengthy justification for the detachment of economic theory from economic reality. Arrow (1972) defended the model on the ground that there is no genuine alternative model. However, Arrow himself had been actively looking for a "genuine alternative model" (Arrow 1973).

Given that the marginal utility theory of Arrow and Debreu was (and is) highly unrealistic, built on extremely restrictive assumptions not entirely satisfactory even to Arrow himself, how did it come to dominate mainstream economic theory? This has little or nothing to do with realism or applicability and much to do with the sociology, culture, and politics of the economics profession in the second half of the twentieth century.

First, as Shubik suggests, and as a matter of mathematics, the Arrow-Debreu model is quite rigorous. It is an axiomatic theory. Debreu (1983) summarized the benefits of axiomatization:

> Axiomatization, by insisting on mathematical rigor, has repeatedly led economists to a deeper understanding of the problems they were studying, and to the use of mathematical techniques that fitted those problems better. It has established secure bases from which exploration could start in new directions. It has freed researchers from the necessity of questioning the work of their predecessors in every detail. Rigor undoubtedly fulfills an intellectual need of many contemporary economic theorists, who therefore seek it for its own sake, but it is also an attribute of a theory that is an effective thinking tool.
>
> Two other major attributes of an effective theory are simplicity and generality. Again, their aesthetic appeal suffices to make them desirable ends in themselves for the designer of a theory. But their value to the scientific community goes far beyond aesthetics. Simplicity makes a theory usable by a great number of research workers. Generality makes it applicable to a broad class of problems.
>
> In yet another manner, the axiomatization of economic theory has helped its practitioners by making available to them the superbly efficient language of mathematics. It has permitted them to communicate with each other, and to think, with a great economy of means. At the same time, the dialogue between economists and mathematicians has become more intense. (Debreu 1983, 99)

Debreu's assessment of the values of rigor and axiomatization are widely accepted by economists; they underpin the discipline of the academic training required to become a professional economist at a high level. Yet not all mathematical economists agree. Roy Weintraub provided a different perspective of axiomatization of economic theory in his book *How Economics Became Mathematical Science*. Weintraub had the following comment on *The Theory of Value*, the definitive volume on the Arrow-Debreu model: "*Theory of Value*... is... a very well-arranged cemetery with a beautiful array of tombstones" (Weintraub 2002, 123). According to Weintraub, the rigorous mathematical models, represented by the Arrow-Debreu model, turn economists into "desiccated robots" (Weintraub 2002, 246).

If a theory is largely consistent with reality, it will be beneficial that axiomatization "has freed researchers from the necessity of questioning the work of their predecessors in every detail." However, the Arrow-Debreu model is highly detached from reality, and so "axiomatization, by insisting on mathematical rigor . . . has repeatedly led economists to" judge research based on mathematical rigor instead of on economic relevance. Axiomatization, with a fixed set of axioms, "has repeatedly led economists to" those problems that were better suited to the mathematical techniques. This is the very opposite of Debreu's claim.

The Arrow-Debreu model does establish "secure bases" for "many contemporary economic theorists, who therefore seek it for its own sake" to generate a large volume of literature, saturating the academic landscape. This makes it difficult for other theories to survive or germinate, even though they are more consistent with reality than the Arrow-Debreu model.

What about simplicity, generality, and the rest, including "aesthetic appeal"? The Arrow-Debreu model is not truly simple. The theory is simple only in the sense that it "has freed researchers from the necessity of" examining the fundamental problems in economics. The Arrow-Debreu model itself is too difficult, too complex, and especially too detached from reality to be used to understand real economic problems. Even extremely simple examples of the Arrow-Debreu model require a high level of mathematical sophistication (Scarf 1960). Few practitioners are at ease with the Arrow-Debreu model, let alone to use it as a "superbly efficient language." The Arrow-Debreu theory has never become "usable by a great number of research workers" to study real economic problems. The Arrow-Debreu model has not permitted practitioners "to communicate with each other, and to think, with a great economy of means." Instead, the Arrow-Debreu theory "fulfills an intellectual need of [a few] contemporary economic theorists," who can showcase their talent of manipulating complex equations.

Nor is the Arrow-Debreu model truly general. It doesn't model new entrants into the economic system; all the firms and all their customers are there from the beginning. It doesn't model exits from the economic system; there are no failures, no deaths, no new generations with changing ideas and preferences. There is no technological change; no new products are invented; no new production processes alter the structure of costs partway through. All production systems are linear; there are no cases of increasing returns, nor even of learning over time. The Arrow-Debreu model doesn't show how monopoly power affects product values. It doesn't have fixed cost in its production systems; there is no fixed capital that must be serviced and maintained and that runs down over time. Everyone in the model simply accepts "equilibrium" from God, or from Arrow and Debreu, even though some participants in the system may get nothing at the "equilibrium" point (Vilks 2021). Behind the facade of mathematical generality, the Arrow-Debreu model confines researchers to problems with little connection to economic reality.

Debreu was keenly aware that mainstream economic theory is highly detached from economic reality. After the Arrow-Debreu model had come to dominate the economics profession, Debreu (1991) tried to present an explanation or excuse for this detachment.

> Before the contemporary period of the past five decades, theoretical physics had been an inaccessible ideal toward which economic theory sometimes strove. During that period, this striving became a powerful stimulus in the mathematization of economic theory.
>
> The great theories of physics cover an immense range of phenomena with a supreme economy of expression. Of this, James Clerk Maxwell (1865) had given a notable example, as he described the electromagnetic field by means of eight equations at the time when mathematical economics was born and came of age in the middle of the 19th century . . .
>
> The benefits of that special relationship were large for both fields; but physics did not completely surrender to the embrace of mathematics and to its inherent compulsion toward logical rigor. The experimental results and the factual observations that are at the basis of physics,

and which provide a constant check on its theoretical constructions, occasionally led its bold reasonings to violate knowingly the canons of mathematical deduction.

In these directions, economic theory could not follow the role model offered by physical theory. Next to the most sumptuous scientific tool of physics, the Superconducting Super Collider whose construction cost is estimated to be on the order of 10^{10} (David P. Hamilton 1990; see also *Science*, 5 October 1990), the experiments of economics look excessively frugal. Being denied a sufficiently secure experimental base, economic theory has to adhere to the rules of logical discourse and must renounce the facility of internal inconsistency. (Debreu 1991, 3)

Debreu pointed out that "the great theories of physics cover an immense range of phenomena with a supreme economy of expression." He cites a famous case: "Of this, James Clerk Maxwell (1865) had given a notable example, as he described the electromagnetic field by means of eight equations." Then he claimed, "In these directions, economic theory could not follow the role model offered by physical theory." The reason? "Next to the most sumptuous scientific tool of physics, the Superconducting Super Collider whose construction cost is estimated to be on the order of 10^{10} . . . the experiments of economics look excessively frugal."

In citing the super collider, Debreu apparently forgot the case of Maxwell he'd just mentioned. Maxwell's theory is based on the experiments of Faraday and others, which "look excessively frugal" by any standard. However, this frugality did not prevent Maxwell from developing "a Grand Unified Theory" (Debreu 1991, 3) of a vast array of electromagnetic phenomena.

Debreu thought that economic theory is "denied a sufficiently secure experimental base." But economic and financial activities are the most practiced and experimented activities in human societies. Economic and financial data are the most frequently recorded and scrutinized data. There is no shortage of data in economics.

Far from stimulating scientific breakthroughs, high spending is the best way to raise entry barriers, the best way to maintain the monopoly of the standard doctrine, the best way to stifle great ideas. Physics became sterile and could no longer generate great ideas after its cost skyrocketed. Indeed, the Superconducting Super Collider mentioned by Debreu became a symbol of waste and extravagance in physics research. It was eventually scrapped by the US Congress. In physics, the age of the Superconducting Super Collider and other expensive machines has produced relatively little, whereas the age of frugality one hundred and two hundred years ago generated many great scientific breakthroughs.

Similarly, economic theory became sterile as its costs rose. When there are so many grants to apply for, there is little incentive to develop great theories to "cover an immense range of phenomena with a supreme economy of expression." Indeed, there is every incentive to ignore and kill new theories to justify numerous expensive grants. Overall, when so much money is at stake, there is little incentive to seek truth. There is a great incentive to seek money.

Fischer Black, like Debreu, was trained as a mathematician. He had the opposite view about the amount of spending and the quality of research. Perry Mehrling quotes him:

> "In my view, the basic problem with research in business (and economics) is not that it's too theoretical, or too mathematical, or too divorced from the real world (though all of these are indeed serious problems). The basic problem is that we have too much research, and the wrong kind of research, because governments, firms, foundations, and generous alumni support it."
>
> The way to create a more free marketplace of ideas was to stop subsidizing the production of new ideas. Professors should be paid for their teaching only, since the ones who are not interested in research will stop producing it, and the ones who are interested in research will do it anyway. The result will be a net gain for society. Fewer noise traders relative to information traders in the marketplace of ideas can be expected to increase efficiency in that market. (Mehrling 2005, 301)

There are some further reasons why the Arrow-Debreu model, and the underlying marginal utility theory of perfectly competitive equilibrium, triumphed and continues to dominate high-level economic theory. These reasons are political. First, as a mathematically rigorous theory, it lends prestige to the profession of economics, giving the impression to outsiders that economic theory is established on the solid foundation. Second, as an abstract theory, it is difficult to understand, so that most economists simply choose to believe it. This gives the Arrow-Debreu model, as well as the larger economic theory built on it, an aura of religion. People defend religion more fiercely than science, especially a religion that gives good jobs. Third, the Arrow-Debreu theory also makes it extremely difficult for outsiders to challenge economic theory. Few would have the patience to take the tremendous effort to understand the model. Many years ago, J. K. Galbraith made a similar observation:

> The very vigor of minor debate makes it possible to exclude as irrelevant, and without seeming to be unscientific or parochial, any challenge to the framework itself. Moreover, with time and aided by the debate, the accepted ideas become increasingly elaborate. They have a large literature, even a mystique. The defenders are able to say that the challengers of the conventional wisdom have not mastered their intricacies. Indeed these ideas can be appreciated only by a stable, orthodox, and patient man—in brief, by someone who closely resembles the man of conventional wisdom. The conventional wisdom having been made more or less identical with sound scholarship, its position is virtually impregnable. The skeptic is disqualified by his very tendency to go brashly from the old to the new. (Galbraith 1958, 11)

Móczár (2020) provided a very systematic review of the Arrow-Debreu model. At the end of his review, he commented,

> Modern economic science requires a paradigm shift. The time of neoclassical economics has ended, as now too many observers can plainly see its lack of connection with reality. The new paradigm can only be non-equilibrium economics. (Móczár 2020, 62)

Arrow and Debreu laid the foundation of modern mainstream value theory, and therefore of economic theory, on a mathematical model of general equilibrium. One can arbitrarily build many mathematical models, which may or may not describe human activities accurately. As for their "aesthetic appeal," that is in the eye of the beholder. We find nothing in the Arrow-Debreu model, or its many derivatives, that suggests beauty to our eyes.

However, all human activities, including mental activities, are consistent with physical and biological laws. Simplicity, generality, and even beauty can all be had by aligning economic theory with basic biophysical principles. In the rest of this chapter and book, we build the foundation of economic theory on thermodynamics, the most universal part of biophysical theory.

SCARCITY AND ENTROPY: FROM WALRAS TO GEORGESCU-ROEGEN AND BEYOND

Leon Walras founded general equilibrium economics but sought to base the theory of value on scarcity rather than utilities. Unfortunately, he lacked a clear definition of what scarcity is—perhaps because the scientific foundation for such a definition was relatively new at that time. Mirowski (1989) has documented Walras's struggles with the formalisms, especially the conservation principle, required to specify his ideas.

Entropy is a measure of scarcity in physics. With this in mind, we can say that an entropy theory of value is a scarcity theory of value. All physical systems tend to move from a less probable state to a more probable state. Entropy is a measure of physical probability at a given time. The tendency of directional movement is what drives, among other things, living organisms. In formal language, systems move from a low-entropy state to a high-entropy state. This is the second law of thermodynamics, the most universal law of nature.

The second law is often understood from an equilibrium perspective, where maximum entropy is a state of equilibrium. This view renders entropy as an image of waste and death. However, from the nonequilibrium perspective, the entropy flow—manifested in heat flow, light flow, electricity flow, water flow, and many other forms—is the fountain of life. Every organism needs to obtain resources for survival. Although resources take many diverse forms, most resources can be understood from a unifying principle. Intuitively, resources are something that are of low probability, or scarce. The movement from low to higher probability is the entropy flow, from the scarcity of a resource to the ubiquity of dust and rubble. Since, for survival, all living organisms need to tap into the entropy flow, entropy is a natural measure of value for living systems, including human beings.

Since entropy tends to increase, it takes effort to maintain a low-entropy state. The ability to do so is naturally attractive. A display of low entropy is therefore the universal sign of attractiveness for animals, including for human beings. We are naturally attracted to the young, the new, the fresh, and the efficient, whether in food, manufactured products, or other people. This explains how subjective utilities are generally entropy-related, so that an entropy theory underpins a utility theory of value. Since all human activities make use of low-entropy resources, human labor is itself a source of low entropy, and an entropy theory of value includes the labor theory of value. But it is broader than the labor theory of value. From the entropy theory of value, other low-entropy resources, such as oil or uranium, will have value, as well as human labor.

An entropy theory of value has, among other virtues, simplicity, generality, and aesthetic appeal. It is, itself, a low-entropy artifact. Others have remarked on the elegance of the idea. In 1971, Nicholas Georgescu-Roegen observed that "there have been sporadic suggestions that all economic values can be reduced to a common denominator of low entropy" (283). Georgescu-Roegen's observation has been often cited since, but there has been little progress in getting through to economists, who were brought up to a theory of utility and general equilibrium.

Georgescu-Roegen had reservations about the prospects for an entropy theory of value. He thought that if an economist linked economic value to low entropy, it would not be of much help because "he would only be saddled with a new and wholly idle task—to explain why these coefficients differ from the corresponding price ratios" (Georgescu-Roegen 1971, 283). In this remark, Georgescu-Roegen was evidently reflecting on the struggles of Marxians with the transformation problem.

To this argument, we may reflect on Claude Shannon's entropy theory of information, the underpinning of modern digital communications. The entropy theory of information does not resolve all important problems related to information, but it does resolve many. Especially, the entropy theory of information provides a measure of the *minimal* cost of information transmission. It measures the smallest file that can carry a given message. The entropy concept of information provides a theory that helps us transmit large amounts of information at low cost.

Similarly, an entropy theory of value will not resolve all problems in economics. It does not explain all transaction prices. But it greatly simplifies our understanding of a broad range of social and economic phenomena, underpinning transactions and much else besides. It provides a simple, general mathematical relation to understand how scarcity, the number of producers or service providers, and market size all affect market values. In parallel with the role of entropy in information theory, an entropy theory of value sets a lower bound on sustainable transaction prices. It tells us the price below which a given economic activity will not be viable over time.

In the entropy theory of value, economic value is defined as a logarithm function, just as information is defined as a logarithm function. In information theory, the base of the logarithm function is 2, as the information is transmitted in a binary system $\{0, 1\}$. In the entropy theory of value, the base of the logarithm function represents the number of suppliers of a product or a service. When the base approaches 1, the market approaches pure monopoly and the value of the product or service approaches infinity. This situation, though actually quite rare in the real world—since most things have some substitutes most of the time and all potential monopolies are subject to regulation—indicates that building monopoly and oligopoly are among the most important ways to increase economic value.

ENTROPY AND MONOPOLY POWER

As noted in the preface, governments have (in principle) a monopoly on violence and taxation. Patents, intellectual property rights, regulation, industry standards, and market dominance help businesses establish and maintain monopolies and oligopolies. Unionization achieves monopoly power in bargaining. Indeed, many of the most important functions in human societies are structured as monopoly or as *oligopoly*, a form where a small number of major producers control the output and distribution of most goods and many services (Michels 1915; Schumpeter 1942; Galbraith 1967). In 1966, Paul Baran and Paul Sweezy argued for the centrality of monopoly power in the capitalist economy:

> Today the typical economic unit in the capitalist world is not the small firm producing a negligible fraction of a homogeneous output for an anonymous market but a large-scale enterprise producing a significant

share of the output of an industry, or even several industries, and able to control its prices, the volume of its production, and the types and amounts of its investments. The typical economic unit, in other words, has the attributes which were once thought to be possessed only by monopolies. It is . . . impermissible to ignore monopoly in construct-ing our model of the economy and to go on treating competition as the general case. In an attempt to understand capitalism in its monopoly stage, we cannot abstract from monopoly or introduce it as a mere modifying factor; we must put it at the very center of the analytical effort. (Baran and Sweezy 1966, 6)

An advantage of an entropy theory of value is that it fully rises to the challenge laid down by Baran and Sweezy. And in this respect, it parts company, in full, with the tradition of basing economic analysis, as a point of departure, on the ideal type of "perfect competition."

SUBJECTIVITY AND OBJECTIVITY
IN VALUE THEORY

A marginal utility theory of value is highly subjective; it interprets value according to the preferences, or *revealed preferences*, of a multitude of independent consumers and business firms. Some argue that utility and scarcity theories are essentially similar, since the latter also has many subjective elements. This is, however, not the case. Although there are many subjective elements in the estimation of scarcities, that is because the objective conditions may not be fully known. This does not change the fact that theories based on scarcity rest (largely) on objective facts about the real world, not on "preferences" that cannot be observed independently of the transactions they are supposed to induce.

We can use an example of petroleum to discuss the measurement issue in a scarcity or entropy theory.

When we estimate the value of petroleum by measuring the scarcity of petroleum, we estimate the amount of petroleum under the ground, which is highly subjective. We estimate the geological conditions of petroleum reserves, which are highly subjective. We estimate the future progress of technology to extract petroleum, which is highly subjective.

We estimate the future progress of technology of substitute energy sources, such as solar panels, which is highly subjective. We estimate the future global population and their consumption of energy, which are highly subjective; these future demands govern the depletion of existing resource pools and determine the cost of producing energy in the future. We estimate many other things of which our measurements are highly subjective.

However, overall, the value of petroleum, under a scarcity theory of value, represented by the entropy theory of value, is still an objective fact. How can this be?

In the entropy theory of information developed by Shannon, the amount of information is measured by the entropy function. When we use different methods to code a message, the sizes of the coded files can be very different, depending on the format of the file.[1] For example, video data can often be compressed one hundred times in transmission, with little loss of quality. The entropy of such a message is *the lower bound of the file size* that can carry the same message. Though we may not know exactly how best to reach this lower bound, it exists as an objective fact. In this way, Shannon's entropy theory of information turned information theory from a subjective theory into an objective theory.

Similarly, when we apply scarcity theory, or entropy theory, to economic valuation in the case of petroleum, there can be large variations in valuations from different parties, due to differing subjective assessments. There can be even larger variations in market price, owing to speculations or short-term shortages or gluts. Entropy theory is not a theory of the current price; it does not explain why a given transaction occurred at a given time at a given price. A theory which purports to do that, such as a marginal utility theory, is empty of real content—a semantic game. It justifies any price whatever from the fact that the transaction was voluntary and represented the best deal between the transacting parties that they could reach at that time.

What the entropy theory asserts is that the variations are all anchored in physical entropy and the real cost of obtaining petroleum (Shiozawa 2016). The value of petroleum is the lowest bound of the real cost associated with obtaining petroleum, taking account of the market power of the producers. It is the lowest price at which production is likely to be sustained. This is an objective fact even if its exact dimensions are not fully known by all or even any of the agents. Thus, an entropy theory of value roots valuation in real costs and market power. It turns the theory of value into an objective theory.

MONEY AND THEORIES OF VALUE

How do theories of value apply to the value of money?

A labor theory of value cannot explain the value of money. Even in the days when money consisted largely of silver (or, more rarely, gold) coin, the value of the coin routinely diverged from the underlying value of the metal. Typically, a silver coin was stamped, or declared, by the king to be worth more than the silver it contained, and this condition induced holders of silver plate or bullion to bring it to the mint to be converted into coin (Desan 2015). The amount of plate or bullion available limited the issuance of coin, although silver and gold could be brought into the kingdom by successful mining or through piracy and pillage. When this happened, there was some relationship between the labor required to obtain precious metals and their value. But the relationship was variable and uncertain.

When paper and then ledger entries corresponding to bank deposits replaced precious metals as the predominant form of money, even the most remote relationship between the labor content of money and the value of money disappeared. It costs no labor to change the denomination on a paper bill, and no labor to add to the value of a bank deposit through the act of making a loan.

Can utility account for the value of money? This is a slightly more complicated matter. It is possible that the mere possession of money can bring pleasure—and to many people, it clearly does. A poet (identity unknown to us) wrote:

> Women and wine are pleasures that cloy,
> But money always brings me joy.

That said, utility theories of economic value, which in turn underpin supply-demand models and the larger construct of general equilibrium, have no independent role for money. In these theories, utility is attached to the possession and consumption of commodities and services, and not to the medium by which those commodities and services are acquired. Money is "a veil"—a unit of account, the determinant of the general level of prices and not of the all-important *relative* prices (values) of goods and services. Moreover, in a world of perfect markets and perfect foresight, the comfort of holding money as a hedge against future troubles (a major feature of the real world) is unnecessary and would be irrational. The problem of fitting money into a model of general equilibrium of the Arrow-Debreu type proved a major sticking point in the development of general equilibrium theories. It is a problem that has never been properly resolved.

If, on the other hand, one considers the problem of money in terms of the utility of the government, a different problem emerges. A government, maximizing its own utility in the issuance of money, would continue to issue money until the marginal benefit equaled the marginal cost. But, as we have seen, the marginal cost of issuing new money, for a government that controls its own money supply—in paper or electronic chits—is zero. So the marginal benefit, and therefore the value, of money would (in a hypothetical equilibrium) be zero. This is a theory that predicts unlimited hyperinflation as a matter of course. But we know that actual hyperinflations are quite rare, and governments rightly try to avoid them as much as possible.

If it fits at all within a theory of value, the value of money therefore fits into the general rubric of scarcity theories of value. And then the question becomes: What makes money scarce? This is a most interesting question. A good deal of monetary theory is tied up with the search for a credible answer.

Partisans of commodity monies—of metallic coins, and in more recent times, of gold and silver standards—understood the scarcity of money to be governed by a fixed relationship between the quantity of metallic reserves held by the government and the amount of circulating medium permitted by the same government. The idea was that the possibility of converting paper into silver or gold would discipline the issuance of paper certificates that could be so redeemed. The most recent articulation of this system was the dollar-exchange standard developed at Bretton Woods in 1944, which underpinned international exchange mechanisms until August 1971. Under this system, the United States promised to redeem US dollars held by foreign central banks into gold at a fixed rate of exchange—$35 per ounce of gold. However, this promise was untenable, as the volume of dollars that fell into the hands of foreign central banks was determined by the deficit in the US current account, which bore no connection to the volume of gold reserves. The notion that the US dollar was "backed by gold" was, in effect, a pleasant fiction, which held up only so long as it was not strongly challenged. When the challenge occurred, President Richard Nixon slammed the "gold window" shut.

The curious consequence, after a decade of turbulence in world money markets, was that the dollar emerged even stronger than before, as the anchor currency of the world system. Why was that? The answer is two-fold, but it comes down to the fact that gold never was the source of scarcity for dollars. Within the United States, the dollar retains value because US residents need dollars to pay taxes to the American state and to service debt on loans taken from American banks (Wray 2006). The United States, unlike many countries, has a very effective tax system, for most people, and a generally functional credit system. *The result is that dollars have a scarcity value.* No matter how many dollars one may have, there is always a need to ensure that fixed dollar commitments can be met. For this, one must work to earn more dollars.

The same is true for those holding dollars outside the United States, even though they are not subject to American taxes. For them, it is debts incurred in dollars that must be serviced by earning dollars. It is a fact, as well, that holding dollars may be a useful way of evading taxes in other countries and their currencies. Thus, the strength of the dollar bleeds strength from other countries, which are then obliged to print their own money to cover their bills. A *relatively* scarce (and therefore valuable) dollar creates a world in which many other currencies are not scarce, and their value declines regularly against the dollar. It is possible that the age of relative dollar scarcity and high value may soon end. So far, however, it has not.

CRYPTOCURRENCIES AND SCARCITY VALUES

The rise and decline of cryptocurrencies provide another example of a scarcity value theory at work. Bitcoin, the original cryptocurrency, was invented in 2009. It was at that time a monopoly product, and the monopoly was enhanced by a feature of the algorithm that promised to limit the issue of Bitcoin to a maximum of twenty-one million units.

Bitcoin thus solved the problem of gold and silver certificates, whose scarcity varied with the success of mining and with the unsteady relationship between the physical reserve and the number of certificates issued against it.

Bitcoin acquired value because it was scarce. It was also regulated, in theory. The Bitcoin system was independent of any government or central bank, but it was designed to have its own regulation, in the form of blockchain, which made it possible to maintain a distributed log of all transactions involving Bitcoins. The quantity of new Bitcoins was also destined to rise slowly, thanks to the enormous amount of energy, and therefore cost, involved in "mining" new Bitcoins, a process requiring large-scale computing power. Prices rose, reaching $20,000 by the end of 2017.

What was uncertain about Bitcoin, however, was the extent of the market, and therefore its scarcity relative to the desire to hold it. This uncertainty contributes the speculative element to Bitcoin. Moreover, beginning in 2011 and accelerating after 2015, other cryptocurrencies were invented and introduced: Litecoin, then Ethereum, with others following. Bitcoins were (and are) inherently scarce, but cryptocurrencies as a class are not. It is straightforward, if not necessarily technically easy, to imitate one cryptocurrency by creating another. From the standpoint of a speculator, cryptocurrencies are similar, though not identical, and they may be substituted, one for another, to a degree. So the effective supply of cryptocurrencies as a group greatly increased with the increasing number of suppliers. As our theory and the log function predict, prices soon fell, hitting $4,000 in 2018.

As we have explained elsewhere (Chen and Galbraith 2012a), a typical response to the financial stress of a low rate of return is an increased temptation to commit financial fraud. Fraud makes performance look much better than it is, so long as the fraud is undetected. It may be hard to commit fraud with cryptocurrencies as such, thanks to blockchain. In principle, every transaction is tracked and recorded and public—even though the identities of those trading and the underlying purposes are concealed. But platforms for trading and exchanging cryptocurrencies are another matter. They operate like unregulated banks, taking deposits and making loans, while providing a service for crypto holders, namely making it much easier to trade them. The terms of loans and the quality of the borrower are not possible to control via blockchain, so this feature of the cryptocurrency system is effectively subverted in the interest of making access and speculation easy. Exchanges also can issue their own cryptocurrency tokens and use those to convey a misleading impression of their own financial condition.

FTX, an unregulated crypto exchange based in the Bahamas, came into existence in 2019. It enjoyed an extraordinary early success, attracting tens of billions of dollars, much of it from untraced sources. The market value of FTX itself rose, ultimately to $32 billion. Binance, another cryptocurrency exchange, had been created in 2017. With new channels making crypto purchases relatively easy, the market for Bitcoin expanded. Bitcoin and other cryptocurrencies recovered their value and went on to a spectacular boom as households became flush with cash during the COVID-19 pandemic. At that point, Bitcoin and other cryptocurrencies were again relatively scarce, in comparison with the means available to buy them. Bitcoin exceeded $69,000 at its peak valuation. But as the normal realities reasserted themselves in the real economy, as free cash diminished, and as doubts about FTX surfaced, there was an even more sensational crash culminating (so far) in November 2022. Over the year to that point, Bitcoin had lost two-thirds of its value. FTX collapsed, investors lost billions, and it became clear that FTX had been suffused with shady practices and with alleged frauds. Bitcoin then recovered once more, surpassing $70,000 in April 2024.

Was there an equilibrium value for Bitcoin, FTX, or other parts of the cryptocurrency ecosphere? Obviously, there was not. In this situation, the scale of the market was the destabilizing factor. But the various cryptocurrency tokens did enjoy a regulated scarcity value—until competition between cryptocurrencies, predictably, eroded that value. And the declining ability to make money by buying and holding Bitcoin or its rivals gave rise to the highly insecure, effectively unregulated, out-of-control, and corrupt entity that was FTX, operating offshore, largely removed from the eyes of regulators in the United States. It is no surprise that when FTX filed for bankruptcy in late 2022, the liquidator (who had experience with major frauds, including Enron) stated that he had never seen a corporation with worse internal management and controls (Ray 2022).

THE VALUE OF LABOR IN RICH
AND POOR COUNTRIES

How does a scarcity theory of value apply to human labor? As we have already seen, for Malthus, labor was paid according to a pure scarcity theory, and the natural course of human reproduction assured that labor was not usually scarce. Hence wages could never rise above the barest subsistence. As we've also seen, Marx rejected Malthus's grim determinism; for Marx, the social minimum was socially determined, which opened the way toward the full expropriation of the product of labor by labor itself. This system, should it ever exist, would be called socialism.

Labor in the United States and other wealthy countries is concentrated in the services sector, meaning that the contribution of machinery and resources to the various activities being bought and sold is relatively small and most of the proceeds are paid out directly as wages. The contribution of services to total output is therefore measured at the price of labor, which is the wage. But what determines the wage? In the US, as in most rich countries, wages in the services sectors are governed by social norms: by laws such as the minimum wage, by salaries in the public sector, and by customs, such as the norms of tipping in restaurants. In practice, in wealthy societies, the minimum value of labor has been determined socially for at least a century, since the rise of trade unions, social insurance, minimum wages, and, in general, the welfare state.

We commonly speak of the low wages in service occupations, but this is a social judgment—a judgment about the degree of inequality of which we may not approve. It is true that working people in the wealthy countries lead difficult lives, marked by instability and precarity. Even so, by long-run historical and international standards, their wages in real terms are quite high. They permit most working people in advanced countries to live in heated dwellings built to code, to shop in grocery stores, and to purchase clothing, computers, televisions, smartphones, and vehicles, most of the time. Few working people in the advanced countries build their own houses, grow their own vegetables, cut their own firewood, or haul their own water—although these are still quite commonplace activities for much of the world's population.

Such standards greatly improve the living conditions of the working population and convey many benefits, including political legitimacy and stability, on the society. They also affect the relationship between the price of goods and the price of labor, giving almost everyone a strong incentive to purchase commodities and machinery rather than labor. For this reason, upper-income households in the industrial countries moved from having full-time servants, just a few generations back, to relying largely on household appliances for the same functions, such as cleaning. In poor countries, servants are still the norm. Servants are willing to accept very low cash incomes, supplemented perhaps by room and board in austere conditions. Social Security and minimum wage laws give people who would otherwise have no alternative to domestic service options that they generally prefer.

So is human labor plentiful, or is it scarce? In many occupations, it is quite scarce, even in services, because human societies set up various functions to be highly restrictive. There is only one president of the United States, corporations have only one chief executive officer, universities have only a given number of slots for tenured professors, doctors and lawyers must qualify to be admitted to their professions, and so on. These scarcities may be artificial, but they exist because society permits them to exist. And they work greatly to the benefit of those who acquire one of the coveted positions. They are consistent with a scarcity theory of value and with the understanding that monopoly and oligopoly are among the most effective ways to enforce scarcity in the real world.

A good deal of the labor in the services sector, on the other hand, is not all that scarce. It is usually quite easy to find new waitstaff, new custodians, new secretaries, and new construction workers willing to work at the offered wage. Opening a service business is not costless, but it is relatively easy, compared to (say) setting up a factory. Young people coming to work for money for the first time often take jobs of this type. Turnover in these occupations is high. In this part of the economy, which covers a large majority of workers in most wealthy societies such as the United States, Canada, or Europe, the compensation is set by society. In rich countries, it is much higher, due to social standard setting, than it would be if there were not such standards. And it is much higher than it is in "developing" countries, where the standards are much weaker, or even nonexistent. There, the meaning of poverty is quite different than in the richer countries.

To restate this point, it is not the case that waitstaff or drivers or custodians or cooks are more productive in wealthy countries than in poorer ones. In fact, they perform the same functions, in close to the same ways—which is why immigrants from poor to rich countries can (and do) readily take these jobs. Service labor in rich countries does not have a strong bargaining position with employers, and employers do not have trouble, most of the time, finding staff. It is simply that rich countries have the means and have—largely for social and political reasons—taken measures to place a floor under the incomes of this large and otherwise vulnerable part of their population and workforce. The floor is *relatively* low, and jobs are precarious, by comparison with those of higher rank. But the floor is what determines the wage.

The mainstream theory of labor markets argues that wages are related to the productivity of each worker or group of workers, which clearly presupposes an absence of overriding social norms. The idea is that pay is determined on a case-by-case basis, and this is true in some selected sectors and industries, for small businesses whose incomes are determined directly by their sales, and for the self-employed. But in rich countries, for most workers, and especially in basic services, wages and compensation are regulatory decisions, and (for this reason) wages in basic services are broadly similar (Galbraith 1998). They are not governed by productivity. Indeed, in most basic services there is no distinct measure of productivity; "output" is absorbed by input costs.

A useful way to think of this is to build labor into the distinction between fixed and variable costs. For an individual business, wages are a variable cost, but only up to a point. A service business cannot reduce its labor indefinitely and keep its doors open. Moreover, in a rich country, if a service business dismisses its workers or closes its doors, the cost of labor does not go away; it is merely shifted onto the public sector. For a wealthy and organized society—given the existence of unemployment insurance, social security, health insurance, and other broad-based supports—labor, practically speaking, is a fixed cost. We can even say that the process of becoming a rich and "developed" country entails moving a large share of the workforce out of the strictly private market system of economic textbooks and bringing it into the regulatory framework of the society at large.

Whether such a society can be successful is a matter of whether the relative incomes of different people and groups is acceptable over a long period of time, whether the real living standards continue to be supported by abundant resources, and—crucially—whether outsiders can be kept outside. Where this is not the case, the result is usually conflict, often expressed as inflation, as each group—business firms and organized workers—seeks to disturb the existing arrangements and gain an advantage over the others. In the longer run, a decline in resource quality and an increase in resource costs will express itself in other problems, notably a decline in the biological return. In the formerly "real-existing" socialist countries, notably the USSR itself, full employment and egalitarian living standards were the norm—until they could not be sustained and the society itself fell into demographic decline, social conflict, and ultimately collapse.

The general result of these arrangements is that in rich countries, the measured contribution of human labor to the gross product is very large. It is large relative to the contribution of many basic commodities, which are plentiful and cheap. In fact, real wages are high because—and *only because*—the underlying resources are abundant and cheap. The large element of fixed costs makes the society look prosperous and detaches our measures of economic activity from the underlying physical activities—mining, farming, manufacturing—that make the prosperity possible. In "developing" countries, by contrast, labor is truly a variable cost, left to its own devices when not needed by an employer. Labor's contribution to the national accounts is therefore generally much smaller.

The use of the national income accounts for comparative purposes, across countries, is thus greatly affected by the rise and now predominance of services labor in wealthy countries. In the United States, the contribution of a gym attendant, tattoo artist, Uber driver, or college professor to the national income is valued precisely at their wage, and the size of the American economy is amplified by the many millions of people in such employments. But while the measures do what they were designed to do, which is to capture the total flow of purchasing power, they make no distinction between these services activities and, say, the extraction of resources or the production of machinery or the production of goods.

By the valuation of the national income accounts, a dollar earned in one occupation makes the same contribution as a dollar earned in any other. A country with a vast pool of well-paid back scratchers looks exactly as rich as a country with mines, factories, and fields yielding minerals, oil, automobiles, and food in the same dollar amount. As mainstream economists sometimes say, dollar for dollar, computer chips and potato chips make the same contribution to GDP. This misses something important. What it misses, exactly, deserves some thought.

HOW ARE THE NATIONAL INCOME ACCOUNTS RELATED TO A THEORY OF VALUE?

We come to a curious fact of life in real economies. Despite the several centuries of thought and debate that went toward elaborations of contested ideas of economic value, the system of national income accounting on which practically all countries rely in practice seems not to be based directly on any of the three classical theories of economic value.

The national income (and product) accounts do not attempt to relate the price of goods and services to the amount of labor involved in the production process. If they did, they would be much simpler; it would be sufficient to add up the labor hours worked per year, make a few adjustments for the depreciation of machinery and perhaps for efficiency of work effort, and report the result, measured in labor-hours. But that is not how gross domestic product or gross domestic income are computed.

The accounts also do not ask whether the products and services produced and consumed contribute to happiness or utility. From the standpoint of textbook economics, this is quite odd. It is still the declared purpose of a well-run economy, according to textbooks, the Arrow-Debreu mainstream, and the United States Constitution, to promote the general welfare. The aggregate of "real" production does not do this. Production may serve no purpose related to welfare: it may be wasted, it may go to the destruction of pointless wars, it may generate lethal side effects that outweigh the perceived benefits of economic activity. All of this is well known. In a speech at the University of Kansas in March 1968, Senator Robert F. Kennedy put it this way:

Our Gross National Product, now, is over $800 billion dollars a year, but that Gross National Product—if we judge the United States of America by that—that Gross National Product counts air pollution and cigarette advertising, and ambulances to clear our highways of carnage. It counts special locks for our doors and the jails for the people who break them. It counts the destruction of the redwood and the loss of our natural wonder in chaotic sprawl. It counts napalm and counts nuclear warheads and armored cars for the police to fight the riots in our cities. . . .

Yet the gross national product does not allow for the health of our children, the quality of their education or the joy of their play. It does not include the beauty of our poetry or the strength of our marriages, the intelligence of our public debate or the integrity of our public officials. It measures neither our wit nor our courage, neither our wisdom nor our learning, neither our compassion nor our devotion to our country, it measures everything in short, except that which makes life worthwhile. (Kennedy 1968)

As we can see, these comments, and the ideas they embody, are not new. Ten years before Kennedy's speech, they were expressed in a book called *The Affluent Society* (Galbraith 1958), which spent many months on the best-seller lists in the first decades of national accounting.

National income accounts were designed in the 1930s, when the ideas of John Maynard Keynes were first being deployed to counter the mass unemployment of the Great Depression. Their purpose was (and is) to keep track of the great forces of total demand, spending, and purchasing power, as these were expressed (mainly) in the behavior of households, businesses, and governments. As Depression turned into war, the national accounts were a tool for managing the flow of purchasing power in relation to the physical supply of goods available for nonmilitary uses, with a view to keeping inflationary pressures in check. In the postwar years, they became a central tool of a new art, macroeconomic management. The objective of macroeconomic management was (and is) to promote growth of total economic activity, and thus of purchasing power, while avoiding (so far as possible) the problems of price inflation and unemployment.

What then are the national accounts about? The dominant factor in the national income accounts is, simply enough, income—the income of households, which are predominantly wages and salaries paid in the services sector by private businesses and by government, plus the profits of business firms. The predominant factor in determining national income is, therefore, the social or regulatory factors as discussed above, which make an abundant factor, human labor, seem to be much more valuable than it would be otherwise.

Since the national accounts are deployed for a particular purpose, one may infer, or impute, a notion of economic value to their creation and use. It is supposedly a unit of "real" or physical production—equivalently, of physical consumption—generated by economic activity. The measure of that unit is a measure of the growth of the economy in money terms but adjusted for a measure of the change in prices—computed mostly, if not entirely, outside of the services sector—to convert the money measure into something that is (apparently) physical or real. Thus, a rapid rate of "real" growth is celebrated as a boom, and a fall is bemoaned as a recession. Booms and slumps have a close association with business profits, so this is a metric that might also be said to reflect a profits theory of value. Moreover, national authorities are prone to judge the economic performance of entire countries by the same metric, thus asking (most recently) whether the economy of the United States is larger or smaller than the economy of China. One might call this an economic size theory of value. This is a far cry from the dominant concepts when the accounts were created.

CONCLUDING REMARKS

A scarcity theory of economic value helps us understand an important part of the construction of national income accounts: namely, the reason why oil, food, and other essential elements of the economy account for such a small part of the accounting measures. That is because, being abundant, they are not scarce. But when it comes to human labor, and in the largest part of the wage structure, in rich countries it is wages and benefits that are fixed rather than specific quantities of employment. In this large domain, physical scarcity and competition are irrelevant in the short run. This is never the case with commodities, which are always cheaper when they are very abundant and more valuable when they are scarce.

To put it another way, wage structures and official interest rates in rich countries are part of the regulatory decisions governing the fixed cost of operating a stable society. They are set so as to distribute the benefits of abundant, low-cost resources in a way that can be sustained for a certain time. If the cost of resources changes, this is not merely a problem for individual households and businesses, whose financial viability and profits are affected. It is a challenge to the whole society, because it becomes difficult, if not impossible, to fulfill the terms of a social contract. Poor countries do not have this problem, since labor is a variable cost, which can be dispensed with, however brutally, when not needed.

A further consequence is that the national accounts cannot give us an accurate sense of another important dimension of economic life, which is national power. Power is the capacity to influence, or dominate, the activities of others. A country with a large GDP based on human services priced highly may lack the material underpinnings required to project power successfully over the long term. A country that produces an abundant material resource, such as oil or natural gas or uranium or nickel, may have a low measured GDP but the capacity to punch far above its weight measured in such terms. Those who think of the United States as the world's most powerful economy, and of Russia as a "gas station," may have fallen into confusions born of mistaking the national income accounts for a measure of economic power.

Economic power is much more readily understood through a theory of production rather than through the theory of value. Power consists in the ability, and willingness, to decide and execute a plan of action. This entails making investments and deploying real resources to cover the variable costs associated with the activities the investments specify and the plans require. For this, it matters little whether there is a large group of relatively comfortable people outside the production process, whether working in services or retired. But the availability of abundant natural resources and the technical capacity to use them matter a great deal.

The national income accounts retain their uses, provided one is quite strict about what those uses are. They measure total spending, in the first instance, which has some bearing, especially on employment. But the national income accounts are not a comprehensive guide to general welfare. They do not measure happiness. They do not give a reliable guide to relative national economic power. And they are not strictly built on relative scarcities, which seems to us to be the way forward for the consideration of the problem of economic value.

In the following chapter, we will present our ideas on scarcity and value in an analytical form. We argue that this is most useful for thinking about one of the most pressing problems we are likely to face as a society, namely the increasing scarcity, and economic value, of basic resources. Hitherto, for several centuries, these have been very abundant and very cheap. When they become expensive, national income will shift from services to resources. If a country produces most of its own resources, GDP may not change all that much in the near term. But the very foundations of modern economic life, which rely on cheap and abundant resources, and on distributing the benefits of these—via service jobs, welfare payments, and pensions—to maintain the fixed cost of a stable society, will be threatened and possibly shattered. Indeed, we are already seeing the onset of this process, and it is causing a great deal of confusion among economists and those who take their cues from conventional economics.

Scarcity, Information, Entropy, and Economic Value

As we've seen, because of the universality of the entropy law, an entropy theory of economic value has been suggested before. The success of Shannon's (1948) entropy theory of information stimulated many research efforts in economics (Hall and Klitgaard 2011; Kimmel 2011; Ayres 2016; Longo 2018). Since information is the reduction of entropy, an entropy theory of value is also an information theory of value, and this point was well understood after Shannon. However, the information/entropy theory of value has not been fully developed or widely accepted. One reason is a simple misunderstanding. Very often, the direction of scientific research is shaped by the thinking of an authority. In an often-cited passage, Arrow concluded,

> The well-known Shannon measure which has been so useful in communications engineering is not in general appropriate for economic analysis because it gives no weight to the value of the information. If beforehand a large manufacturer regards it as equally likely whether the price of his product will go up or down, then learning which is true conveys no more information, in the Shannon sense, than observing the toss of a fair coin. (Arrow 1973, 138)

But the Shannon measure does measure the weight of information. For example, N symbols with identical Shannon measure carry N times more information than a single symbol (Shannon 1948). Similarly, the value of information about a future price is higher to a large manufacturer than to a small manufacturer, other things being equal; the large manufacturer has more at stake. Later, we show that information, as an economic commodity, shares most of the important properties of physical commodities—including the crucial property of "weight."

We can also understand the issue of weight from the perspective of physics. In physics, there are two types of quantity. The first type is called *intensive quantity*, such as temperature and pressure. The second type is called *extensive quantity*, such as volume and mass. You can double the mass of bricks if you put two bricks together. But you can't double the temperature of bricks by putting two bricks together, for temperature is an intensive, not an extensive, quantity. Entropy is an extensive quantity. It naturally carries weight.

If Arrow hadn't made such a simple mistake, he would have found a "genuine alternative model" of value theory long ago. Since low entropy is the measure of scarcity in physics, an entropy theory of value is naturally a scarcity theory of value. Indeed, Arrow's mistake has been pointed out repeatedly (Chen 2005, 2015, 2018). However, academic economists have ignored the issue. In highly authoritarian academia, the silence of authority is often sufficient to prevent new ideas from being heard. This, too, is an indication of the weight carried by information—and the repetition of new information. Ideas that do not spread fade away.

In this chapter, we present a very simple mathematical theory of value-as-scarcity. Value is represented by the logarithm function. The influence on value of factors such as the number of producers and market size can be understood easily from the logarithm function. Scarcity of resources, including human resources, is often regulated by institutional measures, such as immigration laws and patent laws. The number of producers and service providers is also regulated, often by the existence of government monopolies. Because of high valuation of monopoly and oligopoly, attaining and maintaining monopoly or oligopoly is the principal goal of many economic and social activities. Often this is achieved by political means.

MONOPOLIES AND VALUE IN EDUCATION, HEALTH CARE, AND THE ARMS TRADE

Governments have a monopoly on legitimate violence, on legal decisions, and on taxation. Democratic societies maintain multiparty systems and elections, as well as laws and courts to enforce them, with judges appointed for long tenures. This is to control the economic power of governments and the value they can otherwise extract through their monopoly powers. But monarchy, with nearly absolute power in principle, is common in human history. Even in democratic societies, the reach of governmental monopolies tends to grow over time. Today, governmental powers over citizens and businesses are much broader than they were (say) in the nineteenth century in North America. Many important social activities, such as education and (in most countries) medicine, are under effective government control. In many countries, education is mostly funded by the government. Students can go to only one school for their elementary and secondary education. This lack of choice for students greatly increases the power and hence the value of those who control the educational system and the content of the books and curricula. That is why there are major political struggles over the content of textbooks, often involving major abuses of history. But at the same time, the fact that public education is provided freely means that education is a fixed cost to the whole society. In the opposite case of poor countries, education is provided only to those who can pay—and the consumer controls the content of what is provided. Education in poor countries is a variable cost.

Medical systems in some countries, such as Canada, don't allow patients to choose doctors and the types of treatments they can have. Instead, patients can go to only one doctor, who decides what treatment a patient can get and who else the patient can see. With their monopoly over patients, doctors and those who set health policy gain extraordinary power. But the fact that medical care is provided without charge in Canada (and in other countries with national health systems) means that the medical system is a fixed cost for the whole society. This is done to control the value that health-care providers, given monopoly control, would otherwise extract. In this case, the deal is that consumers have access to health care but no control over its content. In the United States, power rests with insurance companies, which hold a monopoly power over their subscribers. Their power is checked only by government regulations, by unions and employers negotiating with insurers, and by the (limited) ability of patients to change insurers before they get sick. Patients in the United States have a little more control over their care and much less over its cost. The opposite situation prevails in poor countries; consumers can choose their health care, but only if they can pay. In poor countries, medical care is a variable cost.

The power of consumers is also negatively related to their numbers. When there is only one dominant customer, that customer can mostly dictate the terms of trade. Producers, on the other hand, would like to increase the number of their customers and to retain their customers for repeat purchases at higher prices. Strategies to "lock in" a base of consumers are thus ubiquitous in the world of designed consumer goods. Likewise, companies that make armaments seek to export them and to sell them to their own governments. A broader base of consumers, each locked-in to a particular set of weapons, increases the market power of the manufacturer and the value of the weapons they produce.

The relation between number of producers and value can help explain many commercial and social phenomena. Each printer manufacturer designs printers so that printer ink from other firms cannot operate well. Customers who buy printers from one company can use ink only from the same company. By restricting customers' choice, producers can sell ink at higher price and obtain higher profits.

Unions form a monopoly of bargaining. With only a single unit of bargaining, a trade union is in a much stronger position than many individuals in bargaining with management. Unions are often formed in stable professions, such as government employees and teachers. Professions such as physicians often are certified by a single organization, which increases their monopoly value. Doctors' notes are famously illegible. When patients are not well informed, the value of the medical profession increases. At the broadest level, the welfare state in all its many manifestations—education, health, retirement—conveys a degree of monopoly power on all qualified citizens in wealthy countries. This imparts economic value and helps make citizenship in wealthy countries desirable to many who come from other parts of the world.

THE SIMPLE MATHEMATICS OF ENTROPY, INFORMATION, AND REPETITION

We turn now to the central task of spelling out an entropy theory of value in mathematical terms. Any reader comparing the section that follows with Arrow-Debreu, or for that matter with any of the hundreds of mainstream economics articles published every year, can verify that our theory is the soul of simplicity by comparison. As we illustrate below, it is also an *analytical* theory. This means that one can obtain numerical estimates of specific economic phenomena by plugging various observed parameter values into the equation. Although no economic theory is likely to give exact answers, given the limitations of economic data and the variability of human behavior, our theory does, in fact, give very plausible numerical predictions in the examples we offer—predictions that can be checked against the facts of what happened. Unlike many theories in mainstream economics, it is not math for math's own sake, or elaborate algebra without any reference to real-world facts.

Discussion of the relationship between information and physical entropy began with Maxwell's demon (Maxwell 1871). In the 1870s, Boltzmann defined the mathematical function of entropy, which Shannon (1948) identified as information many years later, and which, later still, Georgescu-Roegen suggested should be identified with economic value. But information is often regarded as a rather unusual commodity. According to Arrow:

> The algebra of information is different from that of ordinary goods. . . . Repeating a given piece of information adds nothing. On the other hand, the same piece of information can be used over and over again, by the same or different producer(s). (Arrow 1999, 21)

Is it true that repetition of information adds nothing? In information theory, the amount of information received is the information transmitted, minus equivocation. Repeating a signal helps to reduce equivocation, increasing information. Different types of coding generally maintain a certain level of redundancy to reduce errors in transmission. Far from Arrow's claim, repetition adds a great deal to information.

Indeed, and more generally, repetition is the most important method in learning. Reciting poems is one of the most effective ways to study a language or literature. Important genes often have several hundred copies in genetic codes to satisfy heavy demand (Klug and Cummings 2003). A song will survive only if people repeat it over generations. A theory will survive only if researchers continue to discuss it over time. Commercials are repeated many times on TV. From thermodynamic theory, all low-entropy sources tend to dissipate. Repeating the same piece of information is essential to keep it alive and valuable.

The essence of a living organism is to repeat and spread the information encoded in its genes.

Arrow also wrote that the use of information does not involve rivalry, since "the same piece of information can be used over and over again, by the same or different producer(s)." This property is not confined to information. The same hammer "can be used over and over again, by the same or different producer(s)." However, the value of the same information will be different for different users or at different times. For example, if an unexpected surge of corporate profit is known about by very few people, this information would be highly valuable. Huge profits may be made by trading the underlying stocks. But when it is known to many people, the value of such information is very low. In general, when some knowledge is mastered by many people, its market value is low. That is why scarce educational credentials are often valuable, whereas those easily obtained by many people are not.

In an entropy theory of value, as we have said, economic value is a function of scarcity. Scarcity can be defined as a probability measure P in a certain probability space; the more probable an event or a product, the less scarce it is. A product is defined as an economic "good"—something that is desired and can therefore be sold. Its probability can be thought of as the degree of market penetration or market saturation—how much can be sold, with a given degree of effort, at a price that will cover the cost of production, in relation to the size of the market. This is, of course, somewhat related to the intrinsic desirability of the product in the eyes of consumers. But it is also related to objective factors: the scale of the available market, the size and productive power of the company, the degree of competition from other suppliers, the degree of market protection from a friendly government or regulatory agency.

To be considered a "good," the value of any product must satisfy the following properties:

1. The value of two products must be higher than the value of each of them.
2. If two products are independent—that is, if the two products are not substitutes or partial substitutes—then the total value of the two products will be the sum of the two values.
3. The value of any product is nonnegative.

The only mathematical functions that satisfy all the above properties are of the form

$$V(P) = -\log_b P, \quad (1)$$

where b is a positive constant (Applebaum 1996) and P is a probability measure ranging from 0 to 1.

Those who are familiar with Shannon's theory of information will recognize that the function of value is similar in form to the value of information. Indeed, this theory of scarcity was inspired by Shannon's information theory (Chen 2005). In information theory, the base of the logarithm function is usually chosen to be 2 because there are two choices of code in information transmission, namely, 0 and 1 (Shannon 1948). In economics, b, the base of the logarithm function, represents the number of suppliers of a product or a service.

Most of the time, we are only interested in a particular element or component of an activity. When we mine for copper, we are only interested in copper, which is a small portion of Earth's crust, around 0.0068 percent so far as we know. If we calculate the value of copper in relation to the Earth's crust, we may set $P = 0.0068\%$. We are not interested in the rest of the Earth's crust. In such a case, the value of copper in relation to everything else in the crust is adequately represented by formula (1). This makes it immediately apparent that a new, high-quality discovery, reducing the scarcity of copper known to us, will reduce the market value of copper.

However, we need to keep in mind that the Earth's crust—and any copper deposit that we may find—contains other components, including some by-products and many waste products. The number of components may be different, depending on our knowledge of the relevant space and whether we are required to deal with waste products. Suppose there are n components, each with probability measure $\{P_1, P_2, \ldots P_n\}$. Since we include all components in a system,

$$P_1 + P_2 + \ldots + P_n = 1.$$

Earlier on, we only deal with P, the scarcity of one component in a production process. But a more complete description should include

$\{P_1, P_2, \ldots P_n\}$ scarcities or probabilities of all components in a system, or the value of the system (in this case, a mine or deposit) as a whole.

In general, if the scarcity of a service or product, X, can be estimated by the probability measure $\{P_1, P_2, \ldots P_n\}$ across a number (n) of different probability spaces or markets, then the expected value of this product is the weighted average of the value in each space; that is,

$$V(X) = \sum_{i=1}^{n} P_i(-log_b P_i). \quad (2)$$

Therefore, value—just as information—in its general form can be defined as entropy, given that they are the same mathematically.

Formula (2) is a general form of value, where all related elements of an activity are included. This definition provides a more accurate description of value. For example, mining for many minerals (lithium, "rare earths") that are essential for making batteries and electronics generates large volumes of waste. If the mining company is made responsible for cleaning up the waste, the overall scarcity of the outputs decreases and their overall value declines. If the net value approaches zero as a result, the mine will close. Hence mining companies do not want to be held responsible for their waste products. And when we consider the overall consequences, which are more accurately represented by formula (2), a lot of clean energy may not be that clean.

This work is a very primitive study of a new value theory. In what follows, we will focus on formula (1) as the representation of value and leave more detailed study to later investigations.

In the following, we discuss the properties of this simplest version of an analytical theory of value-as-scarcity.

SCARCITY AND VALUE

Figure 4.1 is a graph of formula (1), which shows that value is a decreasing function of probability—or an increasing function of scarcity, which is the same thing.[1] That is why diamonds are worth more than water in most circumstances. In extreme abundance, when $P = 1$ and $-\log P = 0$, the value of a given commodity is equal to zero, even if that commodity is very useful. For example, food is essential for survival. But most countries subsidize food production in various ways to

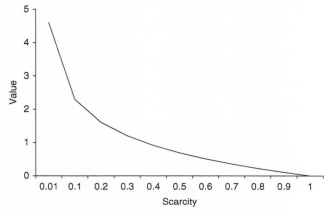

FIGURE 4.1 Value and scarcity.

guarantee the abundance and low cost of food. Among other things, the cost of water usage in agriculture is much lower than in industrial use. Land value in agricultural land is often not taxed. These subsidies generate abundance and low economic value for agricultural products. Economic value and social value can diverge greatly.

Gold is mined at low concentrations, on average, and it takes much energy to grind up the rocks; likewise silver, as compared with copper. In general, a scarce commodity takes more energy and labor to mine than an abundant commodity. The scarcity theory of value is highly consistent with an energy theory of value and the labor theory of value. But compared with the energy theory of value, the entropy/scarcity theory of value can be formulated into a mathematical theory easily. From the perspective of physics, entropy is a more accurate representation of resources than energy. Entropy increases over time, whereas energy is constant.

VALUE AND THE NUMBER OF PRODUCERS OR CONSUMERS

From formula (1), the value of a product is inversely related to the number of producers. Figure 4.2 displays the relation between product value and the number of producers. When the number of producers

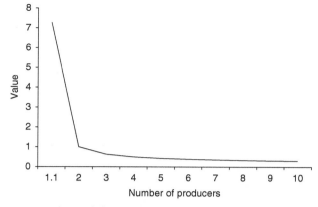

FIGURE 4.2 Value and the number of producers.

is small, the unit value of a product is high. The products of monopolies and oligopolies are valued highly. If the base becomes 1—that is, absolute monopoly without substitution—value approaches infinity. Despite frequent use of the word *monopoly*, this situation is very rare, and such monopolies must always be subject to regulation and control, limiting the exercise of their power.

This concludes the entire mathematical presentation of our value theory.

APPLICATIONS OF AN ENTROPY THEORY OF VALUE

At the beginning of this chapter, we used results from information theory and statistical physics to discuss the relation between physical entropy and economic value. We showed how informational and physical commodities share common properties in the light of an entropy theory of value. We then presented the theory itself. By resolving conceptual difficulties that have confounded economics for many years, we offered a unified understanding of physical entropy, information, and economic value. In the rest of this chapter, we apply the value theory to various economic and a few political activities.

What follows is more technical than most of the rest of the book. The examples we present are all drawn from real life. In some cases, we use actual data from historical experiences. In others, we make the case with hypothetical numerical examples. In all cases, however, we are making direct, practical, quantitative use of the formulas given above and immediate derivative expressions. Contrary to much economic theorizing, we do not appeal to imaginary economic agents operating under imaginary conditions. Ours is an economic theory for the real world.

MARKET SIZE, PRODUCT LIFE CYCLE, AND PRODUCT VALUE

Suppose the potential market size of a product is M. The percentage of people who already have the product is P. P can be understood as a measure of scarcity. If many people desire a product and only a few can afford to buy it, the product is scarce. The unit value of the product can be represented by

$$-\log P. \quad (3)$$

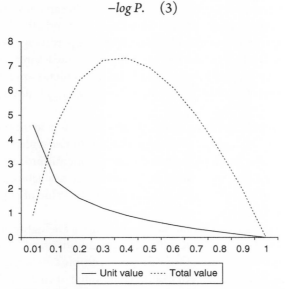

FIGURE 4.3 The unit value and total value of a product with respect to scarcity.

When we are not discussing the relation between value and the number of producers, we may write the formula of value as in the generic form $-log\,P$ instead of the more specified form of $-log_b\,P$.

If the number of people who possess the product is MP, the total value of the product is

$$MP(-log\,P) \quad (4),$$

which we can understand as the market value of the production process at any given time, as P (or market penetration) increases from 0 to 1. From (4), the value of a product is higher with a larger market size, but total value depends also on the proportion of the market that has been penetrated, or on the scarcity/abundance of the product.

From figure 4.3, when a product is new and scarce, the unit value is high, but its total value is low. As production increases, the total value will initially increase even though the unit value decreases. When the production quantity is over a certain level, however, the total value of a product will start to decrease as well. Intuitively, this is easy to understand. General Motors was once the world's most valuable company. As cars became very common, making them became less profitable. Over time, the market values of General Motors and other traditional car manufacturers gradually declined, while the percentage of car ownership trended higher. The market values of manufacturers of mature products are generally low, although their production processes are very efficient. This observation shows that efficiency is not equivalent to value.

As the above discussion shows, the implications of identifying value with scarcity are highly consistent with our intuitive understanding of economic value. It should be noted that in economic processes, a final product embodies many different types of scarcities: labor, raw materials, and equipment. A detailed analysis of the value of any product will be much more involved.

Although economic values of commodities are highly correlated with the level of *physical* scarcity, they are not identical. One reason is that scarcity, and therefore value, of a commodity is regulated by institutional structures. For example, the value of an invention is influenced by how long and how broadly patent protection is granted.

The value of a patent is higher in a system where patents are valid for twenty years than in one where patents are valid for ten years. If patent protection is defined more broadly, the market is larger, and the value of an invention is higher. Thus, economic value, as a function of scarcity, is to a great extent regulated by institutional structures. Among all the institutional measures that regulate scarcity, the most important regulations are the immigration laws that govern the scarcity of the labor force and qualifications for membership in a welfare state. This is what makes persistent large wage differentials across regions possible. Wage differentials can persist for other reasons, such as relocation costs or differences in cost of living. Wages in the cities are higher than in the countryside in the same country, with no legal barriers to migration. But these wage differentials are relatively minor compared with wage differentials where legal barriers to migration are high.

This explains why elites, representing employers, prefer large, borderless regions (such as the European Union), whereas workers in wealthy countries generally prefer borders and restricted immigration, even though they may feel solidarity with immigrant workers already present. In practice, the result is often a large body of workers lacking citizenship, with uncertain legal status and inferior rights of access to social benefits. They help support the welfare state. Exploiting this divided interest among workers helps employers sustain their preferred policy.

COMPETITION, FIXED COSTS, MARKET POWER

Fixed costs are defined as the investments that must be put in place before production can get underway. Higher fixed costs reduce the number of businesses in an industry, which increases the value of their products or services. Regulations and other entry barriers also increase fixed costs. We can analyze how the increase of fixed costs affects profits. Suppose the market size of an industry is M, scarcity is p, and the number of businesses in the industry is b. Then the unit value for the product is

$$-\log_b p.$$

Suppose the fixed cost for each business is K and variable cost of production is C. Assume each business gets the same amount of revenue. The revenue and total cost for each business are

$$\frac{Mp}{b}(-\log_b p) \text{ and } K + C\frac{Mp}{b}(-\log_b p),$$

respectively. The return for each business is

$$\frac{\frac{Mp}{b}(-\log_b p)}{K + C\frac{Mp}{b}(-\log_b p)} - 1. \quad (5)$$

Suppose $M = 1,000$, $p = 0.4$, and $b = 3$. The fixed cost of each business is 35 and the variable cost of each business is 60 percent of the revenue. The rate of return for each business is

$$\frac{\frac{1000 \times 0.4}{3}(-\log_3 0.4)}{35 + 0.6\frac{1000 \times 0.4}{3}(-\log_3 0.4)} - 1 = 0.09.$$

This rate of return is not very high. Now suppose a business persuades the government to increase regulatory measures—say, environmental or safety protections—on this industry. As a result, the fixed cost is increased to 50. Assume other parameters remain the same. The new rate of return for each business, calculated from (5), becomes negative. If the rate of return becomes negative, one business, usually the financially weak one, will drop out of the market. Suppose now there are only two businesses in the industry. Assume other parameters remain the same. The new rate of return for each remaining business is

$$\frac{\frac{1000 \times 0.4}{2}(-\log_2 0.4)}{50 + 0.6\frac{1000 \times 0.4}{2}(-\log_2 0.4)} - 1 = 0.27.$$

This is much higher than the previous rate of return. This shows how financially strong companies can (and do) use regulatory tools to increase fixed cost. In this way, they can reduce the number of competitors and help the remaining players, including themselves, achieve a high rate of return. There are many examples of this process; one known to us personally concerns the pressure brought by the Carter administration in the 1970s on cotton mills to reduce levels of cotton dust in their factories. The new regulations forced the weak producers out of business, while the remaining strong producers adopted new machinery and increased their profitability (conversations with former Secretary of Labor Ray Marshall).

In neoclassical economics, regulation is justified when there is a "market failure." From the above analysis, we can understand why regulations are often driven by strong players in the industries, seeking a higher rate of profit. The theory also explains why biological and chemical weapons are banned by international treaties, whereas nuclear weapons, which can cause much more destruction, are not. Biological and chemical weapons, which are sometimes called poor men's nuclear weapons, are cheap to make. If these weapons are not banned, many countries can make them, which will reduce the value of weapons of mass destruction. To maintain the high value of such weapons, international treaties, which are generally initiated by leading political powers, banned those weapons of mass destruction that are cheap to make. Nuclear weapons, on the other hand, are restricted to the handful of countries that have them and a few that defied the treaties. But they are not banned.

A NUMERICAL EXAMPLE FROM A BANKRUPTCY

An entropy theory of product value applies to the value of the corporation as expressed on the stock market. Since our theory is an analytical theory, it can be tested empirically, using market data. We do not always need to make up illustrative data or run hypothetical simulations.

It is often difficult to determine the exact number of providers of a given good or service. Air travel in vast and thinly populated countries, such as Canada, where alternative modes of transportation are often very time consuming, provides a good testing ground. In the first decade of the twenty-first century, there were three major operators in the air-travel industry in Canada. They were Air Canada,

WestJet, and Jetsgo. There were also regional carriers and international airlines competing for many routes. Most of the profits of airlines, however, come from regional routes where competition is not intense. On March 10, 2005, Jetsgo declared bankruptcy. We can assume four providers for the air-travel service for typical regional routes before Jetsgo declared bankruptcy. From (1), the value of each airline can be represented as

$$-log_4 P \text{ and } -log_3 P$$

before and after Jetsgo declared bankruptcy. The change of value is therefore

$$(-log_3 P)/(-log_4 P) - 1 = log_3 4 - 1 = 0.262.$$

Jetsgo declared bankruptcy in the evening of March 10, 2005, after the market closed. The closing prices of stocks of WestJet and Air Canada on March 10 and 11 are 11.17, 15.6 and 32.19, 37, respectively. The price changes are

$$15.6/11.17 - 1 = 0.397 \text{ for WestJet}$$

and

$$37/32.19 - 1 = 0.149 \text{ for Air Canada,}$$

respectively. The average change of price is

$$(0.397 + 0.149)/2 = 0.273,$$

which is very close to the theoretical prediction of 0.262.

This is just one example. We do not claim that the precise numerical prediction of our theory would hold in all cases. But the fact that it appears to have held in this case is encouraging and points the way to future research and testing. Moreover, the theoretical predictions can be further refined. For example, this theory does not distinguish the sizes of different providers of a service. That and other refinements of the theory are left to future research.

PROTECTIONISM AND FREE TRADE

The most widespread restriction on the number of suppliers for any given product is probably trade policy, including tariffs and quotas. Opening a domestic market to foreign competitors is very likely, in the short run, to produce an increase in suppliers and a reduction in unit values. This reduces prices and improves living standards in the short run in the importing country. What happens in the long run depends on what then happens to the domestic producers, and on the number of foreign producers competing for the domestic market.

Trade policies can be open or restricted. Access to the market can be easy or difficult. What are the effects? Does free trade increase total wealth? Who are the winners and losers in trade? We can use a scarcity theory of value to explore these questions.

In general, trade occurs between regions with differential abundance of a commodity, which could be due to differential concentration of natural resources or the capacity of some manufacturing technology. Most oil exports come from a few leading countries. High-tech industries are highly concentrated in the area of northern California known as Silicon Valley. To examine the quantitative effects of a trade policy, we examine a two-region case and calculate a numerical example.[2] Let the market sizes of two regions be 100 and 1,000, respectively, with resource concentration of 0.9 and 0.2. This indicates that the smaller region is abundant in a particular commodity. In this section, we need to do a lot of calculations of value not related to the number of producers. Nevertheless, we need to specify a number for producers to obtain numerical values. Natural log (ln) seems to be a natural choice here. Any other base for logarithm function will get the same result.

First, suppose the two regions are segregated. Then the commodity prices in the two regions are

$$-ln(0.9) = 0.11 \text{ and } -ln(0.2) = 1.61. \quad (6)$$

The commodity price in the abundant area is much cheaper (think of gasoline prices in Venezuela). The total values of the commodity in the two regions are

$$100 \times 0.9 \times (-ln(0.9)) = 9.48 \text{ and } 1000 \times 0.2 \times (-ln(0.2)) = 321.89. \quad (7)$$

The global total value of the commodity is

$$9.48 + 321.49 = 331.37. \quad (8)$$

When two regions are integrated into a free-trade zone, the global scarcity of the commodity is

$$(100 \times 0.9 + 1000 \times 0.2)/(100 + 1000) = 0.26. \quad (9)$$

The new price of the commodity is

$$-ln(0.26) = 1.33. \quad (10)$$

The global value of the commodity is

$$1100 \times 0.26 \times (-ln(0.26)) = 386.62. \quad (11)$$

The total value of the commodity in the resource-rich region is

$$100 \times 0.9 \times (-ln(0.26)) = 119.99. \quad (12)$$

The total value of the commodity in the resource-poor region is

$$1000 \times 0.2 \times (-ln(0.26)) = 266.64. \quad (13)$$

From (8), the global value of the commodity in a segregated economy is 331.37. From (11), the global value of the commodity in a free-trade environment is 386.62. Thus, free trade increases the total value of a product.

Next, with free trade, producers in resource-rich countries will increase their wealth, whereas producers in resource-poor countries will reduce their wealth. From (12) and (7), total value from the resource-rich region in the free-trade environment is 119.99, which is much higher than 9.48, the total value in a segregated economy. That is why producers from the resource-rich region will promote free trade. From (13) and (7), total value from the resource-poor region in the free-trade environment is 266.64, which is lower than 321.89, the total value in a segregated or protected economy. That is why producers from the resource-poor region will resist free trade.

Third, with free trade, consumers in resource-rich countries will pay higher prices, and consumers in resource-poor countries will pay lower prices. From (6) and (10), the unit value of the commodity in a free-trade environment is 1.33, which is higher than 0.11, the unit value of the commodity in the resource-rich region, and lower than 1.61, the unit value of the commodity in the resource-poor region in a segregated economy. Ordinary consumers in a resource-rich country who do not receive income from the resource industry will resist free trade. Ordinary consumers in a resource-poor country who do not receive income from the resource industry will welcome free trade.

Fourth, from (12) and (7), for the small region, the change of commodity value is from 9.48 to 119.99, which is very large. From (13) and (7), for the large region, the change of commodity value is from 321.89 to 266.64, which is moderate. As a result, small regions have stronger incentive to influence trade policies, although large regions are often more powerful. For example, Canada charges a 270 percent tariff on imported dairy products to deter US dairy imports. By comparison, the US charges a 27 percent tariff on Canadian lumber imports. In general, small social groups often have stronger internal cohesion than large social groups. By no coincidence, empires are often ruled by minority groups, and the most powerful people and most wealthy people in a country are often from social minorities.

The main calculation results are summarized in table 4.1. A similar argument can be made about the effect of removing patent protections; we discuss this below.

In the above calculations, we assume the number of producers is constant. In a real situation with free trade, in the combined trading area, the number of producers will increase, at least at first. As a result,

TABLE 4.1. Summary of value changes with market integration

	Segmented market		Integrated market
	Resource-poor region	Resource-rich region	
Market size	1,000	100	1,100
Scarcity	0.2	0.9	0.26
Unit price	1.61	0.11	1.33
Value in segregation	321.89	9.48	331.37 (sum in segregation)
Value in integration	266.64	120	386.62
Difference in value	−55.25	110.51	55.25

prices will drop. Due to intensified competition, the number of producers will decline over time. It is a dynamic process. A detailed analysis of the dynamics is left to future research.

INTEGRATING THE NORTH AMERICAN OIL MARKET

There are two major price indexes in the crude-oil market: West Texas Intermediate (WTI) and Brent. Historically, WTI and Brent crude-oil prices were very close. However, WTI traded at a deep discount to Brent in recent years as Alberta increased its oil output, most of which was sold in the US. To sell more oil at the international price, proposals were made to build or expand several oil pipelines to the coastal area so Alberta oil could be supplied to the international market. This would increase the value of Alberta oil products. Canada produces about three million barrels of crude oil per day. Canadian oil is often sold several dollars per barrel below the international price (Aliakbari and Stedman 2018). Every year, the Canadian oil industry loses billions of dollars from this price differential; equivalently, customers of the Canadian oil gain billions of dollars from the current situation. From the above analysis, it is easy to understand why there is so much negative publicity and disruption around the pipeline projects—although we do not dispute the high motives of many who organize and participate in the protests. Underlying economic forces can amplify—or ignore—social-protest movements according to economic advantage.

TARIFFS AND THE CASE OF SOFTWOOD LUMBER

Tariff policy can often significantly influence output quantity and hence product value, especially when a certain commodity has one big producer and one big consumer. For example, Canada is a big producer of softwood lumber, and the US is a big consumer. From our value theory, the value of the lumber market is represented by $VP(-lnP)$, where P is the proportion of lumber that is on the market. Assume V, the total volume of the forest, is 10,000. A consumer country will benefit from a trade policy that increases the production of lumber, since it will reduce the value of imported lumber.

Suppose the cost structure of the lumber industry is the following. The total fixed cost in lumber production in country C is 100. The variable cost is 55 percent of product value. The total value of the lumber products is $VP(-lnP)$ and the total cost of production is $100 + 0.55^*V^*P^*(-lnP)$. Suppose every year, 1 percent of all lumber is harvested. The profit on lumber production is equal to revenue minus total cost:

$$VP(-ln P) - (100 + 0.55 * (VP(-ln P)))$$
$$= 10000 * 0.01 * (-ln(0.01))$$
$$- (100 + 0.55 * (10000 * 0.01 * (-ln(0.01))))$$
$$= 107.$$

In 2001, as noted above, the US imposed a 27 percent import duty on lumber from Canada. If the volume of production remained at the same level, the profit for lumber production would be

$$VP(-ln P) * (1 - 0.27) - (100 + 0.55 * (VP(-ln P)))$$
$$= 10000 * 0.01 * (-ln(0.01)) * (1 - 0.27)$$
$$- (100 + 0.55 * (10000 * 0.01 * (-ln(0.01))))$$
$$= -17,$$

which means that the lumber industry would lose money. Production of lumber had to be increased to avoid loss. If the production level is increased to $P = 1.5\%$, the profit for the lumber industry will become

$$VP(-ln P) * (1 - 0.27) - (100 + 0.55 * (VP(-ln P)))$$
$$= 10000 * 0.015 * (-ln(0.015)) * (1 - 0.27)$$
$$- (100 + 0.55 * (10000 * 0.015 * (-ln(0.015))))$$
$$= 13.$$

As production is increased from 1.0 percent of the total reserve to 1.5 percent, the unit value of lumber falls from $-ln(0.01) = 4.6$ to $-ln(0.015) = 4.2$. The United States collected a 27 percent tariff on lumber imports *and* enjoyed lower price on lumber. Table 4.2 gives a summary of softwood lumber futures prices, annual production from Canada, and revenues and profits from Canfor, Canada's largest softwood producer, in 2000 and 2002, one year before and after the US imposed the 27 percent tariff on softwood lumber imports from Canada.

Historical data confirm the theoretical prediction. After the tariff, production increased, prices dropped, and corporate profits from lumber producers tumbled. This shows that tariffs are an effective way to shift wealth from producing countries to consuming countries. It contradicts the standard theory that tariffs hurt importing countries by imposing higher prices on consumers. It is worth noting that the softwood lumber tariffs were imposed by a Republican administration—that of George W. Bush—which had a supposed ideology of free trade, but which also had a sophisticated understanding of business constituencies and a clear desire to promote house construction in the United States. It seems that the economic and political benefits of more construction may be very well understood by those who impose such tariffs, notwithstanding the scolding from economists and the lessons of textbooks.

From the theoretical analysis, as well from the data in table 4.2, trade policies have large effects on the distribution of wealth across borders. This also greatly influences the distribution of jobs across borders. This is why trade policies are such an emotional issue and always have been.

The scarcity of a commodity is influenced by market size. For Canadian lumber, the market size is very much determined by the US housing market, which is much larger than the Canadian market. Market size is also greatly affected by transportation costs. For example, petroleum is relatively light compared with coal for the same amount of energy. Therefore, petroleum is a global commodity, and coal is much less so. Lumber is six times heavier than coal as a fuel. Hence the market for wood as a fuel is highly localized. But the market for wood as lumber, which is higher-priced than fuel, is much larger. Still, the increasing cost of oil decreases the size of the lumber market, since not only do transportation costs increase, but also higher energy prices can make constructing a home more expensive.

TABLE 4.2. Summary statistics of softwood lumber futures price, annual production from Canada[1]

	2000	2002
Softwood lumber futures price (January closing)	346.6	268.7
Production (thousands of m³)	68,557	71,989
Canfor revenue (CA$millions)	2,265.9	2,112.3
Canfor profit (CA$millions)	125.6	11.5

[1] Revenues and profits from Canfor. Sources of data: CME, indexmundi, Canfor annual reports

PATENTS, COPYRIGHTS, AND
INTELLECTUAL PROPERTY

Information is thought to possess yet another quality that makes it difficult to transform into property. According to Arrow:

> The peculiar algebra of information has another important implication for the functioning of the economic system. Information, once obtained, can be used by others, even though the original owner has not lost it. Once created, information is not scarce in the economic sense. This fact makes it difficult to make information into property. It is usually much cheaper to reproduce information than to produce it in the first place. In the crudest form, we find piracy of technical information, as in the reproduction of books in violation of copyright. Two social innovations, patents and copyrights, are designed to create artificial scarcities where none exists naturally, although the duration of the property is limited. The scarcities are needed to create incentives for undertaking the production of information in the first place. (Arrow 1999, 21)

Is it true that "artificial scarcities" are necessary to create incentives to produce new information? We think not. Information is a type of low-entropy resource. Utilization of low-entropy resources—acquired from others—is a universal phenomenon of living systems. Information resources are an example, not an exception, to this rule:

> Once again animals discover the trick first. . . . Butterflies did not evolve their colors to impress the females. Some species evolved to be poisonous or distasteful, and warned their predators with gaudy colors. Other poisonous kinds copied the colors, taking advantage of the fear already sown. But then some nonpoisonous butterflies copied the colors, too, enjoying the protection while avoiding the expense of making themselves distasteful. When the mimics become too plentiful, the colors no longer conveyed information and no longer deterred the predators. The distasteful butterflies evolved new colors, which were then mimicked by the palatable ones, and so on. (Pinker 1997, 501)

The perceived uniqueness of copying information products in human societies is an illusion, or a conceit; copying is quite universal within living systems. Once we look at the living world from the entropy perspective, it can hardly be otherwise. In human societies, the attempt to copy and reproduce valuable assets, whether informational or physical, is also universal.

The fashion industry offers an example that illustrates clearly the dynamics of innovation and copying. When a new fashion style is created, it is scarce and hence valuable. This valuable information will be copied by others. As more people copy the style, P increases, $-\log P$ decreases, and the value of the fashion decreases. To satisfy the demands for high-value fashions, new fashion styles "are designed to create artificial scarcities where none exists naturally." Eventually outmoded fashions end up on the racks of discount stores.

Protection of an organism's source of low entropy to prevent access by others is also a universal phenomenon of living systems. Animals develop immune systems to protect their low-entropy source from being accessed by microbes. Plants make themselves poisonous to prevent their low entropy from being accessed by animals. When space is a limiting factor in survival or reproduction, animals defend their territory vigorously (Colinvaux 1978). Whether to enforce the property rights depends on the cost of enforcement and the value of the low-entropy resource. When information products become an important class of assets, the property rights of physical assets are naturally extended to informational assets.

An unknown singer will be grateful for anyone to play or sing her songs. Only when she becomes famous will she demand copyright and payment. Most singers are unknown. Only a tiny portion of singers demand copyrights and royalties. But this tiny portion of singers, the superstar singers, represent huge commercial values. Hence the pressure for long copyright protections is very strong. By similar logic, musicians who can pack a hall or club with paying customers forbid the making of recordings or videos. Street musicians do not care.

It is often claimed that the protection of property rights in information is essential to the innovation process. Arrow stated, "Two social innovations, patents and copyrights, are designed to create artificial scarcities where none exists naturally . . . The scarcities are needed to create incentives for undertaking the production of information in the first place" (Arrow 1999, 21). But the production and reproduction of information, in the form of genes, occurred billions of years before the advent of human beings and copyrights. Moreover, human societies with no patents or copyrights have produced, and continue to produce, great art, literature, and science.

Contrary to Arrow's argument, within a single market, patents, commercial secrets legislation, and the enforcement of intellectual property rights *reduce* the number of suppliers and *increase* unit value. Software patents are supposed to reward innovation, but in fact they inhibit it (Bessen and Maskin 2009). Yet the information technology (IT) industry has less strict patent protection than the biotechnology industry, and as a result, IT develops much faster than biotech. Antitrust laws and regulations, on the other hand, are intended to lower barriers to entry, reducing product value. Whether this works or not will depend on whether technical conditions favor new entrants. Nations that flout intellectual property rights may enjoy rapid technological gains and low product prices.

During wartime, warring parties show the least respect toward patents and copyrights. Many scientific and engineering breakthroughs are achieved in times of intense conflict. Historically, latecomers that turned into industrial powers, including the United States, displayed little regard toward patents and copyrights in their period of takeoff. The policy of protection and emulation in the nineteenth century was known as the *American system*. The British, at the time, preached Free Trade. They resented the Americans just as the Americans today resent the Chinese.

It is natural for dominant players to proclaim their sovereignty over important assets, whether physical or informational. It is also natural for the nondominant majority to use resources available at the lowest possible cost and to disregard claims of property rights. It is natural for the dominant players to forget, or pretend to forget, that they once did the same.

A POLITICAL ANALYSIS

As we noted in the preface, the ruling class in a society generally adopts the policy of "divide and rule." To achieve this, the ruling class divides the lower classes by race, ethnicity, religion, culture, gender, sexual orientation, and other criteria. So long as no single group becomes too well defined and too powerful, this division will lower the value and power of those who are ruled. Favors and subsidies extended to some groups, but not to others, excite the animosity of those excluded. This creates internal conflicts and makes the people easier to control.

In a biography of Winston Churchill, it was stated that Churchill "naturally had a lively sympathy for the underdog, particularly against the middle-dog, provided, and it was quite a big proviso, that his own position as a top-dog was unchallenged" (Jenkins 2001, 180). This Churchillian practice is quite standard in politics and economics. But there is little academic research about such practices. Churchill has become such an icon for the "top dogs" that "researching less popular episodes in Churchill's life . . . would either finish their careers, preclude them from promotion, or make them outcasts in academia" (Hirsch 2018).

Churchill's method is the standard practice of the top dogs. Top dogs, with low capital gains taxes and many loopholes, enjoy tax havens. Warren Buffett once confessed, or bragged, that his tax rate is much lower than that of his secretary. The incomes of middle dogs are taxed heavily to support the welfare of underdogs. With the help of policies and preferences supported by top dogs, often sold as "progressive," underdogs maul middle dogs viciously and vice versa, while top dogs enjoy their privileges. In the past half century, in North America and Europe, the wealth of the upper class has skyrocketed; the living standards of the lower classes have improved somewhat; but the living standard of the middle class has mostly stagnated.

We can apply value theory to a political analysis of this general type. Suppose 10 percent of the population are upper class, 30 percent are middle class, and 60 percent are lower class. Top dogs are scarce, middle dogs are middling scarce, underdogs are plentiful. Suppose that all voters vote according to their perceived class interest: aristocrats, bourgeoisie, and proletarians. However, the size of the group makes a difference. From our theory, smaller and more compact groups are more conscious of their own interests and therefore more coherent as a political entity, as well as more active. Their political value is higher.

Suppose there are two choices—two candidates—in an election. Then the value, in this election, to each candidate of a member of the upper class is $-\log_2 0.1 = 3.32$, the value or political weight of a member of the middle class is $-\log_2 0.3 = 1.74$, the value of a member of the lower class is $-\log_2 0.6 = 0.74$. Individually, to each candidate, lower-class votes are worth less, by a factor of about 5, even though the lower classes hold a strong numerical majority. That is because the lower classes, being abundant, are less coherent. Overall, taking this into account, the weights of the lower class and of the middle class are each only slightly more than the weight of the small minority in the upper class. And by making an alliance with the lower class—even an inefficient one—the upper class can dominate the outcome of the election.

Now suppose the upper class attempts to increase its distance from the middle class. With political power, it taxes the middle class and increases social subsidies for the lower class. Together, the new middle-and-lower class now represents 90 percent of the total population. You might think this will increase their joint power, but in fact, the value of any one member of the new equalized middle/lower class is now $-\log_2 0.9 = 0.15$. The value of a member of the upper class is unchanged. The new middle/lower class is very numerous but very hard to bring effectively to bear on the election. Even a 9/1 numerical majority is now not enough. In this way, the power of the upper class becomes much greater than the rest of the society.

However, the upper class would not stop here. The middle and lower classes can be divided by their race, religion, geography, gender, sexual orientation, and many other factors. In this way, the lower and middle classes are split into many groups, hostile to each other. If there were still only two candidates, that might raise the salience and value of each group, forcing each candidate to pay more attention to each one. That is the hope of the many middle/lower-class political organizers, each representing a group. But since these groups are mutually hostile, they have a hard time finding common cause.

So now there are many candidates for office, drawn from the different groups, and the base of the logarithm function, instead of the original 2, becomes a much larger number. Suppose the new number is 10. The value or power of a member of the new equalized middle/lower class is now $-\log_{10} 0.9 = 0.05$. This is a further reduction from the already diminished value after implementing the "equalizing" policy. The top dogs strengthen their control.

Divide and rule is effective. And fractious behavior is endemic to opposed elements within the population and (notoriously) to left-wing politics. The policy of fostering sectarian politics among the lower classes greatly reduces the political power of the majority. Meanwhile, power and wealth in society is consolidated into the hands of a small elite. This is how oligarchs rule.

CONCLUDING REMARKS

Jevons developed a simple and elegant mathematical model for the marginal utility theory of value in a two-person economy. That was a great appeal of his theory. But when the theory was generalized into multiperson economy, it encountered many difficulties. These difficulties show that the marginal utility theory of value could not describe reality accurately. The utility theory of value eventually morphed into the Arrow-Debreu model. It is rigorous mathematically. Yet the Arrow-Debreu model has little relevance to economic reality.

The mathematics of the entropy theory of value describe reality accurately. The theory is also very simple. It greatly clarifies our understanding of a broad range of social and economic phenomena. Combined with the social and political determination of wages and interest, it covers most of the problems of price setting with which economics needs to deal.

Some might argue that the entropy theory of value offers fewer answers than the utility theory of value. It doesn't prove the existence of an equilibrium state, whereas the utility theory does. But there is a reason for this. The entropy theory doesn't prove the existence of an equilibrium state because equilibrium states do not exist in real life. We are not at the "end of history." Western countries are not "developed" countries. Most Western countries have aging populations and low fertility rates. Most Western countries, containing aging populations and infrastructure with very high fixed costs, are very vulnerable to pandemics and other disturbances, including wars. Equilibrium theory gives us a false sense of security.

The entropy theory of value doesn't assert the Pareto optimality of any system, and the utility theory does. For example, in North Korea, the Kim family enjoys great power and privilege. Any change of the social system, even if highly beneficial to the North Korean people, will harm the Kim family. Thus, the North Korean system is Pareto-optimal! In a world with eight billion people, a social system that benefits a single person at the cost of eight billion people is Pareto-optimal. Indeed, any existing or once-existing social system benefits the ruling elite and is actively defended by the ruling elite. They are all Pareto-optimal. Whatever the original intention of the early developers of the concept of Pareto optimality, it has become the defender of the most oppressive social systems in the world.

The entropy theory of value lacks the innate appeal of Pareto optimality and general equilibrium. Nothing about it suggests that the beautiful system it describes will last forever. But . . . such a theory has an offsetting advantage. It describes the world as it is.

⊙ 5 ⊙

Resources and the Theory of Production

Great effort has been made, including in mainstream economics, to understand the long-term pattern of economic activities. *The Rise and Fall of American Growth* by Robert J. Gordon is a recent example. At the beginning of this book, Gordon correctly states:

> Growth theory features an economy operating in a "steady state" in which a continuing inflow of new ideas and technologies creates opportunities for investment. But articles on growth theory rarely mention that the model does not apply to most of human existence. (Gordon 2016, 2)

Gordon later summarized the history of US economic performance with the following:

> Put simply, the nation's output grew much more quickly than its capital input between 1928 and 1972 and then much more slowly from 1972 to 2013. The annualized growth rate of the output-capital ratio between 1928 and 1972 was 0.9 percent per year and then fell at −0.8 percent per year from 1972 to 2013. This history raises deep questions. (Gordon 2016, 546)

In Gordon's book, the explanation of this simple pattern, following the standard economic theory, is long and convoluted.[1] But the explanation can be very simple if we base it on the abundance and cost of oil. Around 1928, many giant oil fields were discovered, due to luck and the improvement of exploration techniques. This started the age of cheap oil. After 1973, oil prices became high. Productivity growth slowed down.

There was a short period, from 1996 to 2004, when US productivity gain was once again high. Gordon writes:

> The growth rate of aggregate U.S. productivity soared in 1996–2004 to roughly double its rate in 1972–96. However, . . . after 2004, when growth in labor productivity returned, after its eight-year surge, to the slow rates of 1972–96, despite the proliferation of flat screen desktop computers, laptops, and smartphones in the decade after 2004. (Gordon 2016, 17)

The standard explanation for the high productivity gain from 1996 to 2004 is the advance of information technology. But this explanation breaks down after 2004. Prices of major commodities, such as oil, were low from 1996 to 2004. They started rising again thereafter. This is a much simpler and more parsimonious explanation. Why then does the cost of oil not figure into the analysis given by Gordon or other mainstream neoclassical economists? To understand this, we offer an excursion into the underlying theory of production.

PRODUCTION FUNCTIONS IN NEOCLASSICAL ECONOMICS

Gordon's analysis relies, at least implicitly, on the mainstream, or neoclassical, production theory, which in turn builds on the concept of a production function. This mathematical expression relates the inputs, or factors of production, to the output, typically either a physical flow of goods, a flow of services, or the aggregate value of economic output for the whole system. The factors are either fixed (we call this *capital*) or variable (called *labor*), although there are elements of capital that are variable and elements of labor that are fixed. The technology of the production function is given by the form and the coefficients of the function used. Resources do not figure in the story unless they are subsumed under "capital." That, of course, makes it difficult to consider the possible role of a particular resource, such as oil, which accounts directly for only a small share of total expenditure in the economy.

The most well-known form of the production function is the Cobb-Douglas production function. It is a familiar equation to graduate students in economics, though more complicated versions also appear.

For our purposes, the Cobb-Douglas function is a sufficient representation of the core of mainstream production theory. It can be used to describe both a small-scale production setting, such as that of a firm or factory, or the large-scale production relations of the whole economy. This latter is called a *macroeconomic production function*. The concept is shaky, as a comment from Robert Solow illustrates: "I have never thought of the macroeconomic production function as a rigorously justifiable concept. In my mind it is either an illuminating parable, or else a mere device for handling data, to be used so long as it gives good empirical results, and to be discarded as soon as it doesn't, or as something better comes along" (Solow 1966, 1259).

Nevertheless, the Cobb-Douglas production function continues to be presented to economists as a mathematical representation of production.

The Cobb-Douglas function takes the form

$$Y = AK^\alpha L^{1-\alpha},$$

where Y, L, and K denote output, labor (variable cost), and capital (fixed cost), respectively. Since α and $(1 - \alpha)$ sum to 1, the Cobb-Douglas function (in this form) exhibits constant returns. If we substitute a more generic β for $(1 - \alpha)$, then the sum can be less than 1, indicating diminishing returns, or greater than 1, indicating increasing returns. However, in most treatments, constant returns to scale are assumed. This means that if the two inputs are doubled in quantity, output will also double. Constant returns to scale are very common in economic theory. But they are very hard to find in real life.

The form and parameters of Cobb-Douglas function are given without rigorous justification. In principle, the factor mix is flexible and can respond to changes in the relative price of capital and labor. What role could changing ratios of capital to labor, brought on by changing optimal choices of technique, have played in the history Gordon recounts? Can the production function cast light on this question? It may be helpful to do something we have seldom encountered in textbooks—namely, to give some specific numerical illustrations of how the Cobb-Douglas production process is supposed to work.

To gain further understanding about the Cobb-Douglas function, consider the following calculations. Let A, the constant term, take the value of 2. Let capital and labor inputs sum to unity—the canonical case of constant returns to scale. Let α take values from 0.1 to 0.9. For each value of α, let capital take a value from 0.1 to 0.9, while labor takes a value from 0.9 to 0.1, correspondingly. Thus, our measures of capital and labor are scaled to give a series of capital-labor ratios, from extreme capital intensity to extreme labor intensity of production. The output values of the different scenarios are listed in the following table, with capital values reported along the column headings and the coefficients (α values) reported down the rows.

From this calculation, when α approaches 0 or 1, output reaches a maximum at the highest or lowest ratios of capital to labor. This is the value 1.44 in our example. Assuming that the prices of inputs and the price of output are given to competitive firms, so that profit depends on output alone, this means that either pure labor or pure capital are the optimal production modes under the Cobb-Douglas specification! This is not consistent with empirical patterns.

Also from the calculation, when the ratio of capital to labor is equal to the ratio of α to $(1 - α)$—that is, along the diagonal of the table from northwest to southeast—output is maximized for that value of α. In other words, there is no flexibility in the proportion of capital and labor for any given production technology, represented by α. To survive in a competitive market, one must follow the pre-determined proportions of capital and labor, given by the ratio of the production function coefficients. To put the matter simply, the

TABLE 5.1. Outputs of the Cobb-Douglas function under varying coefficients and K/L ratios

Capital	0.1	0.2	0.3	0.4	0.5	0.6	0.7	0.8	0.9
α									
0.1	*1.44*	1.39	1.29	1.15	1.00	0.83	0.65	0.46	0.25
0.2	1.16	*1.21*	1.18	1.11	1.00	0.87	0.71	0.53	0.31
0.3	0.93	1.06	*1.09*	1.06	1.00	0.90	0.77	0.61	0.39
0.4	0.75	0.92	1.00	*1.02*	1.00	0.94	0.84	0.70	0.48
0.5	0.60	0.80	0.92	0.98	*1.00*	0.98	0.92	0.80	0.60
0.6	0.48	0.70	0.84	0.94	1.00	*1.02*	1.00	0.92	0.75
0.7	0.39	0.61	0.77	0.90	1.00	1.06	*1.09*	1.06	0.93
0.8	0.31	0.53	0.71	0.87	1.00	1.11	1.18	*1.21*	1.16
0.9	0.25	0.46	0.65	0.83	1.00	1.15	1.29	1.39	*1.44*

Cobb-Douglas production function was supposed to represent a world of flexible substitution between capital and labor. But it doesn't even do that. Once you have a specified technology, the maximum output and therefore the mix of capital and labor is predetermined.

In an input-output model, one would assume the input is consumed in the process of producing output. However, in the standard literature, capital (K) is retained from one period to the next, albeit with a reduction owing to depreciation (Nobel Foundation 2018, 9). If that is the case, it would be advantageous to use as much capital as possible in each period. One might argue capital is long-term. However, if capital is long-term, its benefits should be released over the long term, not discharged in every unit of time. But the model fully discharges the benefits of capital in each period. This is most peculiar.

In this theory, labor seems to be independent. Its supply is given exogenously. But in the real world, the labor supply is not independent. When the demand for education level is high, the fertility rate is low. This means that an increase in the share of capital, including so-called human capital, will depress labor input over the long term.

Where, again, are resources in the Cobb-Douglas model? One might say they form part of "Capital." But if they do, they play no special role and are treated exactly like machines. This is not a very useful way to think about the role played by resources in economic processes.

Finally, what about "A," the constant term at the start of the Cobb-Douglas expression? It "has been called, among other things, 'technical change,' 'total factor productivity,' 'the residual' and 'the measure of our ignorance'" (Blaug 1980, 465). Evidently, it is the supposed variability of this number that puzzles Gordon—productivity, independent of any change in factor ratios, speeds up and slows down. But how can a constant term become a variable? One might argue that A is not constant with different production modes. But then we would need to designate A as a function of the production mode, not as a constant. The production function specification gives no guidance on how to do this, and this accounts for the mystery associated with changing rates of productivity growth.

In sum, the Cobb-Douglas production function has little relevance to real economic activities. A recent meta-analysis of research on Cobb-Douglas functions concludes that "the weight of evidence accumulated in the empirical literature emphatically rejects the Cobb-Douglas specification" (Gechert et al. 2021, 55). There is no reason to believe that further elaborations of this functional form (such as the trans-log or constant elasticity of substitution versions) can overcome the basic deficiency of irrelevance.

One might argue that there is no alternative. But there is one. The production theory presented in this book is derived rigorously from the fundamental properties of life systems. It gives simple and clear analytical estimates of returns to investment under different market conditions. It explains in simple terms why the cost of resources is critical to the profitability and measured productivity of any economic system, whether we consider an ordinary business firm, an entire country, or even a humble household. We will present this theory in a mathematical form in the next chapter. In the next sections, we motivate a theory of production that is based on resources, their quality, their cost, and the fixed investments required to obtain them.

TECHNOLOGIES, ENERGY, AND CHOICE OF TECHNIQUE

Resources are low-entropy sources or materials providing a gradient to the environment. But to utilize resources requires structures to harness entropy flows. These structures are called *technologies*. At the most basic analytical level, the periodic table can guide us to see what kinds of chemical elements are the best raw materials for building structures to harness entropy flows. Table 5.2 shows the first three rows of the periodic table without the column for noble gases, which are chemically inactive.

As table 5.2 shows, carbon is the first element of the fourth column (the center column of the periodic table). Carbon is the lightest of a group of elements with four valence bonds that are largely chemically neutral. The chemical neutrality and large number of valence bonds

TABLE 5.2. The first three rows of the periodic table of the elements, minus the chemically inactive noble gases

H						
Li	Be	B	C	N	O	F
Na	Mg	Al	Si	P	S	Cl

makes it easy for carbon to link with many different atoms to form large molecules and complex structures. Large molecules are essential for the preservation of life. They help to withstand random dissipation (Schrodinger 1944). Large molecules are also essential for performing complex and varied tasks. This is why carbon, and carbon alone, is the backbone of life (Atkins 1995). The stable and weak bond of carbon is ideal for storing and releasing energy. For this reason, carbon underpins all carriers of organic energy, including natural gas, petroleum, and coal. Hydrogen is the smallest and the lightest element. That is why hydrogen is a low-cost carrier of energy and building block of an organic system.

For a technology to last, it must be able to utilize energy to make another copy of itself before it wears out. Living systems are technologies that last. Carbon and hydrogen atoms are natural raw materials that make up living systems. Since the buildup of living systems embodies energy resources, living systems themselves become resources that can be used by other living systems. Animals eat plants, other animals, fungi, and bacteria. Bacteria eat plants, animals, and other bacteria. Viruses eat bacteria, plants, and animals. Human beings and many bacteria also consume fossil fuels, which are transformed from the dead bodies of living systems.

The earliest organisms that developed the structure for photosynthesis were probably bacteria. These bacteria utilized solar energy to build up structures with carbon, hydrogen, and other kinds of atoms. Bacteria obtained carbon atoms from carbon dioxide. Initially, bacteria obtained hydrogen from hydrogen sulfide (H_2S) via photosynthesis. Compared with water (H_2O), the chemical bond in hydrogen sulfide is weak. From table 5.2, both oxygen and sulfur are at the sixth column of the periodic table. Their chemical properties are similar. But sulfur is one row lower than oxygen; the sulfur atom is larger than the oxygen atom. Therefore, the electric force from sulfur is weaker than the electric force from oxygen. It takes less effort, or lower fixed cost, to get hydrogen from hydrogen sulfide. Yet there is a problem: "When hydrogen is removed from hydrogen sulfide in the interior of a bacterium, the excrement is sulfur. Sulfur, being a solid, does not waft away, so the colony of organisms has to develop a mode of survival based on a gradually accumulating mound of its own sewage" (Atkins 1995, 22). Eventually, to get the hydrogen they needed, organisms developed techniques to break the strong bond in water. Oxygen is a byproduct of this technology. Since oxygen is a gas, the pollution does not accumulate locally. It spreads out globally. Another advantage of obtaining hydrogen from water is the abundance of water. With water as a raw material in photosynthesis, living systems spread all over the Earth.

Oxygen molecules, the waste product from photosynthesis, are highly energetic. This energy destroyed many early living systems and rusts many materials. Eventually, some organisms evolved the structure to harness the energy from oxygen. These organisms used antioxidant technology to reduce the destructive power of the energy from oxygen to tolerable levels. Animals, whose active lifestyle requires substantial energy consumption, evolved to take advantage of the abundant atmospheric oxygen. All materials with a gradient against the environment have the capacity to destroy. Only after technologies emerge to harness the gradient of these materials and contain their destructive power do these materials become resources.

Photosynthesis is probably the most important technology organisms have ever developed. It transforms the vast amount of light energy, which is difficult to store, into chemical energy, which is easy to store. And the amount of solar energy available to early photosynthetic bacteria was almost infinite. Those bacteria multiplied quickly. Over time, photosynthetic organisms came to cover most parts of the world. Since the invention of photosynthesis, almost all living organisms have come to derive energy available to them from solar energy, directly or indirectly.

If a technology helps an organism to earn a positive return on resource utilization, the technology will be duplicated and will spread. However, not all technologies developed by organisms are able to provide a nonnegative return consistently. Most genetic mutations or innovations are harmful. Even among those mutations where new species are established, more than 99.9 percent of the species eventually went extinct. Technology and innovation do not guarantee prosperity and safety to any biological species, nor to human societies that adopt them. This is obvious when one considers just about any case, from gunpowder to nuclear fission, but it is obscured by words like *productivity* and *progress* in mainstream economics.

A technology is not only expensive to develop; it is also expensive to maintain. Some fish living in dark underground caves become blind because eyes are expensive to maintain. This is also true for the famous blind salamander of Barton Springs in Austin, Texas. When eyes are no more useful, their structures degenerate. Similarly, the sense of smell of human beings is highly degenerated from that possessed by our ancestors. Walking upright increases our dependence on vision and reduces our dependence on smell. As a result, smell is under less selection pressure. A technology will be developed and maintained if its return on investment is positive during that period. Otherwise, the technology or its host will degenerate.

With the continuous multiplication of organisms, resources will become scarce and the limiting factor of growth. Competition for scarce resources is the permanent theme of life. Individual organisms defend themselves or are consumed by other organisms. There are two main strategies: to form social groups for mutual protection and to enhance individual power. Social sciences are generally viewed as being exclusively concerned with humanity. But almost all organisms form social groups (Trivers 1985; Willey, Sherwood, and Woolverton 2011). Bacteria can live alone. They often thrive better in groups. Most organisms need to develop effective means of communicating or coordinating with other organisms. Social biology was developed to study these phenomena.

As with social behavior between organisms, so too is the coordination of functions within organisms. Long ago, some single-celled organisms evolved into multicelled organisms. Multicelled organisms are larger than a single-celled organism. Ultimately, an individual multicell organism can grow into a collection of many trillions of cells. Large animals can often overpower small animals and control more resources. But multicell organisms also need to communicate and coordinate among different cells inside their own body, through hormones and nerve cells. This very much resembles how different individuals in a society need to communicate and coordinate with each other.

Technologies in human societies are generally understood as tools. These tools exist outside our bodies. The making of tools is not constrained by our body's physical and chemical environment. For example, iron smelting requires a temperature above 1,500°C, much higher than our body temperature. Aluminum smelting requires strong electric currents that would kill us instantly. However, all biological and human technologies are bound by the same economic principle. If a technology generates a positive return in any system, it will be developed and maintained. If not, it will decline. Since different technologies require different social structures and bring in different amounts of resources, technical structures and social structures become closely intertwined.

We study past events to estimate the possible patterns in the future and to guide our actions today. The events that greatly affected the lives of people in the past, such as the Industrial Revolution, the Great Depression in the 1930s, the oil crises in the 1970s, and the 2008 Great Financial Crisis, have an especially strong grip on the minds of the public. The interpretation of these events greatly influences the public's vision about the future and the policies adopted by governments. In the following, we examine humanity's abilities to exploit energy and hence other resources over time.

FIRE, COOKING, AGRICULTURE

What is the most important activity that separates human beings from other animals? From an energy perspective, we might say the use of fire and cooking distinguishes humans (Wrangham 2009). Using fire makes us familiar with a chemical process of high energy intensity. This would become crucial in the development of the Bronze Age, Iron Age, and "Silicon Age." Human beings live comfortably in hot tropical areas. The use of fire greatly expands our habitats. Because of the use of fire, we can endure long winters in the deep North. Fire intimidates many fierce animals. This expands the territory of humans against other animals. Cooking kills most of the pathogens in food. Consequently, our bodies don't have to spend as much energy on our immune systems. Cooking, by breaking down large organic molecules, predigests food before it is consumed and, by breaking down cell walls, allows access to much more food. Our bodies don't have to spend as much energy on our digestive systems. The energy savings can be used to nourish other important systems, such as our brain, enabling more complex functions, such as language and abstract thought. Cooking reduces the risk of infectious disease. It enables human beings to live in higher density, with less moving around, which stimulates the need for better communication. Language, culture, and religion flourished to bind people together. All of this, thanks to fire.

Most researchers believe that sedentary lifestyles followed the advent of agriculture. But they could have preceded agriculture, in some places and under some circumstances. Some places have a very high concentration of resources. Along Highway 16 in British Columbia, Canada, there is a canyon at a place called Morristown. In salmon-spawning season, large numbers of salmon wait just below the canyon, preparing to jump over the rapids to reach their final spawning destinations. Anyone can scoop up a fish from the river with a net. The salmon are so abundant that local people can live a sedentary life around the canyon all year round. There are many such places in the Pacific Northwest, where salmon are abundant. Thus, some people could live sedentary lifestyles before the development of agriculture. The same pattern can be found in island fishing and shellfish-eating communities, for instance in the Pacific or the Caribbean. It could be that sedentary lifestyles led to agriculture, instead of the other way around. In general, if this is correct, sedentary lifestyles provided an incentive to practice agriculture, which requires intensive work in fixed fields for prolonged periods.

Although some sedentary lifestyles may have preceded agriculture, large-scale sedentary lifestyles followed the invention of agriculture. Agriculture is the growing of a few selected crops with active exclusion of most competing plants. Crops are mainly selected (and bred) for their nutrition value to humans and not for their competitiveness in the fields. They are usually not very competitive. The growth of crops requires intensive human intervention to remove weeds growing in the same fields. Crops, due to their high resource density, become a favored food source for microbes, other animals, and other people. Farmers must remain vigilant against other animals, including people. The increase of resource density always increases the potential of wars against raiders and poachers, from microbes on up. Because agriculture produces a higher energy yield than hunting and gathering, it can support higher human density. Gradually, farming communities replaced hunting and gathering communities in many places of the world. High human density comes with complex societies with many hierarchies.

BRONZE, IRON, CHARCOAL, COAL

Making bronze tools requires special smelting technology, and the advent of the Bronze Age was a significant step in the mastery of energy resources. Iron was a further, even larger step. The melting point of bronze is 232°C, and the melting point of iron is 1,535°C. It is much more difficult to smelt iron than to smelt bronze, and the technology of making iron was developed much later. Iron is much harder than bronze, so that weapons made from iron are more powerful. Iron tools can be used to cut down trees, from which charcoal is made. Charcoal is used to smelt iron. More charcoal led to more iron and more iron led to more charcoal.

This positive feedback greatly increased the output of energy and of iron equipment, such as swords and plows. Swords enabled iron-making people to expand their territories. Plows enabled iron-making people to get more nutrients from deep soil, improving crop yields and increasing population density. The arrival of the Iron Age generated the greatest burst of military, economic, and cultural activity in human history to that point. However, the amount of iron production was ultimately constrained by the availability of nearby trees to provide fuel for the smelting process. Increases in iron production led to deforestation, which limited the scale of iron output throughout most of the Iron Age. Indeed, deforestation and soil erosion often turned once-prosperous civilizations into desolate areas. A Dark Age, which consumed fewer resources, followed the Iron Age.

The Industrial Revolution has been interpreted in many ways. Here we offer an interpretation based on the interaction between resources and technology, not necessarily inconsistent with other interpretations. Before 1750, the need for charcoal in iron making deforested most of England (Jevons [1865] 1965). The limit to the supply of charcoal limited the supply of iron, which limited the supply of charcoal. Shortly before 1750, a technology of iron making with coal was invented in England, using coal supplies located near Newcastle, on the English coast. Mining and transportation of coal requires considerable iron equipment. After the invention of iron smelting by means of coke, derived from coal, coke replaced charcoal as the main fuel in iron making. Coal is much more abundant than wood and has much higher energy density than wood. More coal led to more iron and more iron led to more coal. The positive feedback between the output of coal and iron, the most important energy source and the most important material of that era, enabled human beings to increase tremendously in number and in prosperity. This was the essence of the Industrial Revolution.

Jevons was very aware of the importance of this invention. In *The Coal Question*, he described it in detail.

THE AGE OF OIL: FROM THE GREAT DEPRESSION
TO THE GREAT FINANCIAL CRISIS

Since the beginning of the Industrial Revolution, the global economy has grown steadily, most of the time. There have been several slowdowns, such as the Great Depression of the 1930s, the oil crisis in the 1970s, and the recent Great Recession or Great Financial Crisis.

The causes of the Great Depression have been long debated. Very often, they were attributed to structural weaknesses in various economic sectors and to policy mistakes by governments, or to monetary disorders resulting from international debts and the decline of British power in the world. From an energy-and-technology perspective, the transformation from a coal-based economy, centered on railways, to an oil-based economy, centered on cars and trucks, was partly responsible for the Great Depression.

Since the hydrogen content of oil is higher than that of coal, oil is a higher-quality energy source than coal. In the decade of the 1920s, the number of cars increased tremendously. But the supply of oil had been quite limited. Automobiles were regarded as a supplement to but not replacement for the railroad economy and the horse-powered agricultural sector. However, around the end of the 1920s and in the early 1930s, many gigantic oil fields were discovered, mainly in Texas, over a short period of time, due to the development of better exploration methods (Deffeyes 2001). It became very clear that the petroleum and car economy would replace the coal and railroad economy. A large part of the railroad economy fell apart upon this realization. But it took time for the car economy to grow enough to replace the railroad economy.

The structure of the railway-centered economy was very different from that of the highway-centered economy. In the railway-centered economy, areas around the train station were often prime real estate and the center of most economic activity in a city. In many cities, the street where the train station locates is called the first avenue. In a highway-centered economy, shopping areas are relocated to malls and residential areas are moved to suburbs. The shift of economic gravity devastated the downtown areas in many cities. Many once-prosperous towns built along railways became ghost towns when highways bypassed them.

Moreover, before 1920 about one-third of American agricultural land was in crops for forage, to feed the horses and other draft animals required to pull plows and other farm equipment. As mechanization reached the farms, those animals declined precipitously, and land previously used for forage could be converted to food crops, including rangeland for cattle. This made food more abundant and reduced the value and profitability of farming. Many farms failed, and many farmhands were forced to migrate to the cities (or to California) seeking work, which was not yet available. The powerful new equipment also broke up the soil on the American prairies, which created the Dust Bowl, an environmental catastrophe of the early 1930s.

The discovery of the giant oil fields around 1930 happened over a short period of time. The adjustment was very sudden and painful. The Great Depression was therefore unavoidable, regardless of government policies. It could be—and was—eventually mitigated by policies aimed at harnessing hydropower and building roads and airfields, but these measures did not immediately replace the activity lost due to the rise of oil and decline of coal.

Still, the abundance of oil, a higher-quality energy source than coal, set the stage for military production of tanks and aircraft during World War II and for the economic boom after the war, when oil from the Persian Gulf joined American oil on the market, and highways and gas stations were built in many parts of the world. The growth of the petroleum- and car-based economy greatly increased the consumption of petroleum. And this brings us to the period of fluctuating productivity growth that is offered as a puzzle by Gordon and other mainstream economists.

In 1956, M. King Hubbert proposed oil output in the US and in the world would eventually peak and decline (Deffeyes 2001). In 1970, US conventional oil production in the lower 48 states peaked, just as Hubbert had predicted. This increased the need for imported oil and worsened the US balance of payments. Under the then-existing monetary arrangements, the US was obliged to redeem dollars for gold, but the prospect of having to import ever-increasing volumes of oil made this untenable. Around the same time, many people became concerned by the increasing consumption of resources. A representative work at that time was *The Limits to Growth*, published in 1972, sponsored by the Club of Rome (Meadows 1972).

In 1971, the US government stopped converting US dollars to gold at the fixed rate of $35 per ounce, thus delinking the value of dollar to gold, a major commodity. After that, the value of the US dollar depreciated sharply against gold. This put heavy pressure on the price of other commodities, such as petroleum (Galbraith 2008). In 1973, the oil price jumped due to the collective action of major oil-exporting countries. This generated a deep recession in many oil-importing countries, including most wealthy countries. In 1979, events around the Iranian Revolution produced another sharp spike in oil prices, provoking a sharp rise in interest rates that caused a short recession in 1980 and a deep and prolonged recession in 1981–1982.

By the mid-1980s, most wealthy countries regained economic growth. The standard explanation is that these countries were able to overcome high oil prices with proper economic policies. Hence, according to the dominant theories, good economic policy can overcome resource scarcity. However, if we understand human society as a biological system, we will observe that in most wealthy countries, where resource consumption was and is high, fertility rates (which had peaked in the early 1960s), dropped below replacement rates after 1973. This shows that the biological rate of return had turned negative.

In turn, the drop in the fertility rate reduced the investment cost of raising the next generation. It also freed up many women to join the workforce. This generated economic growth, mostly due to an expanding services sector. Growth of this type continued for several decades, even as resource and capital-intensive manufacturing declined. Gross domestic product grew, productivity grew very slowly, and the United States and Europe became heavily dependent on foreign energy sources and Asian manufactured goods. They could grow, and largely prosper, only because of their financial preeminence and the sustained value of their monies—backed by military power.

But there is a limit to labor-force participation, especially as a population ages. This limit was reached by the time of the Great Financial Crisis. After that, older workers left the workforce in large numbers and did not return. This helped the unemployment rate come down quickly, even though the lost jobs were not replaced. Eventually, except for immigration from poor countries, negative biological returns will lead to social decline, as we are witnessing in many wealthy countries. Immigrants can fill the gap for a long time, but not indefinitely, and only if the immigrants are able to fill the same social roles that would have been performed by native-born citizens. Generally, this is unlikely; for worse or better, countries with many immigrants will adjust to the cultures that the immigrants bring with them.

Another adjustment for wealthy countries was to move manufacturing activities to poor countries. In most poor countries, ordinary people have minimal political power, and the ruling elites are happy to have new sources of export earnings. So "offshoring" reduced the need for processing waste and mitigating pollution, both of which are very energy intensive. Offshoring also reduced the wages paid to workers in manufacturing trades. Lower wages mean less resource consumption, and factories in subtropical and tropical zones typically operate with less heating, cooling, and other energy demands. Through offshoring, energy consumption in rich countries and indeed energy consumption overall was reduced, per unit of production.

In the 1970s, even though oil production in the (lower 48 states of the) US had peaked, global oil output was still growing rapidly, and the average cost of oil production was low. But the control of price setting for oil shifted from major oil-consuming countries—specifically the United States—to the oil-producing countries. By the end of the 1990s, with the rapid depletion of easy-to-extract oil, the average cost of oil steadily increased. In a now-classic 1998 paper titled "The End of Cheap Oil," Colin Campbell and Jean Laherrère, after carefully examining the oil exploration and production data, concluded, "What our society does face, and soon, is the end of the abundant and cheap oil on which all industrial nations depend" (Campbell and Laherrère 1998, 83).

In 1998, oil prices were in the low teens of dollars per barrel. Since the middle of the first decade of the twenty-first century, the price of oil, as well as other major commodities, has increased substantially. If we had recognized the fundamental importance of resources to the overall economy, we would have stopped measures to "stimulate" the economy after the burst of the internet bubble in 2000. However, the authorities at the time believed they had mastered the proper policy response and were not worried about the steady increase in oil prices. Indeed, they tended to favor a higher oil price because they represented high-cost American oil producers, notably in Texas and Oklahoma. They responded to the burst bubble with tax cuts, low interest rates, and increased government spending, notably for the wars in Afghanistan and Iraq, which also worked to keep oil from Iraq off the world market, while sanctions had a similar effect on Iran.

But the economic system in the United States could not expand in the face of high resource prices. Most economic activities in the US, and other rich countries, use rather than produce resources; high prices are a drain on profits and a disincentive to growth. Nevertheless, Wall Street and the larger culture demand high profits. To mask the failure to earn them, financial and business firms resorted to large-scale cooking of their books—to elaborate forms of financial fraud. Enron—an energy company, but in the pipeline business—was an early example. Tyco and WorldCom followed, and then, in massive form, so did the housing sector. The authorities in each case believed, or pretended to believe, that the growth and profits being reported were real. That is why they were unprepared when the financial crisis broke out in 2007 and 2008, just as oil prices peaked at about $147 per barrel.

During the Great Financial Crisis, oil prices collapsed. But then a new development emerged, which was *fracking*, enhanced recovery of oil and natural gas from oil-bearing shales deep underground in Pennsylvania, North Dakota, and especially the Permian Basin of Texas. Economic recovery occurred from 2009 forward, and there was even recovery of manufacturing in the United States thanks to competitive prices for natural gas, which was not heavily traded intercontinentally and therefore did not have a single world price. The fracking boom ended with the COVID-19 pandemic in 2020. When demand recovered in 2021, supply recovered more slowly, and prices for gasoline in the US soared. In Europe, economic competitiveness was maintained in the first two decades of the twenty-first century by inexpensive Russian gas, supplied over pipelines through Ukraine, Poland, and under the Baltic Sea. This flow was largely cut off in 2022, with serious consequences for European industry, which are unfolding at present writing.

According to neoclassical economic theories, recessions are short-term interruptions from long-term economic growth. After each recession, economic growth will eventually resume. If there is a problem with some resource, such as oil or gas, the price will rise and substitutes will be found. These days, with concern about climate change, large investments are being made in renewable electric power from solar panels and windmills. There is great confidence in some circles that these investments will permit us to cease using fossil fuels, that the cost of producing power from the new technologies will decline, and that growth will resume or continue.

But from a biological and resource perspective, long-term economic growth is not assured. In most wealthy countries, human replacement rates have been below one for almost fifty years, and so the biological rate of return has been below zero. The adjustment of the workforce to the decline of fertility has ended. Since 2008, net immigration to the United States has also been low, in fact collapsing almost altogether in the early 2020s. There is no guarantee that resource costs can be brought down. With high resource costs and the demographic structure of an inverse pyramid, economic activity will eventually decline.

This resource- and technology-based interpretation, together with its demographic consequences, provides a simple and consistent view of numerous major events in human history. There are many other interpretations; some are apparently competitors, but others, on inspection, are quite consistent with ours. For instance, financial crises are often blamed on human greed. There is certainly an element of truth in that accusation. But humans are always greedy, before and after financial crises. However, when resource costs are low, humans can afford to be less greedy, to share more, to leave others in peace. When resource costs rise, they become desperate, and make risky bets and foolish mistakes.

Financial crises are blamed on bad monetary policies—for instance, keeping interest rates too low for too long and "inflating bubbles." But in a system with abundant resources, a low-interest-rate policy only has a mild effect on inflation, while encouraging long-term investments that make even more efficient use of cheap resources. It's only when resources become expensive that long-term fixed investments run into trouble. Finally, financial crises are often blamed on widespread fraud. There was certainly colossal fraud before the crisis of 2008. But why was fraud so systematically practiced on this occasion? In an environment with increasing resource costs, fraud becomes the only viable way to generate a reported high rate of return, which is still expected by the public (and by the markets), which are accustomed to the good old days of abundant resources (Chen and Galbraith 2012b).

CONCLUDING REMARKS

To return to the questions posed by Robert Gordon, an integrated theory of biology and human society enables us to better understand long-term social trends. After the rise of oil prices in the 1970s, many countries regained economic growth only after deep recessions. How did this happen? Neoclassical economic theory contends that markets can overcome a scarcity of resources and directs our attention to changing technologies. But from a biological perspective, a different answer emerges.

Any living system, including human societies, requires above-replacement population fertility to be viable in the long term. Fertility in most wealthy countries dropped below the replacement rate in the 1970s, rendering their rate of return on biological investment negative. The initial drop in the fertility rates reduced the number of dependent children. This reduced the cost and the time required for raising children. Many more adults, especially women, became available as workers. With more workers, economic growth resumed, though at a low rate of productivity growth. This perspective puts the biological, not the technological, implication of more-expensive resources in the spotlight.

Countries in demographic transition often enjoy a high rate of growth in economic output for several decades. But eventually, the scope for more labor-force participation runs out, and as the working population ages, with far fewer next-generation workers to replace them, the ratio of working population to total population declines. Monetary activities will then decline eventually as well. Biological theory foretold the social problems of the former Soviet bloc, Japan, Europe, and many other countries several decades ago, when their biological return turned very negative. The United States and Canada have avoided these problems, for now, by exploiting additional energy resources and accepting many immigrants. Europe had the first option only through Russia, from which it is now cut off, and it has resisted the second. It is not hard to predict that Europe's growth problems will continue, at least for some time, to be more serious than those of the United States and Canada.

Elements of a Biophysical Production Theory

Neoclassical economists assume that human beings and social systems maximize utility, and that businesses try to maximize profits. From our daily experience, when we are hungry, we try to obtain food; when we are thirsty, we try to obtain water; when we are sexually mature, we long for a mate. Our preferences and activities are indeed directed by our short-term needs, or *utilities*. But short-term utilities are ways to achieve long-term goals—they are the means toward the goal of survival and reproduction.

For any biological or social system to survive and prosper, it must provide a nonnegative rate of return and sustain that return over time. In finance theory, the performance of a business is measured by its rate of return on monetary investment. In biological theory, the performance of an organism is measured by its rate of return on biological investment. The return on biological investment is the ability to sustain, reproduce, and grow a population. In energy extraction, the rate of return is measured as *energy return over energy invested*. EROI is defined as the amount of energy one can obtain from a given amount of energy devoted to the extraction of energy from the ground, the atom, or the Sun.

Over the long term, whether a system survives and prospers depends on its rate of return and not on achieving maximum profit or utility in the short run. This is as obvious as the fable of the ants and the grasshopper. A business will fail if it loses money over the long term, whether it maximizes its profit or not. Sometimes the maximum achievable profit is negative; and sometimes (as in the fable) a positive rate of return in the long run requires foregoing immediate gains—the quick buck or easy pleasure. Our investment and production decisions—both real and financial—over the medium and long term are of primary importance. Yet nothing is guaranteed. We all have limited capacity to forecast and to respond to surprises in an uncertain world. In this, we are not alone. After all, most species that have appeared on the Earth have already gone extinct; most powerful and prosperous societies eventually collapsed; most businesses that once existed have failed. This was not for lack of trying to survive and to succeed.

As researchers of biological and social systems, we hope to understand why a system does well or fails. For this purpose, understanding our objective measure—and why "rate of return over time" is different from "utility maximization at all moments and at all costs"—is most useful. We judge success over time. A successful person, firm, or country has arrangements that promote stability over time, even though not every impulse can be, or should be, satisfied at each moment. This is the most basic common sense, familiar to every parent and every business manager. Only small children and economists sometimes take a different view.

Establishing an objective measure of performance does not mean that the human mind and emotion and will are not important. On the contrary, the human mind and emotion have evolved to generate positive biological returns. It is our love of children that enables us to feed and protect helpless babies—even though they do not always make us happy. It is because of the irresistible attraction to the opposite sex—or, for that matter, to another person of the same sex—that two very different individuals live together to raise the next generation. These relationships necessarily work out over time, and we reject and disparage people (for good reason) who insist on instant or constant gratification.

Our emotions, even if they are sound and stable, do not always help us gain a positive return over time. The human mind is an evolutionary product of the past. The environment we live in today is very different from the past. We adapt our behavior to what we think produces success, but we may be wrong. What worked in the past may not work well in the future. A return-based theory allows us to analyze the long-term effects of our own behaviors, the strategies of our businesses, the structure of our societies, and the policies of our governments.

If a return-based theory provides clarity about our society, how can we explain the dominance of a utility-based theory in economics and of "profit maximization" in production decisions? There are many reasons; here we will discuss one. The very first paper that introduced the concept of utility in economics was written by Daniel Bernoulli and originally was published in 1738 (Bernoulli 1738). In that paper, Bernoulli showed that the arithmetic rate of return (simple interest) does not provide a good measure of return. He proposed what he called the concept of *utility* to replace the arithmetic rate of return. But Daniel Bernoulli's logarithmic utility function was equivalent to a geometric (or compound interest) rate of return. The geometric rate of return provides a more accurate measure of return than the arithmetic rate of return over time (or over a probability space). If we adopt the geometric rate of return as our measure of return, we can resolve the problem raised by Bernoulli without resorting to the utility function. The idea of *utility* is simply an unnecessary decoration—a distraction.

By adopting a common measure of performance for our production decisions for both biological systems and social systems, we can understand biology and social sciences as an integrated theory. Social systems, like other biological systems, are enabled and constrained by physical resources and physical principles and require nonnegative returns for their long-term viability.

Production decisions involve many factors. These include—among the most important—fixed cost, variable cost, uncertainty, discount rates, investment life span, and product output. That's quite a list, but with some work we can relate them all to a theory of production. The relations among these factors are subtle and delicate. We discuss the relations of some of these factors qualitatively in the next several sections. In the chapter that follows, we will present a mathematical discussion of the relationships we discuss below.

FIXED AND VARIABLE COSTS

From thermodynamic theory, useful work can be obtained only when a differential, or gradient, exists between two parts of a system. In general, the higher the gradient, the more efficiently energy can be transformed into useful work. This is the famed Carnot's Principle, the foundation of thermodynamics. At the same time, creating and maintaining a high differential is difficult and hence expensive. The economic principle is a consequence of the physical principle.

Plants can utilize sunlight to generate chemical energy because the Sun is much hotter than the Earth. We can utilize water flow to generate electricity when water flows from a higher place to a lower place. Birds exploit the edges of the forest. Fish exploit currents and temperature differentials in the sea. However, fixed investment is required before positive returns can be generated. Plants must make chlorophyll before they can transform solar energy into chemical energy. Humans must build dams and install electricity generators before electricity can be produced and transmitted. In general, all organisms require a fixed set of genes before they can reproduce themselves.

In the language of economics, it requires fixed costs to transform resources profitably. Fixed costs reduce variable costs, making higher profits possible. In general, a lower-variable-cost system requires higher fixed cost, although the reverse is not necessarily true, since a production process can be inefficient. In general, a higher fixed cost and lower variable cost promotes profitability, but this also is not always true. We can give several examples from engineering, biology, and economics to illustrate the trade-off between fixed and variable costs. Some of these we have mentioned before.

In electricity transmission, higher voltage will lower heat loss. But higher-voltage transmission systems are more expensive to build and maintain. The differential of water levels above and below a hydro dam generates electricity. The higher the hydro dam, the more electricity can be generated. But a higher dam is more expensive to build and needs to withstand higher water pressure. In an internal combustion engine, the higher the temperature differential between the combustion chamber and the environment, the higher the efficiency in transforming heat into work. But it is more expensive to build a combustion chamber that can withstand higher temperature and pressure. Diesel burns at a higher temperature than gasoline. The energy efficiency of diesel engines is higher, and the cost of building a diesel engine is higher as well.

Traffic moves more easily on highways with more lanes. But it is more expensive to build highways with more lanes. Shops located near higher traffic flows generate higher sales volumes. But the rental costs in such locations are also higher. Well-trained employees work more effectively. But employee training is costly. People with higher education levels on average command higher income. But education takes time, effort, and money. These are among the many economic examples of the same principle.

The fixed cost of a system is often its defining characteristic. It is often used as a classification criterion in many research areas, although the term *fixed cost* is not necessarily used. In cultural studies, cultures are often classified as high-context cultures and low-context cultures. In ecological studies, species are classified as K species (high fixed cost) and r species (low fixed cost). In the study of social systems, societies are often classified as complex (high fixed cost) or simple (low fixed cost). Many debates in our societies are about the level of fixed cost. When we say education is a right, we really mean that education should be part of the fixed cost of the society and that the state should pay for public education out of tax revenue, or more precisely, that the state's whole population should pay, according to tax law.

For any living organism to be viable, its cost to obtain resources cannot exceed the value of those resources, over the life cycle of the organism. Similarly, for a business to be viable in the long term, its average cost of operation cannot exceed its average revenue. The main feature of an organism or a business is the structure of its fixed and variable costs; this determines whether the total cost can be lower than revenue in specific environments. Historically, lower-fixed-cost systems often appear earlier than higher-fixed-cost systems. Single-celled organisms appear earlier than multicellular organisms. Cold-blooded animals appear earlier than warm-blooded animals. Small family-owned shops appear earlier than large global companies.

Fixed costs in wealthy societies are also higher than fixed costs in poor societies. As we have discussed, wealthy societies often have compulsory secondary education and easy-to-access postsecondary education, whereas people in poor societies often start working at an early age. Wealthy societies often have well-maintained roads, free public libraries, and relatively open and fair legal systems, all of which require high maintenance costs; poor societies usually don't have many of these things. Many people feel that the world will continue to evolve toward more complex, higher-fixed-cost systems, with only occasional setbacks. However, if we look at longer time spans and broader scales, the evolutionary patterns are subtler.

> The "Doctrine of the Unspecialized" ... describes the fact that the highly developed, or specialized types of one geological period have not been the parents of the types of succeeding periods, but that the descent has been derived from the less specialized of preceding ages ... The validity of this law is due to the fact that the specialized types of all periods have been generally incapable of adaptation to the changed conditions which characterized the advent of new periods ... Such changes have been often especially severe in their effects on species of large size, which required food in great quantities ... Animals of omnivorous food-habits would survive where those which required special foods would die. Species of small size would survive a scarcity of food, while large ones would perish ... An extreme specialization ... has been, like an overperfection of structure, unfavorable to survival. (Cope 1896, 173–174)

We often have the impression that higher-fixed-cost systems are better than lower-fixed-cost systems. Simple organisms or societies are generally called *primitive*, whereas complex organisms or societies are generally called *advanced*. However, biologists now recognize that systems of different fixed costs are adapted to different kinds of environments. Indeed, all life forms, simple or complex, are successful outcomes of unbroken chains of almost four billion years of survival and reproduction. The proper amount of fixed investment depends on the amount of resources available. In an environment of abundant resources, large, high-fixed-cost systems dominate; in an environment of scarce resources, small, low-fixed-cost systems break even more easily.

In the past several hundred years, with the large-scale use of fossil fuels, higher-fixed-cost social systems did well most of the time, expanding to global scale. Population also grew rapidly, since with good infrastructure and abundant resources the cost of raising children was quite low. Biological returns were high; at the peak we had the "baby boom" in the industrial West. To most economists, demographic changes are not the fundamental determinant of long-term economic activities. But as we have observed several times, the demographic boom ended with the age of cheap resources.

During the 2008 financial crisis and ensuing recession, policymakers injected large amounts of money to pump up the financial and automotive sectors, two of the highest-fixed-cost industries. Policymakers expected these sectors to generate high profits and good jobs once the economy started to grow again. However, from the perspective of resource scarcity, the bailout of these high-fixed-cost industries only delayed the necessary adjustments toward a lower-fixed-cost society. After 2008, US financial markets enjoyed the longest bull market in history. During the same period, fertility in the US dropped even further below the replacement rate.

The increase of fixed cost is often associated with the division of labor. Instead of a single cell handling all biological functions, a multicellular organism often consists of many different organs, such as heart and liver, each responsible for specific functions. Unspecialized stem blood cells reproduce easily. But once these unspecialized stem cells become red blood cells and various white blood cells, they cannot reproduce themselves anymore. In general, specialized cells, such as red blood cells and neuron cells, are infertile or less fertile. Similarly, in human societies, highly trained professionals tend to have smaller families. Being a parent requires a lot of general skills—such as changing diapers, feeding the babies, and cooking—that are possessed by so-called unskilled workers but are valued less by many highly trained specialists. If the fixed cost of a system becomes too high and many people in the system become overspecialized, once again the average fertility of the social system will decline. This can help us understand why fertility rates remain higher in some poorer parts of the world, such as sub-Saharan Africa, which currently enjoy the highest population-growth rates.

The trade-off between fixed cost and variable cost is universal in economic activities. However, this trade-off is often not explicitly discussed in the economics literature and often not considered in policy discourse. Fixed cost is frequently ignored. For example, electricity generated from solar panels is considered clean energy because the solar panel does not need fuels that will cause environmental problems. But the manufacturing of solar panels is highly resource-intensive and polluting. Electric cars are considered clean because driving an electric car does not emit carbon dioxide or other pollutants. But the manufacturing of car batteries is very resource intensive and very polluting.

The pollution from manufacturing solar panels and car batteries—the fixed-cost part of solar electricity and electric cars—is rarely mentioned in policy discussions. Although it is in the interest of the promoters of "clean" energy and "renewable" energy to avoid discussing such issues, a good economic theory should provide guidance on them. It is not the job of a scientist to go along with good feelings and public relations.

DIMINISHING AND INCREASING RETURNS

Since all use of resources requires a prior fixed investment, there is a fixed cost for any production system. As output increases, the fixed cost is shared across a higher production volume. In a pizza shop, one must first build a hot oven. This is a fixed cost. As orders increase, that cost is spread over more customers and more pizzas. Average cost declines. There is an increasing return to scale. Another source of increasing returns comes from the relationship between oven volume and surface area. The volume of the oven increases more rapidly than the surface area, or cost of building the oven, so that larger ovens (up to a point) have lower per pizza costs, if they are fully used. If they are not fully used, then the pizza shop may fail.

Low-cost, easier-to-access markets are usually served first. For a pizza-delivery store, the delivery costs to nearby customers are usually lower than those to distant customers. As the store expands its business to larger areas, its delivery cost per pizza will increase. This is a source of diminishing returns to scale.

Diminishing and increasing returns are practically universal characteristics of all business activities, and indeed of all life processes. Constant returns to scale, the foundation of the mainstream production function, are a mathematical approximation that is practically never observed exactly in real life, except over very short periods and small changes. To assume constant returns is like taking the tangents of an ever-changing curve.

For any business, both increasing and diminishing returns are at work. The specific cost curves for specific businesses will be different for different businesses at different times. Increasing returns are generally associated with larger fixed costs; diminishing returns are generally associated with rising variable costs. We will capture these differences, and the presence of both increasing and diminishing returns as a general matter, in mathematical form in the next chapter. Here, we merely note that a realistic production theory should take account of both types of returns—whereas mainstream economics concentrates on the special case of constant returns, which is by and large unrealistic.

RISK AND UNCERTAINTY

Risk and *uncertainty* are two distinct concepts in economics and finance (Knight 1921). Risk is supposedly objective and quantifiable; uncertainty is not. However, it can be very difficult to distinguish these two concepts in practice. People have different perceptions about many things, different backgrounds, different access to information, and differing levels of confidence in the information they read or hear. They may make very different judgments on the same issues. Because of the difficulty in distinguishing between risk and uncertainty in practice, we will make no distinction between risk and uncertainty in our discussion. Although mainstream economics often deals only with risk, we treat both as uncertainty, the more general construct.

Uncertainty is integral to all living systems. To a degree, the future is always unknown, and some changes are always unanticipated. But different systems respond to uncertainty in different ways. In general, simple systems with low fixed costs and short life spans are quicker to adapt to environmental changes than complex systems with high fixed costs and long life spans. However, high-fixed-cost systems often possess more resources to work with. To reduce uncertainty, they often have, and spend, more resources to maintain stability in internal and external environments. They also evolve mechanisms to adjust themselves periodically. But broadly, low-fixed-cost systems adapt because they can, whereas high-fixed-cost systems try to control—and adapt only if they must. Some examples can illustrate the differing strategies adopted by systems with different levels of fixed cost.

Lower-fixed-cost systems in general have shorter life spans than higher-fixed-cost systems. Therefore, the mutation rates or the rates of change of lower-fixed-cost systems are higher. This gives lower-fixed-cost systems advantages in initiating and adapting changes. For example, the novel coronavirus is much smaller than human beings and can mutate much faster. This makes it difficult for humans to develop a natural immune response to fight against coronavirus infections. In the space of a few years, the novel coronavirus has developed multiple variants with differing levels of severity and contagiousness. In the case of flu, it is generally thought that a new variant tends to develop each year, which gives us a concept of the "flu season."

DNA is made from RNA with an extra step of chemical reaction. DNA is therefore more costly to make than RNA, and DNA molecules are more stable and last longer than RNA molecules. DNA is thus the preferred molecule to carry genetic information from one generation to the next.

The only organisms to use RNA to carry genetic information are some viruses, which are very small and mutate very fast. The novel coronavirus and HIV are examples. But RNA molecules are used in our bodies for many functions that do not require high levels of precision and do not last very long. The chemical properties and biological functions of DNA and RNA show that fixed cost, uncertainty, and duration are intimately correlated in biological systems. They also show that economic properties of living systems, including human societies, are ultimately derived from physical and chemical properties of molecules.

Higher animals develop a general strategy in immune systems that has been very effective most of the time. Instead of developing one kind of antibody, our immune systems produce millions of different types of antibodies. It is highly likely that for any kind of bacteria or virus, there is some suitable type of antibody to destroy them. This strategy is very effective but very expensive, because our bodies produce many different antibodies that are useless most of the time. When we are too young, too old, too weak, or too stressed, our bodies don't have enough energy to produce large amounts of antibodies. That is when we become vulnerable to infection. Many studies have shown that when challenged with pathogens, organisms divert energy to combat the invader, but at an overall cost in energy to the organism, leaving less energy available for other contingencies. That is why fatigue is a common consequence of even a mild illness.

Organisms also try to regulate their internal, and sometimes their external, environment. In general, higher-fixed-cost systems spend more resources to regulate the environment, to reduce the level of uncertainty. Human beings, as warm-blooded animals, regulate our body temperature around 37°C, regardless of the external temperature.

The constancy of body temperature greatly reduces the uncertainty for our body's many chemical and physical processes. However, the maintenance of constant temperature is energy intensive. For this reason, warm-blooded animals have higher metabolisms and require more food than cold-blooded animals of the same size. When they cannot find any food for several days, their body functions weaken seriously. This causes a great increase in uncertainty. Cold-blooded animals can get along without food for quite some time by going dormant if conditions are not favorable.

Among all animals, human beings have the greatest capacity to modify our external environment to reduce the risks and uncertainties of life. We clear land for agriculture, which provides a much more certain supply of foods than hunting and gathering. We build houses to shelter us from the uncertainty brought by wind, rain, and snow. When we lose jobs, we receive unemployment benefits. When we are disabled, we get disability insurance payments. Our buildings are cooled in summer and heated in winter to maintain a near-constant indoor temperature. Water is chlorinated to eliminate bacteria. Populations are vaccinated to reduce infectious diseases. Many measures are taken to make life as predictable and as pleasant as possible. In general, uncertainty in wealthy countries is very low compared with poor countries. In an environment with low uncertainty, investments with high fixed costs and long durations often generate high rates of return. But measures to reduce uncertainty require resources. For example, to keep buildings warm in winter, we need natural gas to provide heat. Natural gas is supplied by pipes, powered by gas turbines, which cannot be adapted to other fuels. If the supply of natural gas is disrupted, it is very difficult to find workable substitutes in a short period of time; there is only so much firewood, and many modern houses lack fireplaces or woodstoves.

Generally, it is more difficult for high-fixed-cost systems to change. But high-fixed-cost organisms do develop mechanisms to change periodically to adapt to changing environments. Most complex animals reproduce sexually. Sexual reproduction is very expensive compared with asexual reproduction. Just consider how much effort we humans spend on relationships—and how difficult relationships can become and how stressful it is when they come to an end, especially through divorce or death. However, by reproducing sexually, the genes of our offspring are reshuffled. The genetic diversity of our offspring makes some of them more adaptable to the changing environment. The genetic changes also make parasites in our bodies less able to get established in our offspring, giving them renewed resilience from one generation to the next. In social systems, democratic countries have elections periodically to change their leaders. This makes such societies more resilient—if elections provide actual alternatives that can produce change. Unfortunately, in many cases, ruling elites work to ensure this is not the case, so that elections become mere rituals, devoid of the power of making change happen. In this way, ruling elites work to reduce uncertainty about their own positions.

In general, mature industries with low levels of uncertainty are dominated by large, established companies. For example, the household-supply industry is dominated by Proctor & Gamble; the soft-drink industry is dominated by Coca Cola and Pepsi Cola. Fast-changing industries, such as IT, are pioneered by small and new firms. Microsoft, Apple, Yahoo, Google, Facebook, and many other successful businesses were started by one or two individuals, not by established firms with capital and expertise, although many of these firms are currently establishing themselves as oligopolies. Similarly, in scientific research, mature areas are generally dominated by top researchers from elite schools, while fundamental ideas are often initiated by newcomers or outsiders. Neoclassical economics, the dominant economic theory today, was founded around 1870 by Jevons, Walras, and others. Jevons and Walras, considered by many as the greatest economists in the nineteenth century, were trained in science and engineering. Their ideas came to supplant those of, say, John Stuart Mill, who was trained in political economy largely by his father, James Mill, also a political economist. Most economists today receive very narrow training in the neoclassical perspective, often to the exclusion of physical and biological sciences. Mainstream economists work to control the ideas and resources in economics and find it very difficult to adapt.

LIFE SPAN, OBSOLESCENCE, FAILURE, RENEWAL

How do the life spans of different organisms evolve? How are project durations determined? Are long-lived systems necessarily better?

Uncertainty is an unavoidable part of nature. But the same level of uncertainty will have different effects on systems with different fixed costs and durations. The fixed costs are incurred or committed at early stages of an organism's or a project's life. But the expected payoffs, which occur in the future, are only estimates. Therefore, expected payoffs from investments are subject to discounting. How should discount rates be determined? What are the consequences of different levels of discount rates? When market size is large, then high-fixed-cost systems, with low variable cost, will generate a high rate of return. But are larger market sizes always better?

If the duration of a project is too short, we may not be able to recoup the fixed cost invested in the project. If the duration of a project is too long, the variable cost may become too high, and the rate of return will turn negative. For example, if a taxi driver keeps a car for too long, the maintenance cost may become very high. As a result, the total cost may become higher than the revenue. The same is true for all forms of equipment, from airplanes to power plants. And it is also true of biological equipment—of living bodies.

This is why individual life does not go on forever. Instead, it is preferable—of higher rate of return—for animals to have finite life spans and to produce offspring. In social sciences and policy discussion, a longer average life span (life expectancy) is often used as an indicator of the higher quality of a social system. However, societies that enjoy long life spans, such as Japan, often struggle with below-replacement fertility, and conversely, societies with relatively short life spans often have many children and a young (and therefore relatively robust) population. This is in part why, in the COVID-19 pandemic, Italy—a wealthy country with the oldest population in Europe—was hit hard, whereas sub-Saharan Africa (subject to limitations of available data) seems to have escaped relatively lightly.

When the level of fixed cost increases, it often takes longer time for a project to break even. Large animals and large projects, which have higher fixed costs, often have longer life spans. There is an empirical regularity that larger, heavier animals generally live longer (Whitfield 2006). The relation between fixed cost and duration can be also applied to human relations. In childbearing, women spend much more effort than men. On average, women value long-term relationships, whereas men often seek shorter-term relationships (Pinker 1997).

When the duration of a project keeps increasing, variable cost will keep increasing, and the return of a project will eventually turn negative. Hence the duration of a project or an organism cannot become infinite. For life to continue, there must be a systematic way to generate new organisms from old organisms; in other words, the old must make a fixed investment in the new before the new can hope to generate positive returns on their own. Thus, a universal necessity: there must be a resource transfer from one generation to the next generation in biological and social systems. "Higher" animals, such as mammals, generally provide more investment to each child than "lower" animals, such as fish. In human societies, parents provide for their children for many years before they become financially and physically independent. In general, wealthy societies provide and require more investment in children before they are released to compete in "the market." In business, new projects are heavily subsidized at their beginning stages by cash flows from profitable mature projects. This is called *venture capital*.

Empirical evidence illustrates the inverse relationship between life span and fertility. Lane (2002) provided a detailed discussion about the trade-off between longevity and fecundity in biological systems.

> With a few exceptions, usually explicable by particular circumstances, there is indeed a strong inverse relationship between fecundity and maximum lifespan. Mice, for example, start breeding at about six weeks old, produce many litters a year, and live for about three years. Domestic cats start breeding at about one year, produce two or three litters annually, and live for about 15 to 20 years. Herbivores usually have one offspring a year and live for 30 to 40 years. The implication is that high fecundity has a cost in terms of survival, and conversely, that investing in long-term survival reduces fecundity.
>
> Do factors that increase lifespan decrease fecundity? There are number of indications that they do. Calorie restriction, for example, in which animals are fed a balanced low-calorie diet, usually increase maximum lifespan by 30 to 50 per cent, and lower fecundity during the period of dietary restriction . . . The rationale in the wild seems clear enough: if food is scarce, unrestrained breeding would threaten the lives of parents as well as offspring. Calorie restriction simulates mild starvation and increases stress-resistance in general. Animals that survive the famine are restored to normal fecundity in times of plenty. (Lane 2002, 229)

Lane went on to provide many more examples of the inverse relation between longevity and fecundity.

The necessity of fixed-cost investment and the finiteness of life spans determine that resource transfer from old generations to new generations is essential for the long-term viability of a system. However, the details of resource redistribution are often the source of many conflicts between generations and within the members of the same generation. Each child wants more resources from his or her parents. But parents prefer children to become independent early, so resources can be distributed to younger or unborn children. Old mature industries, which need little R&D expense, prefer low-tax systems. But young high-tech industries, which rely heavily on universities to provide new technologies, employees, and users, strongly advocate government support for new technologies. Businesses generally prefer lower tax rates. But educational institutions, which mainly train the younger generation and receive much of their incomes from governments, prefer higher taxes, government revenues, and spending to support education.

In our daily lives, we all experience conflicts between generations. When contraception technology is available, many people decide to delay raising children, which delays the transfer of resources to the next generation. With aging parents, more children are born with genetic defects. An increase in children with birth defects raises pressures for government to support the affected population—transferring the burden from the parents to the society. We all observe these processes at work, with understandable sympathy, but often without reflecting on the underlying dynamics.

An increase in retirement age is often advocated as the solution for potential labor shortages in societies with a low fertility rate. But many countries with low fertility rates have very high youth unemployment rates—this is very characteristic of modern Europe. Younger people are more energetic and more productive in most employments. Economic performance will therefore improve if more young people can have jobs, while older people are permitted to retire. In general, systems with below-replacement-rate fertility and high youth unemployment need to shorten the duration of the work period, and increase employment and wages for young people, if they wish to restore the viability of the systems. A system with strong job prospects for young people will also attract more immigrants, who are generally young and adaptable, and this too will strengthen the demographic viability of the society in the long run.

If older people can retire earlier, as, for example, they did in France before the most recent neoliberal "reforms," more young people can move out of unemployment. With financial security, young people in their prime reproductive age can have more children. However, in a society with low fertility and long life spans, the proportion of seniors will be very high.

Furthermore, younger people will grow old but old people will not turn young. Since everyone expects or hopes to grow old, but the old do not hope to become young, resources allocated to seniors generally get less resistance than resources allocated to young people. Since unborn and small children have little political clout, their interests are often underrepresented in public discussion. Since immigrants do not enjoy political rights, their interests are often also neglected, or suppressed. Societies dominated by the old have great difficulties in adjusting policy for the benefit of future generations.

CONCLUDING REMARKS

In this chapter, we have tried to motivate a theory of economic decision-making suitable for analyzing the problem of production. We have illustrated the concepts of expected returns, fixed and variable costs, uncertainty, increasing and diminishing returns, and life spans and discount rates. We have shown that these concepts are pervasive in biological, mechanical, and social systems. In our view, these are the core concepts that any economic actor—government, business, households, and individuals—must and generally does consider when deciding whether to act in the economic sphere. In the next chapter, we show how to bring all these concepts together in a mathematical theory of production.

A Biophysical Theory of Production in Mathematical Form

In this chapter, we present a mathematical theory of production decisions. We will show how a biophysical production theory provides a simple, systematic understanding of investment activities and economic policies, including taxation and regulation.

As we have said several times, there are two fundamental properties of life. First, living organisms must extract resources from the environment to compensate for the continuous diffusion of resources required to maintain various functions of life (Schrodinger 1944). Second, for an organism to be viable, the total cost of extracting resources must be less than the value of resources extracted (Odum 1971; Hall, Cleveland, and Kaufmann 1986; Rees 1992). The second property may be understood as natural selection rephrased as an economic principle. The purpose of this chapter is to show that a self-contained mathematical theory of production can be derived from these two fundamental properties of life.

As we and others have said before, from a physics perspective, resources are low-entropy materials (Georgescu-Roegen 1971). The entropy law holds that systems tend toward higher entropy states spontaneously. Living systems, as nonequilibrium systems, need to extract low-entropy materials from the environment to compensate for their continuous dissipation. Such processes can be represented mathematically by lognormal processes, which contain both a growth term and a dissipation term. A lognormal process is a stochastic process. It can be represented by a deterministic thermodynamic equation, which is an evolutionary equation. Therefore, a biophysical theory of economics is naturally an evolutionary theory.

According to the entropy law, the thermodynamic dissipation of an organic or economic system is spontaneous. However, the extraction of low-entropy sources from the environment depends on specific biological or institutional structures that incur fixed or maintenance costs. Additional variable cost is also required for resource extraction. Higher-fixed-cost systems generally have lower variable costs. Fixed cost is largely determined by the genetic structure of an organism or the design of a project. Variable cost is a function of the environment. An organism survives if the total value of resources it extracts is higher than the total cost, both measured in appropriate energy units. Similarly, a business survives if its revenue is higher than the total cost of production.

Product value, volume of output, fixed cost, variable cost, project duration, discount rate, and uncertainty are major factors that determine the viability and success of production. These factors naturally became the center of investigation in early political economy. However, because of the difficulty in forming a compact mathematical model about these factors, discussion about many of them became peripheral to what is now termed *mainstream* economics. With the help of the production theory presented here, theoretical investigation in economics may refocus on these issues. In this way, our theory is linked to the major concerns of classical political economy, which was developed to cope with an age of scarce resources.

Our procedure is as follows. We set the initial condition so that total cost is equal to the value of resources extracted and revenues generated. Thus, in the initial condition, profits are zero. Then we derive a formula for variable cost as a function of product value, fixed cost, uncertainty, discount rate, and project duration. From this formula, together with fixed cost and volume of output, we can compute and analyze the returns and profits of different production systems under various environmental conditions—such as differences in resource costs and uncertainty—in a simple and systematic way. The results are highly consistent with empirical evidence obtained from the vast literature in economics and ecology. Furthermore, by putting major factors of production into a compact mathematical model, the theory provides precise insights about the trade-offs and constraints of alternative business or evolutionary strategies.

We begin with the crucial relation between fixed cost and variable cost. Useful energy comes from the differential or gradient between two parts of a system. In general—Carnot's Principle again—the higher the differential, the more efficient the work. At the same time, it is more difficult to maintain a system with a high differential. In other words, a lower-variable-cost system requires higher fixed cost to maintain it. This is a general principle. Our production theory provides quantitative measures of return and profit at different levels of fixed cost and variable cost under different circumstances.

When the fixed cost is zero, variable cost is equal to product value. In the Garden of Eden, there was only variable cost, and each fruit returned the value of taking it from the tree; there was no economic profit. This means that any organisms or organizations must make fixed investments before they can earn a positive return. This simple thought has broad implications—it was, after all, what got Adam and Eve thrown out of the Garden. To repeat, any viable organization, whether a company or a country, needs fixed investment as a point of departure. This principle has a direct bearing on the question of taxation, among other issues.

In mainstream economics, taxes are often described as a type of distortion or imperfection. If this were true, a society that abolished taxation would remove the distortion and become less imperfect. Over time, through a process of natural selection, such a society would crowd out social systems that collect taxes. However, this has not happened. Montesquieu ([1748] 1949) observed long ago, "In moderate states, there is a compensation for heavy taxes; it is liberty. In despotic states, there is an equivalent for liberty; it is the modest taxes." From the mainstream economic theory, one might infer that despotic states are more perfect than moderate states.

In our production theory, taxes (like wage standards) are considered as a fixed cost of the whole society. They are also a form of regulation, affecting the general distribution of well-being. Therefore, a lower tax rate does not automatically mean a better society. The proper level of taxation should be determined by other factors, such as the desired living standard of the population, including the physical and social security that make economic endeavors possible, and the degree of inequality that society chooses to tolerate.

In neoclassical economics, the *market* is a very abstract concept.

> The "market" in modern usage is not some physical location. . . . The market is the nonstate, and thus it can do everything the state can do

but with none of the procedures or rules or limitations. . . . Because
the word lacks any observable, regular, consistent meaning, marvelous
powers can be assigned. The market establishes Value. It resolves conflict. It ensures Efficiency in the assignment of each factor of production to its most Valued use . . . From each according to Supply, to each
according to Demand. The market is thus truly a type of God, "wiser
and more powerful than the largest computer" . . . Markets achieve
effortlessly exactly what governments fail to achieve by directed effort.
(Galbraith 2008, 20)

In our production theory, the market is a concrete concept, with precise parameters including, notably, market size. If a market is very
small, then its structure will be very simple, to reduce fixed cost. If a
market is very large, then its structure will be very sophisticated, to
reduce variable cost. For example, a village or farmers' market has little formal structure or regulation. But the New York Stock Exchange
has very expensive computer systems and highly complex regulatory
structures to ensure the smooth flow of a large volume of transactions.
In this concrete structure, it is meaningless to discuss whether "the
market" is "efficient" or not. Markets differ. A market that provides a
positive return will survive and prosper. A market that yields negative
returns will shrink and disappear.

For any organism or organization, part of fixed cost is used to regulate the internal environment. For example, the human body is regulated at around 37°C. When a person is infected, body temperature is
raised, to attack more effectively the infecting bacteria or virus. However, a temperature that is too high will damage the brain's information-
processing capability, which is sensitive to thermal noise (Gisolfi and
Mora 2000). In general, regulation is a compromise between different
parts of an organism. When a part of a biological organism escapes
regulation, that part of the organism will grow rapidly. This is called
cancer. In the end, the unregulated growth, if it is not stopped, will
drain all the available resources and destroy the organism. In human
society, if an economic sector gains control of many resources and escapes regulation, becoming a "free market," it will grow rapidly and
generate profits for the insiders. But the process will drain resources
from the whole society, leading to crisis and collapse. This is what we
witnessed in the 2007–2009 financial crisis.

Although mainstream economists pay little attention to the biophysical foundation of human society, thinking about biophysical constraints is a very effective way to understand social phenomena (Galbraith 2008). A biophysical approach puts the physical conditions facing human society at the center of its analysis. The validity of a physical theory of economics is best shown by mathematical expressions derived from the most fundamental properties of life, consistent with a wide range of patterns observed in both economics and ecology. After all, all physical laws are represented by mathematical formulas. With an analytical theory based on biophysical principles, many philosophical and verbal problems can be turned into scientific and quantitative inquiries. The computability of the mathematical theory will transform biological science, which includes social science as a special case, into an integral part of physics.

The next section presents the derivation of the production theory. We then present basic results from this theory and discuss how different environments will affect the decision to invest, which is fundamental to the choice between fixed and variable costs and so to the structure of production. We conclude by exploring interdependencies between the various parameters of the theory.

DERIVATION OF A BIOPHYSICAL PRODUCTION THEORY

The theory described in this section can be applied to both biological and economic systems. For simplicity of exposition, we will use the language of economics. However, the extension to biological systems is straightforward.

The most fundamental property of organisms and organizations is their need to obtain resources from the environment to compensate for the continuous diffusion of resources they engender. This fundamental property can be represented mathematically by lognormal processes, which contain both a growth term and a dissipation term.

Suppose S represents the quantity of resources accumulated by an organism or the unit price of a commodity; r, the rate of resource extraction or the expected rate of change of price; and σ, the rate of diffusion of resources or the rate of volatility of price change. Then the process of S can be represented by the lognormal process

$$\frac{dS}{S} = rdt + \sigma dz, \quad (1)$$

where $dz = \varepsilon\sqrt{dt}$, $\varepsilon \in N(0, 1)$ is a random variable with standard Gaussian distribution.

The process (1) is a stochastic process. In this book, we assume r to be positive and constant. But r can change over time. For example, after a living system dies, r turns negative during its decomposition. Similarly, r turns negative when a firm fails and its assets are dismantled and sold for scrap.

Although a stochastic process will generate many different outcomes over time, we are mostly interested in the average outcomes from such processes. For example, although the movement of individual gas molecules is very volatile, air in a room, which consists of many gas molecules, generates a stable pressure and temperature. We usually study the average outcomes of stochastic processes by looking at the averages of the underlying stochastic variables and their functions. These investigations often transform stochastic processes into their corresponding deterministic equations. For example, heat is a random movement of molecules. Yet the heat process is often studied by using heat equations, a type of deterministic partial differential equation.

Feynman (1948) developed a method of averaging stochastic processes under very general conditions, which is usually called a *path integral*. Kac (1951) extended Feynman's method into a mapping between stochastic processes and partial differential equations, which was later known as the Feynman-Kac formula. According to the Feynman-Kac formula (Øksendal 1998, 135), if

$$C(t, S) = e^{-qt} E(f(S_t)) \quad (2)$$

is the expected value of a function of S at time t, discounted at the rate q, then $C(t, S)$ satisfies the following equation:

$$\frac{\partial C}{\partial t} = rS\frac{\partial C}{\partial S} + \frac{1}{2}\sigma^2 S^2 \frac{\partial^2 C}{\partial S^2} - qC \quad (3)$$

with

$$C(0, S) = f(S). \quad (4)$$

It should be noted that many functions of S satisfy equation (3). The specific property of a particular function is determined by the initial condition (4). This resembles the Black-Scholes option theory (Black and Scholes 1973). The Black-Scholes equation is satisfied by any derivative security. It is the end condition at contract maturity that determines the specific property of a particular derivative security.

Once again, for an organism or an organization to be viable, the total cost of resources must be less than the gain from the resources extracted. In economic terms, the total cost of operation must be less than the total revenue. Costs include fixed cost and variable cost. In general, production factors that last for a long time, such as capital equipment, are considered fixed costs, and production factors that last for a short time, such as raw materials, are considered variable costs. If employees are on long-term contracts, they may be better understood as fixed costs, although in the economic literature they are usually classified as variable costs. Typically, a lower-variable-cost system requires a larger investment in fixed costs, although high fixed costs do not necessarily guarantee low variable costs. Organisms and organizations can adjust their level of fixed and variable costs to achieve a high return on their investment. Intuitively, in a large and stable market, firms will invest heavily in fixed cost to reduce variable cost, thus achieving a higher level of economy of scale. In a small or volatile market, firms will invest less in fixed cost to maintain a high level of flexibility.

Suppose there is a project with a duration that is infinitesimally small. It has only enough time to produce one unit of product. To avoid an arbitrage opportunity, if the fixed cost is lower than the value of the product, the variable cost should be the difference between the value of the product and the fixed cost. If the fixed cost is higher than the value of this product, there should be no extra variable cost needed for the product. Mathematically, the relation between fixed cost, variable cost, and the value of product in this case is the following:

$$C = max \; (S - K, 0), \quad (5)$$

where S is the value of the product, C is the variable cost, and K is the fixed cost of the project. When the duration of a project is of finite value T, relation (5) can be extended into

$$C(0, S) = max(S - K, 0) \quad (6)$$

as the initial condition for equation (3). Equation (3) with initial condition (6) can be solved to obtain

$$C = Se^{(r-q)T} N(d_1) - Ke^{-qT} N(d_2), \quad (7)$$

where

$$d_1 = \frac{ln(S/K) + (r + \sigma^2/2)T}{\sigma\sqrt{T}}$$

$$d_2 = \frac{ln(S/K) + (r - \sigma^2/2)T}{\sigma\sqrt{T}} = d_1 - \sigma\sqrt{T}.$$

The function $N(x)$ is the cumulative probability distribution function for a standardized normal random variable. From (6), the solution of the equation (3) can be interpreted as the variable cost of the project. We will investigate shortly whether the function represented in formula (7) has the common properties of variable cost.

For a given investment problem, different parties may select different discount rates. To simplify our investigation, we will make the discount rate equal to the expected rate of growth. This is to set

$$q = r. \quad (8)$$

This choice of discount rate can be understood from two perspectives. From a biological perspective, fast-growing organisms also have a high probability of death, and in a steady state, the growth rate will be equal to the death rate. So, in the biological literature, the discount rate is usually set equal to the growth rate (Stearns 1992). From the perspective of economics, in option theory, the discount rate is set equal to the risk-free rate. The level of risk of an option contract is represented by implied volatility, which does not necessarily equate with past volatility or future expected volatility. Some people do not agree with the economic logic behind the mathematical derivation of the Black-Scholes equation, which made the risk-related discount rate disappear (Treynor 1996). However, the disappearance of a separate discount rate greatly simplifies our understanding of how option values are related to market variables. From both a biological and economic perspective, this choice of discount rate provides a good starting point.

With q equaling r, equation (3) becomes

$$\frac{\partial C}{\partial t} = rS\frac{\partial C}{\partial S} + \frac{1}{2}\sigma^2 S^2 \frac{\partial^2 C}{\partial S^2} - rC \quad (9)$$

and solution (7) becomes

$$C = SN(d_1) - Ke^{-rT}N(d_2), \quad (10)$$

where

$$d_1 = \frac{\ln\left(\frac{S}{K}\right) + \left(r + \frac{\sigma^2}{2}\right)T}{\sigma\sqrt{T}}$$

$$d_2 = \frac{\ln\left(\frac{S}{K}\right) + \left(r - \frac{\sigma^2}{2}\right)T}{\sigma\sqrt{T}} = d_1 - \sigma\sqrt{T}.$$

Formula (10) provides an analytical expression for C, variable cost, as a function of S, product value, for K, fixed cost, for σ, uncertainty, for T, duration of project, and for r, the discount rate of a firm. As in physics, the calculated variable cost is the average expected cost of the variable inputs. With this formula, we can calculate how variable cost changes with respect to other major factors in economic and biological activities. Formula (10) takes the same form as the Black-Scholes formula for European call options. But the meaning of parameters in this theory differs from those in option theory.

We now briefly examine the properties of formula (10) as a representation of variable cost. First, when fixed cost is positive, variable cost is always less than the value of the product. No one will invest in a project if the expected variable cost is higher than the product value. Second, when the fixed cost is zero, the expected variable cost is equal to the value of the product, and profit is therefore zero. This means that businesses must make a fixed investment before they can expect a profit, just as organisms must develop a fixed structure before they can extract resources profitably.[1] Third, when fixed costs, K, are higher, variable costs, C, are lower. Fourth, for the same amount of the fixed cost, when the duration of a project, T, is longer, the variable cost is higher. This shows that investment value depreciates with time. Fifth, when risk, s, increases, the variable cost increases. Sixth, when the discount rate falls, variable cost also decreases. This is due to the lower cost of borrowing. These properties are all consistent with our intuitive understanding of, and empirical patterns in, production processes.

After obtaining the formula for the variable cost in production, we can calculate the expected profit and rate of return of an investment. Suppose the volume of output during the project life is Q, which is bound by production capacity or market size. During the project's life, we assume the present value of the product to be S and the variable cost to be C. Then the total present value of the product and the total cost of production are

$$SQ \text{ and } CQ + K \quad (11),$$

respectively. The net present value of the project is

$$QS - (QC + K) = Q(S - C) - K \quad (12)$$

The rate of return of this project can be represented by

$$\frac{QS - (K + QC)}{K + QC} = \frac{QS}{K + QC} - 1 \quad (13)$$

It is often convenient to represent S as the value of output from a project over one unit of time. If the project lasts for T units of time, the net present value of the project is

$$TS - (TC + K) = T(S - C) - K \quad (14)$$

The rate of return of this project can be represented by

$$\frac{TS - (K + TC)}{K + TC} = \frac{TS}{K + TC} - 1 \quad (15)$$

TABLE 7.1. Variables in the production model

S	Unit value of output	
K	Fixed cost	
R	Discount rate	
T	Duration of investment	
Σ	Uncertainty	
C	Variable cost	formula (10)
NPV	Net present value	formula (14)

TABLE 7.2. Representative values in the production model

S	Unit value of output	1
K	Fixed cost	3
R	Discount rate	0.08
T	Duration of investment	10
Σ	Uncertainty	0.5
C	Variable cost	0.51
NPV	Net present value	1.94

Unlike a mere conceptual framework, this analytical theory enables us to make quantitative calculations of returns of different projects in differing environments.

Table 7.1 summarizes the names of the variables in the equations above and gives a representative calculation.

Table 7.2 gives an example of what calculated values of the main variables may look like.

Since our theory is very similar to Black-Scholes option theory, we may compare the basic equations of Black-Scholes theory and our theory. The Black-Scholes equation is

$$-\frac{\partial C}{\partial t} = rS\frac{\partial C}{\partial S} + \frac{1}{2}\sigma^2 S^2 \frac{\partial^2 C}{\partial S^2} - rC. \quad (16)$$

The basic equation in our theory is

$$\frac{\partial C}{\partial t} = rS\frac{\partial C}{\partial S} + \frac{1}{2}\sigma^2 S^2 \frac{\partial^2 C}{\partial S^2} - rC. \quad (9)$$

The Black-Scholes equation has a negative sign in front of the time derivative. From a physics perspective, our equation represents a thermodynamic process, whereas the Black-Scholes equation represents a reverse thermodynamic process. From the economic perspective, the Black-Scholes equation solves the current price of derivative securities when the future payout is determined; our equation solves the expected variable cost in the future when the current fixed cost is determined. The two theories solve different economic problems.

A thermodynamic equation, such as (9), is of first order in time direction. It is an evolutionary equation. Therefore, our theory is an evolutionary economic theory.

BASIC RESULTS OF THE THEORY

Our theory provides quantitative measurements of how major factors in economic and biological systems affect costs and returns in those systems. In this section, we present numerical calculations based on the equations presented above and illustrate them with a series of diagrams, as follows:

- Fixed cost and variable cost under different conditions of uncertainty.
- Rate of return and volume of output under different levels of fixed cost.
- Fixed cost and net present value (or rate of return).
- Project duration and net present value.
- Variable cost and discount rates under different levels of fixed cost.
- Profits at low and high discount rates as project duration changes.
- Discount rates required for breaking even as project duration increases.
- Variable cost as discount rates fall, at different levels of uncertainty.
- Volume of output and rate of return when uncertainty increases with output.
- Effect on returns of increasing fixed cost to reduce uncertainty.
- Rate of return and output scale at differing levels of resource cost, with different levels of fixed cost.
- Rate of return and market size of a system with a given fixed cost, at different levels of resource cost.

Each of these relationships can be calculated from the model. In the text accompanying the graphics, we provide relevant examples from biological, mechanical, and economic systems.

The calculations illustrate the relationships that exist between the major economic concepts of the theory. The fact that we can use the equations to make these calculations is what we mean when we say that ours is an *analytical* theory. The mathematics are not for show! They permit us to illustrate simple but important relationships in ways that we believe are generally valid in the real world. Much of what follows corresponds to common sense—and that (in our view) is a cardinal virtue of this approach. Economic activity is very commonplace; in fact, it is universal. A good theory should give results that most businesses and households can understand and find intuitively clear.

FIXED COST AND UNCERTAINTY

By calculating variable costs from (10), we find that, as fixed costs are increased, variable costs decrease rapidly in a low-uncertainty environment and change very little in a high-uncertainty environment. To put it another way, high-fixed-cost systems are very sensitive to the change of uncertainty level, and low-fixed-cost systems are not. This is illustrated in figure 7.1.

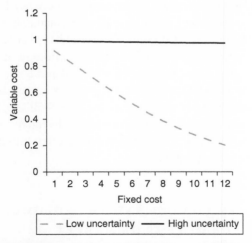

FIGURE 7.1 Fixed cost and uncertainty: In a low-uncertainty environment, variable cost drops sharply as fixed costs are increased. In a high-uncertainty environment, variable costs change little with the level of fixed cost.

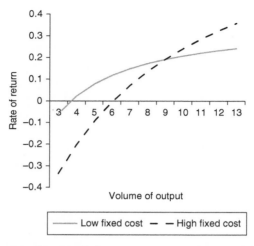

FIGURE 7.2 Fixed cost and the volume of output: For a high-fixed-cost investment, the break-even market size is higher and the return curve is steeper. The opposite is true for a low-fixed-cost investment.

The above calculation indicates that systems with higher fixed investment are more effective in a low-uncertainty environment and systems with lower fixed investment are more flexible in a high-uncertainty environment. As we've said before, mature industries, such as household supplies, are dominated by established large companies, and new industries, such as information technology, are pioneered by small and new firms. Despite the financial and technical clout of large firms, small firms account for a disproportionately high share of innovative activity (Acs and Audretsch 1990). Similarly, in scientific research, mature areas are generally dominated by top researchers from elite schools, while scientific revolutions are often initiated by new-comers or outsiders (Kuhn 1996).

FIXED COST AND THE VOLUME
OF OUTPUT OR MARKET SIZE

Figure 7.2 is the graphic representation of (14). In general, higher-fixed-cost projects need higher output volumes to break even. At the same time, higher-fixed-cost projects, which have lower variable costs in production, earn higher rates of return in large markets.

We can see that the proper level of fixed investment in a project depends on the expectation of uncertainty and the size of the market. When the outlook is stable and the market size is large, projects with high fixed investment earn higher rates of return. When the outlook is uncertain or market size is small, projects with low fixed costs break even more quickly.

In an ecological system, market size can be understood as the size of the resource base. When resources are abundant, an ecological system can support large, complex organisms (Colinvaux 1978). Physicists and biologists are often puzzled by the apparent tendency for biological systems to form complex structures, which seems to contradict the second law of thermodynamics (Schneider and Sagan 2005; Rubí 2008). However, once we realize that systems with higher fixed costs provide higher returns in resource-rich and stable environments, this evolutionary pattern becomes easy to understand. An example from physiology will highlight this trade-off:

> An increased oxygen capacity of the blood, caused by the presence of a respiratory pigment, reduces the volume of blood that must be pumped to supply oxygen to the tissues. . . . The higher the oxygen capacity of the blood, the less volume needs to be pumped. There is a trade-off here between the cost of providing the respiratory pigment and the cost of pumping, and the question is, which strategy pays best? It seems that for highly active animals a high oxygen capacity is most important; for slow and sluggish animals it may be more economical to avoid a heavy investment in the synthesis of high concentrations of a respiratory pigment. (Schmidt-Nielsen 1997, 120)

For high-output systems (highly active animals), investment in fixed cost (respiratory pigment) is favored, whereas for low-output systems (slow and sluggish animals), high variable cost (more pumping) is preferred. Pumping is variable cost compared with respiratory pigment because respiratory pigment lasts much longer.

With a volatile commodity market, people become aware of the problem of resource depletion. Many people have advocated the increase of efficiency as a way of reducing energy consumption. Will the increase of efficiency reduce overall resource consumption? Jevons made the following observation more than 150 years ago.

> It is credibly stated, too, that a manufacturer often spends no more in fuel where it is dear than where it is cheap. But persons will commit a great oversight here if they overlook the cost of improved and complicated engine . . . is higher than that of a simple one. The question is one of capital against current expenditure . . . It is wholly a confusion of ideas to suppose that the economic use of fuel is equivalent to the diminished consumption. The very contrary is the truth. As a rule, new modes of economy will lead to an increase of consumption according to a principle recognized in many parallel instances. (Jevons [1865] 1965, xxxv and 140)

Put another way, the improvement of technology is to achieve lower variable cost at the expense of higher fixed cost. Since it takes a larger output for higher-fixed-cost systems to break even, to earn a positive return the total use of energy must be higher than before. That is, technological advances in energy efficiency will increase total energy consumption. Jevons' statement has stood the test of time. Indeed, the total consumption of energy has kept growing almost uninterrupted for several centuries, along with continuous gains in the efficiency of energy conversion (Inhaber 1997; Smil 2003; Hall 2004).

Hybrid cars are an example. Hybrid cars have two engines, an internal combustion engine and an electric engine. This adds to the manufacturing cost (and hence resource consumption) of hybrid cars. If the owner of a hybrid car drives very little, the total resource consumption from a hybrid car is higher than a conventional car. Only when a hybrid car is used extensively, burning a lot of fuel, does it become less wasteful than a conventional car. Therefore, the use of a hybrid car, when manufacturing cost is included, guarantees high resource consumption.

FIXED COST AND RETURNS

We next examine how different levels of fixed investment affect the value of a project. From figure 7.3, as the fixed cost of a project is increased, the net present value of the project will increase initially.

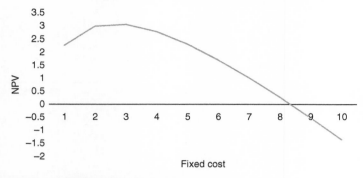

FIGURE 7.3 Fixed cost and returns.

When the level of fixed cost is at a certain level, its further increase will reduce the value of the project. Eventually the value of the project will become negative. Education is a type of fixed cost in our lives. We generally regard education as a worthwhile investment. But most people, for good reason, will not pursue PhD degrees.

DURATION OF THE PROJECT AND RETURNS

How does the duration of a project affect its return? If the duration of a project is too short, we may not be able to recoup the fixed cost invested. If the duration of a project is too long, the variable cost, or the maintenance cost, may become too high. On this point, the calculation of formula (14) is illustrated in figure 7.4. As in figure 7.3, when the life span of a project increases, the net present value of the project will increase initially. When the life span is at certain level, its further increase will reduce the value of the project. Eventually, the value of the project will become negative. This, again, explains why individual life does not go on forever. Instead, it is more profitable for animals to have a finite life span and to produce offspring. The calculation also explains why most businesses fail in the end (Ormerod 2005).

The formula also shows that when fixed cost increases, the duration required for a project to earn a positive return also increases. This suggests that large projects and also large animals, which have higher fixed costs, often have longer lives (Whitfield 2006). Since higher-fixed-cost

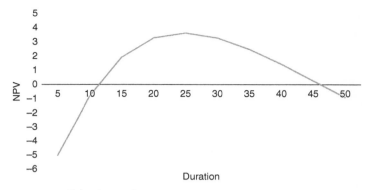

FIGURE 7.4 Duration and returns.

systems have longer life spans than lower-fixed-cost systems, the mutation rates of lower-fixed-cost systems are faster.

When the duration of a project keeps increasing, the return of a project will eventually turn negative. Hence duration of a project or an organism cannot become infinite. For life to continue, there must be a systematic way to generate new organisms from old organisms. From our calculation, for a system to have a positive return, fixed assets must be invested first. To achieve this, old organisms must transfer part of their resources to younger organisms, before the younger organisms can maintain a positive return. The need for seed capital explains the universal necessity of resource transfer from the old generation to the younger generation in the biological world. This necessity increases with wealth. In human societies, parents provide for their children for many years, and in general, wealthy families and wealthy societies make greater investments in children than poor families and poor societies. Similarly in business, promising new projects are heavily subsidized at their beginning stages by cash flows from profitable mature projects and previous capital gains.

Since project life or organism life cannot last forever, resource transfer from organism to organism or from project to project is unavoidable. However, the process of transfer is often the source of many conflicts. Businesses prefer lower tax rates. Educational institutions prefer higher subsidies. Each child wants more attention from its parents. Parents, however, would like to distribute resources more or less evenly among different children. Mature industries, which need little

R&D, prefer low-tax systems. High-tech industries, which rely heavily on universities to provide new technologies, employees, and users, strongly advocate government support of new technologies. In good times, financial institutions preach the virtue of free markets. In bad times, the same institutions will remind the public how government support can ensure financial stability of the nation. The amount of resource transfer and the method of resource transfer often define the characteristics of a species or a society.

FIXED COST AND DISCOUNT RATE

The level of fixed cost affects the preference for discount rates. When discount rates decrease, the variable costs of high-fixed-cost systems decrease faster than the variable costs of low-fixed-cost systems (fig. 7.5). This indicates that high-fixed-cost systems have more incentive to maintain low discount rates or lending rates. This result helps us understand why prevailing lending rates are different in different places and at different times.

In poor countries, lending rates are very high; even the vaunted "microcredit" institutions celebrated in development economics often charge effective rates exceeding 100 percent per year. In wealthy countries, lending rates charged by regular financial institutions, other

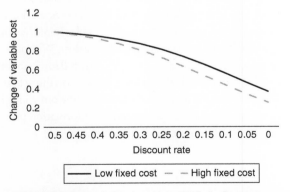

FIGURE 7.5 Fixed cost and discount rate: When discount rates are decreased, the variable costs of high-fixed-cost systems decrease faster than variable costs of low-fixed-cost systems.

than unsecured personal loans such as credit card debts, are generally very low. To maintain a low level of lending rates, many credit and legal agencies are needed to inform and enforce standards, which is very costly. As wealthy countries are of high fixed cost, they are willing to put up with the high cost of credit and legal agencies because the efficiency gain from a lower lending rate is higher in high-fixed-cost systems. In the past several hundred years, there is in general an upward trend in living standards worldwide. There is also a downward trend in interest rates (Newell and Pizer 2003). This is well explained by our calculations.

The human mind intuitively understands the relation between the discount rate and different levels of assets. In the field of human psychology, there is an empirical regularity called the *magnitude effect*—small outcomes are discounted more than large ones. In Thaler's (1981) study, respondents were, on average, indifferent between $15 immediately and $60 in a year, $250 immediately and $350 in a year, and $3,000 immediately and $4,000 in a year, implying discount rates of 139 percent, 34 percent and 29 percent, respectively. Since the human mind is an adaptation to the needs of survival and reproduction, evaluating the relation between discount rates and amounts of fixed investment must be a common task in our evolutionary past.

Our understanding of discount rates and fixed costs resembles an earlier work by Ainslie and Herrnstein:

> The biological value of a low discount rate is limited by its requiring the organism to detect which one of all the events occurring over a preceding period of hours or days led to a particular reinforcer. As the discounting rate falls, the informational load increases. Without substantial discounting, a reinforcer would act with nearly full force not only on the behaviors that immediately preceded it, but also on those that had been emitted in past hours or days. The task of factoring out which behaviors had actually led to reward could exceed the information processing capacity of a species. (Ainslee and Herrnstein 1981, 481)

DISCOUNT RATE AND PROJECT DURATION

When the discount rate becomes lower, the variable cost of a project will decrease, and profit will increase. Projects with different durations

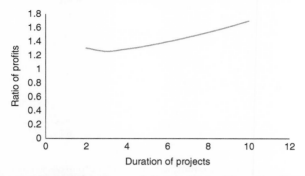

FIGURE 7.6 Project duration and discount rate: The ratio of profits between projects at low and high discount rates at different levels of project duration.

will be affected differently by the reduction of discount rates. Figure 7.6 presents the ratio of profits between projects at low and high discount rates, for different levels of project duration. As durations increase, the ratio mostly increases as well. This indicates that projects of longer duration benefit more from a reduction of interest rates. Keynes made a similar argument: as interest rates increase, the optimal duration of a production process is shortened (Keynes 1936, 216).

We can calculate the break-even point of a project with respect to project duration and the discount rate. Let us assume that project output per unit of time is 1. Formula (14) shows that it requires a lower discount rate to break even when the project duration is lengthened. The calculation is illustrated in figure 7.7. Many empirical studies have shown that humans—as well as other animals—often discount long-duration events at lower rates than short-duration events (Frederick, Loewenstein, and O'Donoghue 2004). This pattern is called *hyperbolic discounting*. The calculation provides a possible explanation for hyperbolic discounting. Since it takes lower discount rates for long-duration projects to break even, the human mind—and those of other animals—will discount long-duration projects at a lower rate.

In human society, we often use longevity, or duration of human life, as an indicator of the quality of a social environment. At the same time, societies that enjoy long life spans, such as Japan, are often concerned about below-replacement fertility. Intuitively, an aging population needs many resources to maintain its health, and this reduces the resources available to support children. Hence there is a natural

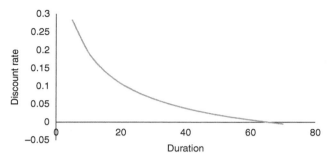

FIGURE 7.7 Required discount rate for a project to break even at different project durations: As project duration increases, the required discount rate for a project to break even decreases. This provides a possible explanation for hyperbolic discounting.

trade-off between longevity and fertility. This result has important policy implications. In a society with below-replacement fertility and low immigration, it is a great challenge to maintain a sustainable society over a long period of time.

DISCOUNT RATE AND UNCERTAINTY

Variable cost is an increasing function of the discount rate. When uncertainty is low, variable costs are much lower with a low discount rate. When uncertainty is high, variable costs are not very sensitive to the discount rate. Therefore, it is often more effective to reduce the discount rate in a stable environment. Figure 7.8 presents the change of variable costs at different levels of discount rates when levels of uncertainty are low and high. It shows that the reduction of variable cost is more significant at a low uncertainty level. This explains why simpler species, such as algae or grasses, which have high discount rates, often thrive in highly uncertain environments. It may show why in economic crises low interest rates have little effect on the level of perceived profitability and therefore on activity. This is called "pushing on a string."

This idea about the relationship between discount rate and uncertainty is, by the way, not new. "The same discount curve that is optimally steep for an organism's intelligence in a poorly predictable

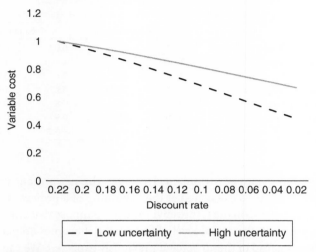

FIGURE 7.8 Change of variable costs with discount rate at different levels of uncertainty.

environment will make him unnecessarily shortsighted in a more predictable environment" (Ainslie 1992, 86). Our theory gives this insight a precise quantitative expression.

DECISION-MAKING IN DIFFERENT ENVIRONMENTS

Decision-makers will attempt to maximize the value or return of an investment in any given environment. Very often, the discount rate and uncertainty are external environmental factors not controlled by businesses. Businesses therefore choose the level of fixed cost and life span of projects to maximize the value or return of a project in that specific environment of uncertainty and discount rates that they confront.

Let the discount rate take two different values at 3 percent and 10 percent per annum, respectively, while keeping uncertainty unchanged. We will choose the level of fixed cost and life span of the project to maximize formula (14), the net present value of the project. The left two columns of table 7.3 list the maximization results.

From table 7.3, we find that when the discount rate is lower, the amount of fixed investment is larger, investment duration is longer, and the net present value is higher. So investors normally prefer a

TABLE 7.3. Discount rates, investment, uncertainty, and rates of return

	Initial expectation		Sad result	
Discount rate	0.03	0.1	0.03	0.1
Annual output	1	1	1	1
Fixed cost	7.1	3.9	7.1	3.9
Duration of project	35.7	13.6	35.7	13.6
Uncertainty	0.3	0.3	0.8	0.8
Variable cost	0.46	0.42	0.97	0.86
NPV	*12.3*	*4.0*	*−6.2*	*−2.0*

low-interest-rate environment. However, the net present values are expected returns calculated at the beginning of a project. The actual returns depend on the future environment. Suppose that after the projects are built, the actual level of uncertainty becomes 80 percent per annum instead of the 30 percent previously expected. We can recalculate the net present values from (14) to find the net present value of the first project, built in the low-interest-rate environment of 3 percent, becomes −$6.2 billion, while the net present value of the second project, built in the high-interest-rate environment of 10 percent, becomes −$2.0 billion. The right side of table 7.3 lists all the results in the new environment. Both projects suffer losses, but the first project suffers much greater losses. When environmental conditions change, returns on investment in low-interest-rate environments experience larger fluctuations. In other words, the monetary policy of low interest rates will generate greater business cycles. This theory provides a simple and clear understanding of the relation between the level of interest rate and the magnitude of business cycles.

STABILITY IS DESTABILIZING

Hyman Minsky's work is often summarized in the phrase, "stability is destabilizing." What does this mean, exactly? From our formula, we can obtain a very clear understanding. Suppose in two countries, A and B, annual output is $1 billion. Suppose the interest rate is 5 percent per annum in both countries. Uncertainty rate is 30 percent per annum in country A and 55 percent per annum in country B. Decision-makers attempt to maximize the net present value of an investment

TABLE 7.4. Stability is destabilizing

Uncertainty	0.3	0.55	0.8	0.8
Annual output	1	1	1	1
Fixed cost	5.8	2.1	5.8	2.1
Discount rate	0.05	0.05	0.05	0.05
Duration of project	25.3	12.1	25.3	12.1
Variable cost	0.44	0.64	0.94	0.82
NPV	*8.5*	*2.3*	*−4.4*	*0.0*

project. How much will be the desired fixed cost and how long will the expected project last? What are the net present values of projects in countries A and B?

We attempt to maximize the net-present-value expression in (14) by changing fixed cost, K, and duration, T, when uncertainty rates are set at 30 percent and 55 percent per annum, respectively. The left side of table 7.4 lists the calculated results.

From table 7.4, we find that when uncertainty is lower, the amount of fixed investment is larger, investment duration is longer, and the net present value is higher. So investors normally prefer low-uncertainty environments. However, the net present values are only the expected returns, which were calculated at the beginning of a project. The actual returns depend on future conditions. Suppose again that after the projects are built, the actual level of uncertainty becomes 80 percent per annum in both countries due to circumstances unforeseen by decision-makers, such as a global financial crisis. We recalculate formula (14) to find the new net present values. The net present value of the first project, built in the low-uncertainty environment, is −$4.4 billion and the net present value of the second project, built in the high-uncertainty environment, is −$0.0 billion. These results are listed on the right side of table 7.4. The first project suffers heavy losses, and the second project barely breaks even. When environmental conditions change dramatically, values of investment in formerly stable environments experience large fluctuations. In other words, "stability is destabilizing."

With this analytical theory, simulation is very simple. It enables us to perceive long-term consequences of economic policies and social structures clearly. Detailed discussion of monetary policy and business cycles is presented in Chen (2012, 2015). Many economists and policymakers do sense the long-term implications of their policies. However, without a simple tool to communicate these long-term impacts, most people naturally focus their attention on short-term outcomes.

INTERDEPENDENT PARAMETERS

So far, we have assumed the parameters in the production processes—fixed cost, duration of the project, discount rate, uncertainty, and quantity of output—to be independent variables. In reality, these parameters often have complex and varying relations. It takes detailed knowledge and deep insight about each system to model these relations well. In the following, we will present some simple attempts to model such relations.

All parameters in our theory, except uncertainty, correspond to directly observable quantities. This is very similar to option pricing theory, in which all parameters, except volatility, correspond to directly observable quantities. In option pricing theory, volatility is often called *implied volatility* because volatility is implied from the option prices. Similarly in our theory, uncertainty is implied from the expected variable cost. Indeed, the value of uncertainty can involve many factors. The meaning of the *rate of uncertainty* can be very different in different applications.

ECONOMIES OF SCALE AND THE
LAW OF DIMINISHING RETURNS

All economic systems experience economies of scale and the law of diminishing returns at the same time. This can be modeled by setting uncertainty, σ, as an increasing function of the volume of output. Specifically, we can assume

$$\sigma = \sigma_0 + lQ,$$

where σ_0 is the base level of uncertainty, Q is the volume of output, and $l > 0$ is a coefficient. Intuitively, when the size of a company

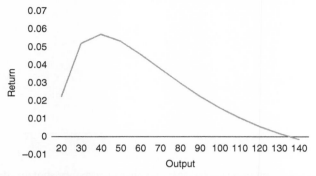

FIGURE 7.9 Volume of output and the rate of return: The rate of return of a project with respect to volume of output, when uncertainty is an increasing function of volume of output.

increases and the business expands, internal coordination and external marketing become more complex. With this new assumption, we can calculate the rate of return of production from formula (13). The result is presented in figure 7.9. The figure shows that the rate of return initially increases with production scale, which is well known as the economy of scale (Romer 1986). When the size of the output increases further, the rate of return begins to decline. This is the law of diminishing returns.

INCREASING FIXED COST
TO REDUCE UNCERTAINTY

When the fixed cost of a system increases, the increased fixed cost can often help reduce uncertainty. Many organisms, from stegosaurus to turtles, invest in armor to decrease predation. Air conditioning and heating systems can reduce the uncertainty of temperature in a building. But air conditioning requires an increase in electricity consumption. Insurance can reduce uncertainty of large losses for the policyholders. Yet insurance premiums must be paid. This pattern can be modeled with uncertainty, σ, as a decreasing function of the fixed cost. Specifically, we can assume

$$\sigma = \sigma_0 + e^{-lK},$$

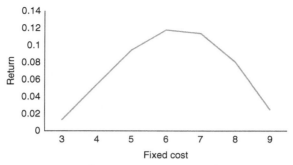

FIGURE 7.10 Increasing fixed cost to reduce uncertainty, showing the relation between level of fixed-cost investment and rate of return.

where σ_0 is the base level of uncertainty, K is the fixed cost, and $l >$ 0 is a coefficient. Assume the unit product value is 1, discount rate is 5 percent per annum, and duration of the project is 10 years. Assume σ_0 is 20 percent per annum and l is 0.2. The calculated rate of return with different levels of fixed cost is shown in figure 7.10. When the level of fixed cost is increased, the rate of return increases initially and then declines.

Many decisions involve the spending of fixed cost to reduce uncertainty; this is true of unemployment insurance, old-age insurance, medical insurance, and government guarantees to financial institutions. People often take polar positions in debating these issues. A good quantitative model may help us reach compromise among various parties.

RESOURCE ABUNDANCE AND INVESTMENT DECISIONS

One way to represent the relationship between resource abundance and resource quality is by the level of uncertainty. In physics, the term representing uncertainty in a lognormal process is often called the *diffusion rate* or the *dissipation rate*. A higher dissipation rate means that more energy is wasted as heat and less energy is available to do useful work, indicating low quality of energy fuels. For example, when a dry cell gets discharged, its internal resistance gradually increases, and more energy turns into unusable heat. The quality of the dry cell declines over time. So the quality of resources can be represented by the (inverse of) uncertainty or (the inverse of) the dissipation rate.

We next model the increase of processing costs for natural resources through the increase of the diffusion rate, to understand how these costs affect the structure and size of economic systems. From equation (10), when the diffusion rate is higher, the variable cost becomes higher. Intuitively, higher diffusion rates mean more effort is needed to process a given volume of resources. Specifically, the level of diffusion will be modeled as

$$\sigma = \sigma_0 + lQ.$$

The base level of diffusion is σ_0, which corresponds to the lowest cost in production when a resource of highest quality is used. The total output of economy is Q, and $l > 0$ is a coefficient. The value of l represents the abundance of low-cost resources; when a low-cost resource is abundant, l is small. In that case, an increase of output will not increase processing costs substantially. When low-cost resources are scarce, l is large. An increase of output will require high-cost resources, which increases the processing cost.

For simplicity, we set $S = 1$, $r = 0.1$, $T = 15$, and $\sigma_0 = 0.4$. We let l take the values of 0.0025, 0.005, and 0.01 to represent different levels of resource abundance. By maximizing formula (13) with respect to the fixed cost and volume of output at different values of l, we obtain the highest possible rate of return from investment projects in different environments. When $l = 0.0025$, projects obtain the highest possible rate of return of 28 percent when the fixed cost is 9.5 and market size is 56. When $l = 0.005$, projects obtain the highest possible rate of return of 15 percent when fixed cost is 4.5 and market size is 33. When $l = 0.01$, projects obtain the highest possible rate of return of 6 percent when fixed cost is 1.7 and market size is 20. Figure 7.11 displays the rates of return with respect to different sizes of output by three different projects with different fixed costs, corresponding to different levels of resource abundance.

As the figure shows, when resources are abundant and cheap, there is an economic incentive to increase fixed cost and market size. As a result, the rate of resource consumption is high. When the low-cost resources are gradually depleted, the return from the same high-fixed-cost system will decline gradually. To understand the precise relation

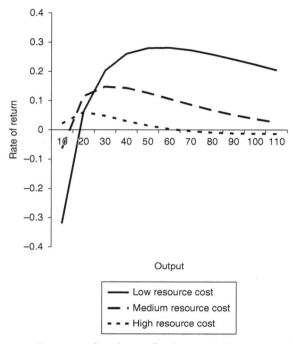

FIGURE 7.11 Resource abundance, fixed cost, market size, and rates of return: The rates of return with respect to different output scales for three different projects with different fixed costs corresponding to different levels of resource abundance.

between resource abundance, economic structure, and rate of return, we calculate the rates of return for the same high-fixed-cost system, which provides the highest possible rate of return, at $l = 0.0025$, when $l = 0.005$ and 0.01. Figure 7.12 displays the rates of return with respect to different output scales by the same high-fixed-cost production system, at different levels of resource abundance. Compared with figure 7.9, when the cost of resource production is moderately higher, represented by $l = 0.005$, the difference of return between the existing high-fixed-cost production system and the potential optimal production system is not large. Furthermore, developing new projects with different levels of fixed cost may require new skills and equipment. Therefore, the incentive to change is small. But when low-cost resources are further depleted, represented by $l = 0.01$, rates of returns of the high-fixed-cost production system turn negative at all levels of output, as shown in

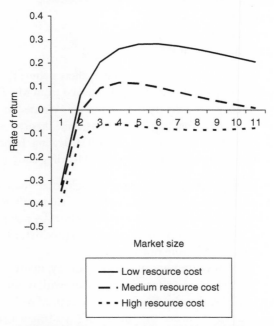

FIGURE 7.12 Resource abundance and rates of return: The rates of return with respect to different output scales for the same high-fixed-cost production system corresponding to different levels of resource abundance.

figure 7.12. Reduction of fixed cost and output size are then required to restore economic activities to positive returns.

ON THE UNIVERSALITY OF THE
THERMODYNAMIC EQUATION

Because of the similarity between our production theory and Black-Scholes option theory, some suggest that the production theory develops out of the universality of the mathematics, having little to do with biophysical and evolutionary principles. Indeed, the pioneers of the option theory had anticipated new theories with very broad scope. Fischer Black once said:

> I like the beauty and symmetry in Mr. Treynor's equilibrium models so much that I started designing them myself. I worked on models in several areas:

Monetary theory
Business cycles
Options and warrants

For 20 years, I have been struggling to show people the beauty in these models to pass on knowledge I received from Mr. Treynor. In monetary theory—the theory of how money is related to economic activity—I am still struggling. In business cycle theory—the theory of fluctuation in the economy—I am still struggling. In options and warrants, though, people see the beauty. (Mehrling 2005, 93)

The above statement shows that Black thought that financial instruments and real economic activities can be modeled with very similar methods. However, despite the tremendous effort by many researchers, including Fischer Black himself, no general production theory has been developed directly from options theory.

Soon after the development of options theory, many researchers applied the theory to project investments. This work is often grouped under the name of *real option theory*. The concept of real options has become an important part of the theory of investment decisions. It has been included in many corporate finance textbooks. The methodologies involved in the works of the real option theory are diverse and often very complicated. Is it possible to develop a simple theory of project investment that is general enough to capture the relation among major factors in economic activities?

Investment under Uncertainty by Avinash Dixit and Robert Pindyck is the standard reference book on the real option theory. In a footnote, they made an intriguing observation about Feynman's path integral method:

In quantum electrodynamics the result proves to have immense practical utility. In fact, it underlies Feynman's (1949) diagrammatic technique for summing probabilities over all possible paths of a particle. His approach, developed before dynamic programming and Ito's Lemma had been thought of, was an amazing achievement. Since the dependent variable—the probability amplitude—in quantum electrodynamics is complex valued, the analogy with dynamic programing and contingent claims valuation may not extend beyond the mathematical formalism. If it does, then in addition to all his achievements in physics, Feynman could be claimed as the father of financial economics. (Dixit and Pindyck 1994, 123)

The Feynman path integral, as an integral, is a general averaging method. It is not restricted to complex-valued functions. As an averaging method, the Feynman path integral naturally applies to economic activities. By applying the Feynman-Kac formula, an extension of Feynman's method, we obtain a differential equation that is central to our production theory. We were able to do that because we regard Feynman's method not merely as a mathematical formalism but as a description of physical reality. It is also out of physical considerations that we seek a new equation other than the Black-Scholes equation, which is a reverse thermodynamic equation.

In Dixit and Pindyck, several partial differential equations related to production theory were obtained. Then the authors sought solutions under equilibrium, in which changes along time dimension become zero. Therefore, partial differential equations become ordinary differential equations. The solutions of these ordinary differential equations don't provide much insight about project investment and economic production. However, if we keep an evolutionary perspective, we will not attempt to seek solutions under equilibrium. This is why we could find an analytical formula connecting major factors in economic activities.

The equation in our production theory is a thermodynamic equation. A thermodynamic equation is first order in time dimension. Hence a thermodynamic system is naturally evolving. The physical world, as a thermodynamic system, is naturally evolving. The physical world includes living systems, which include human societies. Human societies, as part of the physical and biological systems, are naturally evolving. When we state that our production theory is biophysical and evolutionary, we merely acknowledge the obvious fact that human societies are part of the physical and biological world. Such a statement seems odd only because the standard economic theory is an equilibrium theory, a theory that is not consistent with physical and biological laws.

Overall, the differential equation in our theory is indeed very universal. But why is this equation universal? More generally, there can be billions of equations. But only very few of them, such as Maxwell's equations, have universal applications. Why? This is because the Maxwell equations and a few other equations accurately describe a broad range of physical activities. In our case, our equation is universal because it accurately describes a broad range of biophysical activities. A biophysical and evolutionary perspective is essential for us to develop this production theory.

CONCLUDING REMARKS

Many pioneering works have applied physical and evolutionary ideas to economic theory. These works generally use ordinary differential equations to describe economic activities (Chen 1987). Because biophysical and economic activities are thermodynamic processes, we expect thermodynamic equations, which are partial differential equations, to describe economic activities more accurately than conventional expressions commonly used in economics.

In this chapter, we have presented an analytical theory of production by solving a thermodynamic equation. The generality of this theory is a consequence of the generality of physical laws, which apply equally to physical, biological, and economic systems. This allows us to develop a unified production theory that can be applied to many different fields. Historically, some economic principles in physics, such as the principle of least action and maximum entropy principle (Jaynes 1957), have been very fruitful in providing unified foundations to very diverse areas of investigation. The production theory presented in this work provides a unified understanding for a wide range of problems in economics and biology. It can be (and has been) applied to project investment, corporate finance, trade and migration, resource and social structures, language and cultures, evolutionary and institutional economics, fiscal and monetary policies, business cycles, firm size and competitions, software development economics, and other problems (Chen and Galbraith 2011, 2012a, 2012b; Chen 2012, 2015; Liu, Kong, and Chen 2015). However, much more work needs to be done to provide a more accurate and detailed understanding of the implications of our theory for economic and social behavior.

Life in a World without Equilibrium

In this closing chapter, we reprise some of the major themes of this book, to reflect a bit on the implications for our human future. Energy, climate, and demography are the major themes.

The standard economic theory states that natural resources are only one factor in economic activities, that they can be easily substituted by other factors, and that output can be augmented by increases in technology. The depletion of natural resources is of little concern for neoclassical economists for this reason. This was the essence of the mainstream response to *The Limits to Growth* back in 1972 (Meadows 1972). And that is also why mainstream economists find it acceptable to model production as a matter of constant returns to scale, with ever-increasing use of resources yielding ever-increasing output. In the real world, this does not happen except over a very limited range of scales. In the real world, returns may increase or decrease with scale, and usually both factors are working at the same time.

To understand better the relation between resources and technology, we may examine regions where the resource base is very narrow. In such regions, the impact of resource depletion can be assessed more clearly. Sunlight is the most universal resource to the world. Many other resources, such as fresh water and fertile land, are derived from abundant sunlight. Consider, then, the case of population changes in a mining town in the deep North, where solar energy, the most important and universal natural resource, is scarce. Suppose in one mining town, there are 10,000 residents, of which 20 percent are miners or mining-related service providers. The remaining 80 percent are policemen, teachers, doctors, pastors, bakers, grocery-store cashiers, and other service providers. Can we conclude from this census that only

2,000 people in the town depend on the mining activities? No. Suppose that after some years, the mine is exhausted. Can new technologies provide additional job opportunities or at least support the nonmining population? A historical example will offer a hint. In its heyday of gold rush, Barkerville, in northern British Columbia, Canada, had more than 5,000 residents. It was once the largest town in the west of North America. Its population dwindled to zero when the gold mines were exhausted. This is not an isolated example. In almost all mining towns in the deep North, once mines are exhausted, the towns become ghost towns. Any region requires resources to support its residents.

When the resource base is narrow, it is easy to recognize that natural resources are the ultimate source of all economic activities and that technology is a means for using resources. But often there are many different natural resources in the same place. People will move on to other natural resources after the depletion of one natural resource. For example, with the depletion of gold mines in California, people moved on to agriculture and other activities that require different kinds of resources, such as fertile soil, fresh water, sunlight, and petroleum. Some cities, such as New York, may not have a large resource base themselves. But these cities provide services to large areas, regionally and even globally. It is the resources they can control that determines the level of consumption that is possible. It is not unfitting that New York refers to itself as the "Empire State"; without empire, there would not be much in New York.

With increasing volatility of commodity prices, the importance of natural resources becomes more visible to most people. However, for most people the total cost of gasoline and other commodities is still quite small in relation to their incomes. Measured in terms of gross domestic product, output from resource industries is still only a small part of overall economic activity, even for major commodity producers, such as Canada. This gives the impression that natural resources constitute only a small part of overall economic activity. But this is only a matter of definition. The transportation industry, for instance, is not defined as a resource industry. However, the manufacture and operation of vehicles, ships, and planes are totally dependent on the availability of energy resources.

To better understand the extent of our dependence on natural resources, we will view our use of natural resources through the lens of thermodynamic theory.

RESOURCES AND ENERGY

Most of the natural resources on the Earth can be attributed to the temperature differential between the Sun and the Earth. The surface temperature of the Sun is 6000 K, and the surface temperature of the Earth is around 300 K. The high-temperature solar surface emits sunlight, which carries high-quality energy. The Earth receives high-quality solar energy and emits low-quality waste as infrared light energy. This temperature differential is what drives most things, including living organisms, on the Earth. Intuitively, this temperature differential is like the differential in water levels at a hydro dam, which drives turbines to produce electricity.

Part of the solar energy is captured by plants through photosynthesis and converted into chemical energy, which can be stored for a longer time than photons. The chemical energy stored in plants can be released to work for plants when and where it is needed to maintain various life activities, including photosynthesis. Animals, by eating plants, obtain some of the chemical energy stored in plants. Almost all the energy sources in the food web on the Earth ultimately come from solar energy.

Fresh water is so common that we often take it for granted. In many places, its economic value is very low. However, fresh water is vital for our survival. Fresh water is also very scarce compared with salty water. It comprises only 2.5 percent of all water. The rest, 97.5 percent, is salt water. Salt water has a lower free-energy level than fresh water. Hence salt water is stable and in chemical equilibrium, whereas fresh water is unstable and in a nonequilibrium state. The nonequilibrium state is maintained by solar energy. Solar energy distills salt water into vapor and returns fresh water to the Earth, and especially to higher-elevation areas, in the form of rain or snow. Since fresh water has higher free energy, the intake of fresh water instead of salt water saves living organisms a lot of energy. That is why areas with abundant fresh water have higher levels of biomass density than areas with little fresh water, such as deserts and oceans, where water is salty. Most cities are located by rivers or lakes, where fresh water is abundant. Fresh water is another gift from the Sun.

Water will flow from high to low places due to gravity. Without solar energy enabling water vapor to escape the pull of gravity, all water would remain at low elevations. Clouds would not form, and rain would not fall. The whole Earth would be a desert. Rivers would not flow. Rivers are vital to human life. Most early civilizations originated by the riverside—the Tigris, Euphrates, Nile, Ganges, and Yangtze are among the examples. Rivers formed the major channels of transportation before the age of cheap fossil fuels. With rivers comes hydropower, which generates great amounts of electricity for human society.

Today, most energy needs of human society are provided by fossil fuels. We often call our civilization the *fossil fuel civilization*. Coal, oil, and most of the natural gas are from ancient biological deposits. These biological deposits, which were formed over millions of years, were transformed for use by human societies over the past several hundred years. The abundant use of fossil fuels is the foundation of economic prosperity for many people the world over.

More detailed and systematic discussion about natural resources can be found from the standard references, such as Hall, Cleveland, and Kaufmann (1986) and Ricklefs (2001). Although the forms of natural resources are diverse, most natural resources can be categorized into two classes. The first class includes low-entropy sources, more popularly understood as energy sources. The second class includes raw materials that can be used as building blocks to harness energy sources for our use. The second class includes most metals. Many resources belong to both classes. Wood can be used as cooking fuel or building material. Petroleum can be processed into vehicle fuels or vehicle parts. Proteins, fats, and carbohydrates can be used as energy sources or as building blocks for organisms.

CARBON AND HYDROGEN AS ENERGY SOURCES

Carbon and hydrogen are the main components of living organisms. They are also the main component of the energy sources in organisms and in fossil fuels. Most energy sources we encounter, from foods we eat to gasoline we use to power our cars, are mainly combinations of carbon and hydrogen atoms. Hydrogen is lighter and has much higher energy density than carbon. Hence hydrogen has a lower cost of transportation than carbon. At the same time, hydrogen energy is more costly to produce. For animals, because of their mobile lifestyle, the cost of transportation is high. So animals store a lot of energy as fat, which has a high hydrogen content. Plants, because of their sedentary lifestyle, find it more economical to use carbon energy directly. They contain little fat in their bodies, except in seeds, which have high energy demand and need to be more mobile than the plants themselves. This pattern applies to human society as well. Automobiles and airplanes, as transportation tools, are highly mobile. Their energy comes from petroleum products such as gasoline, jet fuel, and diesel, which have high hydrogen content and are relatively light. Electricity generators are not mobile, except on vehicles such as trains and ships. The main energy input in electricity generation is coal, which is mainly carbon, heavy but cheap. The transportation of electric energy moves electrons, which are much lighter than atoms. So transporting electricity is also cheap. This is one reason electricity, a direct product largely of carbon, is universally used in most daily activities.

Among main energy resources, natural gas has the highest hydrogen content. That is why natural gas is preferred over coal as the energy source in homes for cooking and heating. The past century can be thought of as the transformation from a carbon economy represented by coal to a hydrocarbon economy represented by oil and natural gas. Therefore, people moved toward a hydrogen economy long before official mandates from governments. This is also why natural gas and oil, which have much higher hydrogen content than coal, deplete much faster than coal. With the fast depletion of high-quality (high hydrogen content) fossil fuel sources, can we create a man-made hydrogen economy?

Compared with coal, oil and natural gas burn more completely and emit fewer pollutants. In general, an energy source that reacts with the environment more easily will leave less harmful residue. At the same time, since clean energy reacts easily in the natural environment, it will be more difficult to preserve. For this reason, coal is much more abundant than oil and natural gas. In the end, after the depletion of oil and gas, we will have to rely on coal as our main energy supply. The twenty-first century, or perhaps the twenty-second, will become more a carbon economy instead of the hydrogen economy envisioned in some literature. We see this happening already in Europe, which is trying to abandon oil and natural gas from Russia for political reasons—and being forced, in part, to return to coal, from which for environmental reasons it was just recently trying to escape.

When the supply of high-hydrogen-content energy sources, such as oil and gas, is depleted, a man-made hydrogen energy can be produced from three possible sources. One is nuclear power. Another is renewable energy, such as solar, wind, and biomass. The third option is low-quality energy sources, such as coal. The thermodynamic law tells us that to produce a certain amount of high-quality energy will require more low-quality energy. Hence a hydrogen economy, derived from coal, will produce more, not less, pollution on the global level. The consequence of a hydrogen economy can be seen from the electricity economy we already have. Electricity is a very clean form of energy at end use. Its cleanliness enables average households to utilize a huge amount of energy without feeling its negative impact. But electrical power plants are the largest consumer of coal and other energy sources and the largest concentrated producers of greenhouse gases.

A parallel understanding can be made from the separation of residential and industrial areas. The separation makes residential areas cleaner but adds extra pollution from transportation, because people now need to commute between residential areas and work areas. The longer the distance between residential and industrial or commercial areas, the cleaner the residential areas are. But the total pollution will be higher because the extra pollution caused by transportation will be higher. At the global level, trade allows heavily polluting industries to be moved to poor countries, where the general population has little political power. Although the rich countries enjoy a cleaner environment, total pollution on the Earth will increase because of the added transportation and communication costs. The concept of *ecological footprint*, which represents the consumption level of each country, provides a better measurement of the burden of human society on the environment (Wackernagel and Rees 1995). On a global basis, our ecological footprint exceeds biocapacity, a situation that cannot be maintained indefinitely.

The prevailing wisdom on energy consumption is that hydrogen-based energy should be promoted and carbon-based energy should be suppressed. However, hydrogen-based energy sources are scarce and have already been depleted at a fast pace because of their high quality. A further restriction on carbon as an energy source will accelerate the depletion of high-quality energy sources and leave future generations in worse shape. In a more sensible strategy, different energy sources should be utilized in different ways according to the differing physical and chemical properties of hydrogen and carbon. Natural gas, with the highest hydrogen content among carbohydrate fuels, is the cleanest. It can be used as fuel in densely populated residential areas. Gasoline, being a liquid and high-energy-density fuel because of its high hydrogen content, can be primarily used as transportation fuel, where energy supply must be carried on vehicles. Coal, being largely carbon, is heavy, abundant, and hence cheap. It can be economically used to generate electricity. Utility companies are large companies that can afford to make high-fixed-cost investments. Since power plants use large amounts of fuel, they are in the best position to use expensive equipment to reduce the pollution from coal burning. Before the large price increase of oil during the oil crisis in the 1970s, many power plants used oil as fuel. But since that time, most power plants use coal as fuel (Dargay and Gately 2010).

STORAGE VERSUS EASE OF USE

Almost all the energy sources on the Earth ultimately come from the Sun. However, not all living organisms use solar energy directly. Several factors determine the pattern of energy use. The first important factor is energy density. Solar energy is vast. But the net return from transforming light energy into chemical energy, which organisms can store and transport easily for their further use, is low. Plants, whose sedentary lifestyle requires only a low level of energy consumption, can effectively utilize solar energy directly through photosynthesis. Most animals, whose mobile lifestyle requires high levels of energy input, could not support themselves through photosynthesis internally. Instead, some animals consume plants, which store high-density chemical energy transformed from solar energy. Other animals eat plant-eating animals. Fossil fuels, which are a further concentration of biomass in large scale, provide much higher energy density than biomass. The consumption of high-energy-density fossil fuels is the foundation of economic prosperity enjoyed by human societies in the past several hundred years. This is the first factor in energy economics.

The second factor of energy economics is the relation between ease of storage and ease of use. Electricity, which is very easy to use, is very difficult to store. The energy of biomass and fossil fuels is stored in the form of chemical energy, which is less easy to use compared with electricity but is easier to store. Nuclear energy, which requires very expensive systems to harness, can be preserved for billions of years. This fundamental trade-off is determined by the potential well of an energy source. The deeper the potential well, the easier to store the energy and the harder to use it. For this reason, attempts to reduce the storage costs of some easy-to-use energy sources, such as electricity, are elusive. On the other hand, it is often difficult for easy-to-store energy, such as fat, to be used easily. That is why it is so difficult for people to lose fat in their bodies. It is also difficult to achieve high energy density for easy-to-use energy sources, which react easily due to a low potential well. Electricity is easier to use than gasoline. But the energy density in a battery, a form of chemical energy, is generally low. For example, the energy density of a lead battery is $0.16 * 10^6$ J/kg and the energy density of gasoline is $44 * 10^6$ J/kg (Edgerton 1982, 74). Great progress has been made to increase the energy density of batteries by utilizing smaller atoms, such as lithium. Currently, the highest energy density for a battery is about 10^6 J/kg. This is still much lower than the energy density of gasoline. Therefore, electric cars must have very large batteries, and even so, they have relatively less range than gasoline-powered cars. The potential for further increase of energy density of batteries is limited by the physical properties of electrical energy.

Because the energy density of batteries is low, battery weights must be high to provide enough energy for cars. This makes electric vehicles much heavier than internal combustion engine vehicles. For this reason, electric vehicles will cause much more damage to others in accidents.

Because the activation energy of a battery is low, batteries also may explode easily from a strong impact, such as in a car crash. When (or if) the energy intensity of batteries is further increased, the likelihood and force of explosions may increase as well.

Because of the physical properties of batteries, development progress for electric cars has been slow, although batteries have a much longer history as a power source than internal combustion engines.

The third factor of energy economics is the efficiency of energy use and the total consumption of energy. Many people have advocated the

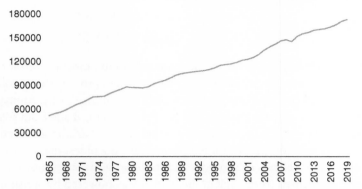

FIGURE 8.1 Global energy consumption (million-ton oil equivalent) from 1965 to 2019. Source: *Our World in Data.*

increase of efficiency to reduce energy consumption. To put it another way, the improvement of technology is to achieve lower variable cost at the expense of higher fixed cost. But since it takes a larger output for higher-fixed-cost systems to break even, to earn a positive return for higher-fixed-cost systems, the total use of energy must be higher than before. That is, technology advances in energy efficiency will increase total energy consumption. Jevons's statement, quoted in the previous chapter, has stood the test of time. Indeed, the total consumption of energy has kept growing, almost uninterrupted, decade after decade, in the past several centuries, along with the continuous efficiency gain of the energy conversion (Inhaber 1997; Hall 2004).

Figure 8.1 displays the total primary energy consumption worldwide from 1965 to 2019, a period of rapid technological progress. During this period, energy consumption grew steadily, with only two brief interruptions. From 1979 to 1982, the period of the Iranian Revolution, oil prices jumped from US$13.60 per barrel in 1978 to US$35.69 in 1980, causing a serious recession in the industrial world. The drop of energy consumption from 1979 to 1982 was due to the sharp jump in oil prices and the ensuing contraction of economic activities, not to technological progress. Another brief interruption occurred in 2009. In 2008, the oil price rose sharply, reaching US$147 per barrel at its peak, just as the Great Financial Crisis broke over the "advanced" world. The ensuing Great Recession diminished energy consumption. But the decline of energy consumption only lasted for one year.

RENEWABLE RESOURCES AND
THE RETURN ON RESOURCES

As we have said many times, the most important, most universal resource is sunlight. All plants use photosynthesis to transform solar energy into chemical energy, which plants can utilize easily. Animals eat plants or other animals to survive. Fresh water is made from solar energy. Oxygen is a byproduct of photosynthesis. No animal will survive without oxygen. In addition to sunshine, the oldest fuel, modern civilization is largely driven by coal, petroleum, and natural gas, which are transformed from ancient life, which was powered by sunshine. Without sunshine, the Earth would be a very cold, lifeless ice ball.

We survive and grow on sunshine and other resources. But it takes resources to obtain and process resources. Plants need to make chlorophyll to collect solar energy. Solar cells must be produced before they can transform solar energy into electricity. For a resource to be truly a resource, the cost of the resource must be lower than its economic value. Coal, petroleum, and natural gas became the main energy sources for modern life because the energy required to extract these resources is much lower than the energy obtained—most of the time. However, high-quality resources are generally extracted first; as time goes on, the quality of ores declines and the cost of finding oil and gas tends to increase. The depletion of high-quality oil and gas, along with the pollution associated with coal, raises a question about the long-term viability of fossil fuels, the most important resources in modern life. Governments worldwide therefore adopt policies to subsidize research and production of renewable energy.

To understand the effectiveness of these policies, we need to clarify the concept of *renewable energy*. Solar energy is renewable—from the standpoint of life on Earth. Almost all life forms depend on solar energy directly or indirectly and have for billions of years. The use of renewable energy is not a new adventure. Instead, it has been practiced for billions of years by all life forms.

Almost all the energy sources produced ultimately by the Sun are renewable to some degree. Fossil fuels are generally considered to be nonrenewable because of the time, heat, and pressure needed to transform dead organisms into fossil fuels. They are produced every day in various geological structures. However, the rate of production of fossil fuels is much lower than the rate of consumption in today's world. A resource is renewable when its consumption rate is lower than or equal to its regeneration rate. Otherwise, it is not renewable. Hence the concept of renewability is intrinsically linked to the level of consumption. For example, many supposedly renewable resources, such as fisheries, collapsed when consumption rates became higher than regeneration rates. Only when the harvesting of fish was reduced by regulation did fisheries become renewable again.

It takes resources to produce resources. Likewise, it takes energy to produce energy that can be used by human beings. Like any other viable investment, investment in energy and other resources should yield a positive rate of return or it will not be viable. Only when energy return is higher than the energy invested does that energy source provide net energy for the society.

We usually measure the performance of an investment by monetary return. This measurement often provides a good indicator of performance. The underlying assumptions are that the market, which gives us the relevant prices, is efficient and that using it is costless. In standard economic theory, financial return in a free market provides the optimal measurement of return. However, markets are not free. If they are not free, they cannot be "efficient," even under the terms of the standard theory—and we must therefore modify our notions of performance.

Since monetary returns—especially in societies with large elements of monopoly power—do not always provide an accurate measure of return on investment in resources, we can seek help from a measurement of physical returns. The energy return on energy investment is an example of a physical rate of return. Technically, the ratio is called *Energy Return over Energy Invested* or *Energy Return on Investment* (EROI). When and only when EROI is higher than one, or equivalently, only when the return on energy investment is positive, an energy source provides net energy to society. However, such measurements are not immune from the intervention of powerful groups, as huge sums of money are associated with such measurements.

The concept of EROI is simple enough and universal enough. But the measurement of EROI has always been a great challenge. Estimates of energy return on investment of many renewable energy resources have been produced by experts in different areas over different times. These estimates can vary. The production of energy, such as through photovoltaic technology, directly and indirectly involves complex steps that no one knows completely. Inevitably, many steps are missed in accounting for the cost of production. Calculated EROIs are often much higher than real ones.

Two prominent forms of renewable energy production are corn-based ethanol production and photovoltaic technology. Corn-based ethanol production is an important part of the renewable energy industry. Pimentel and Patzek (2005) reviewed past research on the production of ethanol from corn and found the following results.

1. The total energy input to produce a liter of ethanol is higher than the energy value of a liter of ethanol. Thus, there is a net energy loss in ethanol production from corn. Therefore, ethanol is not a renewable energy source.
2. Producing ethanol from corn causes major air and water pollution and degrades the environment. Therefore, there are unrecorded social costs associated with ethanol production.
3. There are more than three billion people in the world who are malnourished. Expanding ethanol production, which diverts corn needed to feed people, raises serious distributional and ethical issues.

Despite these facts, government subsidies for bioenergy have been expanding rapidly over time. Why is that? There could be several reasons.

1. Because of government subsidies, companies participating in bioenergy production have been very profitable. (The monetary rate of return to private investment is high.) Hence they will lobby hard for this type of subsidy. And agricultural interests are overrepresented in land-based legislatures, such as the US Senate. Hence there is a distribution of power that favors ethanol producers over both consumers and those who pay the price in pollution and malnutrition.
2. The term *renewable resources* provides a psychological satisfaction for the general public. People can continue a lifestyle that requires high levels of resource consumption while still feeling morally superior, because they have invested in renewable resources, which are supposedly beneficial to future generations.
3. Government officials are eager to be seen as doing "something" for the environment. Spending on environmental projects conveys a positive image and satisfies an activist constituency, which may be backed by

industries engaged in "green" energy. As in other areas, government actions are channeled into policies with maximum political support and minimum political resistance. Such policies often benefit the current generation at the expense of future generations, who are not here to vote and lobby. Voices from those generations might point out the cynicism involved—but they are not yet around to be heard.

Because of the practically infinite amount of solar energy, great efforts have been devoted to the deployment of photovoltaic technology for many years. In the standard literature, the EROI is significantly higher than one. However, Ferroni and Hopkirk provide a detailed calculation on the performance of photovoltaic technology in regions of moderate insolation, such as Germany. They conclude,

> The calculated value for [EROI] is ... 0.82 ... significantly below 1. The methodology recommended by the expert working group of the IEA appears to yield EROI levels which lie between 5 and 6 ... but which are really not meaningful for determining the efficiency, sustainability and affordability of an energy source. The main conclusions to be drawn are:
>
> 1. The result of rigorously calculating the "extended [EROI]" for regions of moderate insolation levels as experienced in Switzerland and Germany proves to be very revealing. It indicates that, at least at today's state of development, the PV technology cannot offer an energy source but a net energy loss.
> 2. Our advanced societies can only continue to develop if a surplus of energy is available, but it has become clear that photovoltaic energy at least will not help in any way to replace the fossil fuel ... since it involves an extremely high expenditure of material, human and capital resources.
> 3. Research and development should, however, be continued in order in future to have more efficient conversion from sunlight to electricity and a cheaper, more reliable PV-technology offering increased efficiency and a longer, failure-free lifetime. The market will then develop naturally. (Ferroni and Hopkirk 2016, 343)

These results have been heavily criticized by a large group of authorities (Raugei et al. 2017). We will not go over the technical details from the literature. Instead, we discuss the practical implications of different estimates of efficiency of photovoltaic technology.

Any investment with highly positive return will spread rapidly if raw materials are not constrained. In photovoltaic technology, sunlight, the major input, is almost infinite. If the energy returns of photovoltaic technology are highly positive, as stated in the standard literature, photovoltaic projects will spread, with or without government subsidies. However, we observe that photovoltaic projects spread rapidly only in places with government subsidy. This suggests that the energy return on photovoltaic technology, if positive, must be very low.

The amount of solar energy received by the Earth is almost infinite compared with our current energy consumption. If photovoltaic technology provides a significant positive return, it will expand rapidly to satisfy our energy demand. There will be no more problem of energy shortage in the world. However, this is not what has happened. Germany has been one of the most aggressive promoters of photovoltaic technology for many years. Yet at the time of writing in the fall of 2023, Germany is still very vulnerable to the disruption of the supply of natural gas. And while Germany has reduced its coal consumption over 30 years, it still produces more than 40 percent of its electricity from coal.

The current biosphere is the result of more than three billion years of evolution. The most-discussed forms of renewable energy, such as solar, wind, and bioenergy, have been around for many millions of years and have been extensively explored by many species, including human beings. It is difficult to rule out the possibility that human beings can develop new technologies that have significantly higher overall efficiency in energy use than other living organisms and our own ancestors. But if research and development costs are included, the likelihood will be low. Human beings, like other dominant species, excel at extracting resources, not at using resources more efficiently (Colinvaux 1980). Furthermore, research activities are very resource intensive and accelerate the depletion of natural resources. Hence government policies about future energy-investment patterns should not rest on the assumption that technological progress will automatically substitute the demand for natural resources, as mainstream economic theory asserts (Samuelson and Nordhaus 1998, 328).

CLIMATE, DEMOGRAPHY, AND THE
FUTURE OF CIVILIZATION

The end product of all forms of activity is waste—waste heat and chemicals, including especially carbon dioxide. In the past century, the increasing concentration of carbon dioxide in the atmosphere has been linked to increased global temperatures. This is the climate crisis of which many scientists have warned, which the world's governments are now struggling to contain. How do these matters look from our perspective of thermodynamic law and entropy economics?

The study of past data and our long-term experience show that the increase of carbon dioxide in the atmosphere is highly beneficial to living organisms in general—and to human civilizations. However, changes do not benefit everyone. Global warming will not benefit everyone. To be a bit glib, it may well be much better for plants and microbes than for humans. That is because carbon dioxide is a waste product for industrial civilizations, but it is a raw material, or resource, for other forms of life.

The end of the most recent ice age about ten thousand years ago was a global warming. It generated great floods in many places. The Bible recorded the story of Noah, a story of global warming and a great flood. Noah (if he existed) lived in a time of global warming. Warming generates a huge melting of ice. Warming generates huge amounts of rain. Warming generates floods. At the time of Noah, floods did devour some low-lying areas. (Among other things, the melting of the ice sheet covering much of North America carved out the St. Lawrence River.) But the warming ended the ice age. The warming energized the globe and greatly increased the carrying capacity of Earth. After Noah, the Earth greened, and human civilizations flourished.

We can expect some of this process to be repeated as the Earth warms some more. Evaporation and rain should increase. More fresh water, along with more carbon dioxide, should feed the plant life of the planet. More plants should mean better soil, and more food from the natural processes of biological reproduction and growth. What then is the problem? The problem is that this will take a very long time. And meanwhile, the present world has been built on other lines. We have made fixed investments that changing circumstances will render unprofitable on a massive scale.

It is obvious that *the current structure* of human civilization is not well adapted to the coming world. It is not just that we are accustomed to certain temperature ranges in certain places. Among other things, we have built our population on our food supply. We have built our food supply on fossil fuels, which are becoming scarce and expensive, and the benefits of climate change for agriculture—if they arrive—will arrive slowly and will not fully replace the low-entropy sources on which we now depend. Climate change, together with resource depletion, portends a food crisis.

In 1930, the human population of the entire world was just two billion. Today it is around eight billion and rising toward ten billion. This vast increase in carrying capacity, at unprecedented levels of prosperity in many countries, is due to the use of high-quality resources: oil, gas, and nuclear energy in addition to coal (which dates from the eighteenth century), as well as minerals and other components of chemical fertilizers. The warm, wet Earth to come will be a greener place. But it will not be green enough, or biologically rich enough, to support the food we presently need for the population we currently have.

Quite likely, as high-quality fossil fuel resources are depleted, the industrial basis of food production will decline long before the richer foundations of new plant life are present. The competition for food is existential for human populations. If the food supply falters, the world's population will fall, in a general biological depression.

And not only that. It is also that we have built major cities by the seaside. We have a vast fixed investment in global trade at existing ports. We have calculated the effect of floods and storms and sea-level rise, as well as riverine floods, and the melting of glaciers in the Himalaya and elsewhere, on our constructions. We've assumed supplies of fresh water for our farms and cities. We've built our health systems to treat chronic rather than infectious diseases. And we've calculated wrongly. These are among the problems that climate change poses for humans.

Can climate change be stopped? Like everyone else, we would like to think so. But so far, the evidence as we see it suggests otherwise. We have not slowed the use of fossil fuels or the increase in CO_2 emissions. Even the massive investments underway in renewable energy sources—in harvesting sunlight directly—are both intensive in their own use of fossil fuels and serve as an addition to, not a replacement for, the consumption of fossil fuels in their present ordinary uses. This is just as Jevons predicted, a century and a half ago. For this reason, we are not optimistic.

As the climate warms, sea-level rise could be as much as 10 m. That much could take centuries, if it ever happens. But with just a few meters of rise, along with other changes such as shifts in ocean currents in the Atlantic, quite a bit of what we have built will be destroyed, and much more will become unprofitable to operate. London, New York, and Shanghai are among the most threatened, and wealthiest, places. Further, the rising cost of fossil fuels will destroy the profitability of many existing industries, especially in transportation, on which trade and commerce depend. Uncertainty and fear will discourage further fixed investments. Existing supply chains will break down, and integrated global industries will shrink or collapse. Mitigation and adaptation to climate change will take second place to the requirements of survival, if there are not enough resources for both.

In short, we have a gigantic backlog of fixed investments, which are likely to become increasingly hard to maintain and unprofitable to operate. Retreat and rebuilding will occur, but these cost resources, require planning and organization, and are unlikely to be carried out at the same standard as in the past. Indeed, our civilization, the fossil fuel civilization, is in difficulty and will get into more difficulty as the costs of extracting and transporting fossil fuels rise and as the existing infrastructure ages. This difficulty is not caused by the increase in carbon dioxide in the atmosphere. But it will make dealing with climate change more challenging.

There is yet another grave difficulty ahead. This is the biological depression that is already underway. In every high-income country, and most of the developing world as well, fertility rates have fallen below replacement levels. This process has been going on for at least fifty years. In extreme cases, such as Japan, China, and some countries in Europe, population will likely decline quite rapidly as the present century unfolds. In others, notably the United States, immigration will mitigate the loss of fertility—but only for a time.

The decline in individual fertility rates means that overall human population growth will slow, stop, and eventually start falling. Why is that? Human reproduction rates are a personal decision. And in overwhelming numbers, those making the decisions are opting to have fewer children. The most likely explanation, in our view, is economic.

In wealthy countries, children are expensive—in economic terms they are a fixed cost—and they reduce the income and wealth opportunities available to young adults. A rising cost of resources, on top of this, simply means that the free resources available to families decline, and with them the margin of maneuver that makes having children attractive. Austerity and precarity compound these problems.

The billions of micro decisions that underlie population growth have macro consequences. With fewer children, human populations age. The burden of caring for the elderly increases. Investments tend to go to meet that challenge, rather than toward easing the cost of having children. As women age, birth cohorts decline, so the number of potential parents further limits the number of potential children. A decline in population begets a further decline. There is little basis for optimism that this process can or will be reversed, even when populations are much smaller, in a few centuries, than they are today.

Human society has become complex, rigid, and fragile. Whether *present* human society can withstand even relatively small changes in the operating conditions laid down by previous human societies under the earlier conditions is an open question. You may recall how the change from coal to oil helped precipitate the Great Depression. The phenomenon we may be facing is similar, but on a much larger and more serious scale, over a longer time, and without an early off-ramp toward renewed prosperity. Although life will continue to prosper on planet Earth, existing civilizations and especially some of their wealthier elements will tend to crumble away.

It seems likely that, in the distant future, most humans will live in tropical and subtropical conditions, with far fewer amenities and comforts than we enjoy today. And with the intervening decline of fertility and populations, fewer humans will inhabit this warmed-up Earth. They will, very probably, look back on our civilizations with curiosity and, perhaps, regret.

CONCLUDING REMARKS

Our society is not supported by the stock market. Our society is supported by food, electricity, and fuels. Our society is supported by grocery stores, cashiers and stockers, farmers, truck drivers, and factory workers. This becomes plain and simple during a crisis. We need more people, more young people with strong immune systems, more young people who can work effectively under stress. To achieve a younger population, we can't keep our eyes glued to the financial indicators or to such measures as gross domestic product, conceived in another age for an entirely different purpose. We should pay attention to birth rates, to public health, to the cost and quality of education, and to other vital biophysical indicators. This is the first step we need to take. We may not succeed in any event, but this is what we should do. It will be the next generations, not the present ones, that will have to cope with the world to come.

Because of the importance of energy in our lives, people have pursued the dream of convenient and cheap renewable energy since time immemorial. In the course of history, many people have believed they discovered an inexhaustible source of energy or invented one or another kind of perpetual motion machine. They think their discoveries or inventions can be put to practical use in large scale once necessary technical improvements can be made. However, more rigorous investigation led to the development of thermodynamic theory, which rules out the possibility of a perpetual, or renewable, energy source without external input.

In this chapter, we investigated further how the physical environment enables and constrains living organisms and economic systems by integrating the economy of human society into the economy of nature. We explored the relation between natural resources and technology in human society. This helps us envision the future of human society in an environment of increasingly scarce and costly natural resources.

The main results can be summarized as follows. First, the survival and prosperity of human society depends entirely on the availability of natural resources. Second, although the forms of natural resources are diverse, they can be understood from the unifying principle as low-entropy sources. Third, to utilize natural resources, fixed structures are required, which consume resources themselves. Fourth, when certain structures can generate positive returns on the use of natural resources over an indefinite period, these structures are called living organisms. Fifth, it is the unique chemical properties of carbon that enables it to become the backbone of life. The major nonrenewable energy resources that our industrial civilization builds on, such as coal, oil, and natural gas, are generated from the remains of the living organisms. They all contain carbon. Sixth, our industrial civilization is bringing on a combination of increased high-quality resource costs, a warming climate, rising sea level, and declining human fertility.

A warmer climate will, very likely, green the Earth. But the other factors will make much of our current civilization obsolete and much of our economic activity unprofitable. So the future of human society is likely, for a long time, to devolve back to smaller populations, shorter life spans, higher variable costs, and lower fixed costs, along with smaller countries and harsher inequalities both within and between them. Social arrangements, advance planning, new energy sources, and new investments can mitigate the suffering from this transition, up to a point. But this, very likely so far as we understand it, is the biophysical reality with which future economists, engineers, and planners will have to engage.

Acknowledgments

This project is the fruit of a collaboration between a mathematician-turned-economist and a policy economist with limited scientific training. We have worked together for many years, and the ideas in this book have been expressed, in various forms, in the *Journal of Economic Issues*, the *Cambridge Journal of Economics*, *Structural Change and Economic Dynamics*, the *Review of Evolutionary Political Economy*, and in several prior books by Jing Chen and one by James Galbraith. We thank the editors of those periodicals, anonymous referees, and our publishers for their help.

We would like to thank Chad Zimmerman of the University of Chicago Press for his support of this project and Wendy Strothman for her ever-efficient work as our agent. Jayashree Vijalapuram assisted with editing. Alexandra Proskurina and John Bailey read the manuscript and provided useful comments and corrections. James Galbraith would like to thank the physicists he has known at the University of Texas at Austin, especially Michael Marder, Ping Chen, and the late Steven Weinberg and Roy Schwitters. Discussions over the years with Yanis Varoufakis, Gael Giraud, Philip Mirowski, and the late Barkley Rosser Jr. have been helpful. We acknowledge the leadership of other economists who have championed an evolutionary and biophysical perspective. We especially thank two referees for careful reading and detailed advice.

James Galbraith would like to acknowledge the influence of his father, John Kenneth Galbraith; of his teachers, especially Nicholas Kaldor, Wassily Leontief, Luigi Pasinetti, Sidney Winter, and Adrian Wood; and the cordial friendship of leading mainstream economists of the previous generation, especially Kenneth Arrow, Paul Samuelson, and Robert Solow.

James Galbraith expresses his deep thanks and love to Ying Tang.

Jing Chen is very grateful for the kind help from his family, friends, colleagues, and students.

Errors are, as always, our own.

Notes

Preface

1. These phenomena were analyzed in Galbraith (1952), Galbraith (1998), and Ahmari (2023).

Chapter One

1. An example from the real world appears in a report by the law firm Paul, Weiss, Rifkind, Wharton, and Garrison on the investment losses of Credit Suisse, a large Swiss bank, in late 2022: "The Archegos-related losses sustained by [Credit Suisse] are the result of a fundamental failure of management and controls. . . . The business was focused on *maximizing short-term profits* and failed to rein in and, indeed, enabled Archegos's voracious risk-taking. . . . a lackadaisical attitude towards risk and risk discipline; a lack of accountability for risk failures; risk systems that identified acute risks, which were systematically ignored by business and risk personnel; and a cultural unwillingness to engage in challenging discussions or to escalate matters posing grave economic and reputational risk" (quoted in Martens and Martens 2022, emphasis added).

2. Some neoclassical economists, including Frank Hahn at Cambridge (Saith 2022), Sir John Hicks at Oxford, and to a degree even Paul Samuelson at MIT, came to acknowledge the defects in their own doctrines at the end of their careers—when indeed they could enjoy a measure of reconciliation with critics who they had long, more or less privately, acknowledged. Late in his life, Milton Friedman also admitted that his long-standing call for strict rules to govern the growth of the money supply had been ill-advised, and in the aftermath of the 2008 financial crisis, Alan Greenspan confessed to a "flaw" in his prior understanding of the efficiency of free markets. Greenspan, however, quickly reverted to his libertarian ideology, suggesting that his confession was merely in response to the pressures of a congressional hearing.

Chapter Two

1. However, even supposedly simple theories such as the laws of motion and gravity have regulatory features in the real world. For an obvious example, consider the solar system. It is a "system" in which the motion of the planets is regulated by the mass, and therefore gravitational force, of the Sun. Einstein's theory of relativity makes this very clear: massive objects warp the space-time continuum to ensure that the principle of least action generates motion along curving pathways. In economics, the assumption of "perfect competition" does a nice job of obscuring this very basic reality.

2. The title of Black's 2005 book, *The Best Way to Rob a Bank Is to Own One*, tells it all.

Chapter Three

1. For example, this endnote can be transmitted as a picture file (e.g., JPG), a PDF, a Microsoft Word file, or a text file.

Chapter Four

1. Scarcity on the diagram increases from right to left.
2. The proof of the general case is available from the authors.

Chapter Five

1. It also assumes an adequate definition of *capital*—another thorny issue.

Chapter Seven

1. Some do not agree with this statement and provide examples of low-fixed-cost investment with high profits, such as J. K. Rowling writing Harry Potter books. However, although a small percentage of authors earn high incomes from blockbusters, an average author does not earn a high income, and our results are about the statistical average.

References

Acs, Z., and D. Audretsch. 1990. *Innovation and Small Firms*. Cambridge, MA: MIT Press.

Ahmari, S. 2023. *Tyranny, Inc.: How Private Power Crushed American Liberty and What to Do about It*. New York: Penguin Random House.

Ainslie, G. 1992. *Picoeconomics: The Interaction of Successive Motivational States within the Person*. Cambridge: Cambridge University Press.

Ainslie, G., and R. Herrnstein. 1981. "Preference Reversal and Delayed Reinforcement." *Animal Learning and Behavior* 9:476–482.

Aliakbari, E., and A. Stedman. 2018. "The Cost of Pipeline Constraints in Canada." Fraser Research Bulletin, *Fraser Institute*, Vancouver, BC, May. https://www.fraserinstitute.org/sites/default/files/cost-of-pipeline -constraints-in-canada.pdf.

Applebaum, D. 1996. *Probability and Information: An Integrated Approach*. Cambridge: Cambridge University Press.

Arrow, K. J. 1972. "General Economic Equilibrium: Purpose, Analytic Techniques, Collective Choice." Nobel Memorial Lecture, Harvard University, Cambridge, MA, December 12.

Arrow, K. J. 1973. *Information and Economic Behavior*. Cambridge, MA: Harvard University Press.

Arrow, K. J. 1999. "Information and the Organization of Industry." In *Markets, Information, and Uncertainty*, edited by G. Chichilnisky. Cambridge: Cambridge University Press.

Arrow, K. J., and G. Debreu. 1954. "Existence of an Equilibrium for a Competitive Economy." *Econometrica: Journal of the Econometric Society* 22 (3): 265–290.

Atkins, P. W. 1995. *The Periodic Kingdom: A Journey Into The Land Of The Chemical Elements*. New York: Basic Books.

Ayres, R. 2016. *Complexity and Wealth Maximization*. Berlin: Springer-Verlag.

Baran, P., and P. Sweezy. 1966. *Monopoly Capital*. New York: Monthly Review Press.

Bernoulli, D. 1738 (1954). "Exposition of a New Theory on the Measurement of Risk." *Econometrica* 22 (1): 23–36.

Bessen, J., and E. Maskin. 2009. "Sequential Innovation, Patents, and Imitation." *RAND Journal of Economics* 40 (4): 611–635.

Black, F., and M. Scholes. 1973. "The Pricing of Options and Corporate Liabilities." *Journal of Political Economy* 81:637–659.

Black, W. 2005. *The Best Way to Rob a Bank Is to Own One.* Austin: University of Texas Press.

Black, W. 2009. *Bill Moyers Journal,* April 3. Transcript of video interview. https://www.pbs.org/moyers/journal/04032009/transcript1.html.

Blaug, M. 1980. *Economic Theory in Retrospect.* New York: Cambridge University Press.

Bonner, B., and A. Wiggin. 2006. *Empire of Debt: The Rise of an Epic Financial Crisis.* New York: John Wiley & Sons.

Campbell, C. J., and Laherrère, J. H. 1998. "The End of Cheap Oil." *Scientific American* 278 (3): 78–83.

Cannon, W. B. 1932. *The Wisdom of the Body.* New York: W. W. Norton.

Chadha, P. 2016. "What Caused the Failure of Lehman Brothers? Could It Have Been Prevented? How? Recommendations for Going Forward." *International Journal of Accounting Research* S1:002. https://doi.org/10.4172/2472-114X.S1-002.

Chen, J. 2003. "Derivative Securities: What They Tell Us?" *Quantitative Finance* 3 (5): C92–C96.

Chen, J. 2005. *The Physical Foundation of Economics: An Analytical Thermodynamic Theory.* Hackensack, NJ: World Scientific Publishing.

Chen, J. 2012. "The Nature of Discounting." *Structural Change and Economic Dynamics* 23:313–324.

Chen, J. 2015. *The Unity of Science and Economics: A New Foundation of Economic Theory.* New York: Springer.

Chen, J. 2018. "An Entropy Theory of Value." *Structural Change and Economic Dynamics* 47:73–81.

Chen, J., and J. Galbraith. 2011. "Institutional Structures and Policies in an Environment of Increasingly Scarce and Expensive Resources: A Fixed Cost Perspective." *Journal of Economic Issues* 45 (2): 301–308.

Chen, J., and J. Galbraith. 2012a. "Austerity and Fraud under Different Structures of Technology and Resource Abundance." *Cambridge Journal of Economics* 36 (1): 335–343.

Chen, J., and J. Galbraith. 2012b. "A Common Framework for Evolutionary and Institutional Economics." *Journal of Economic Issues* 46 (2): 419–428.

Chen, P. 1987. "Origin of the Division of Labour and a Stochastic Mechanism of Differentiation." *European Journal of Operational Research* 30 (3): 246–250.

Clark, W. 2008. *In Defense of Self: How the Immune System Really Works.* Oxford: Oxford University Press.

Cochran, G., and H. Harpending. 2008. *The 10,000 Year Explosion: How Civilization Accelerated Human Evolution.* New York: Basic Books.

Colinvaux, P. 1978. *Why Big Fierce Animals Are Rare: An Ecologist's Perspective.* Princeton, NJ: Princeton University Press.

Colinvaux, P. A. 1980. *The Fates of Nations.* New York: Simon and Schuster.

Cope, E. 1896. *The Primary Factors of Organic Evolution.* Chicago: Open Court Publishing.

Curran, E., and C. Anstey. 2021. "Pandemic-Era Central Banking Is Creating Bubbles Everywhere." *Bloomberg,* January 24. https://www.bloomberg.com/news/features/2021-01-24/central-banks-are-creating-bubbles-everywhere-in-the-pandemic.

Dargay, J. M., and Gately, D. 2010. "World Oil Demand's Shift toward Faster Growing and Less Price-Responsive Products and Regions." *Energy Policy* 38 (10): 6261–6277.

Debreu, G. 1959. *Theory of Value: An Axiomatic Analysis of Economic Equilibrium.* New York: John Wiley & Sons.

Debreu, G. 1983. "Economic Theory in the Mathematical Mode: Nobel Memorial Lecture." *Economic Science* 8:87–102.

Debreu, G. 1991. "The Mathematization of Economic Theory." *American Economic Review* 81:1–7.

Deffeyes, K. S., 2001. *Hubbert's Peak: The Impending World Oil Shortage.* Princeton, NJ: Princeton University Press.

Desan, C. 2015. *Making Money: Coin, Currency and the Coming of Capitalism.* New York: Oxford University Press.

Dixit, A., and R. Pindyck. 1994. *Investment under Uncertainty.* Princeton, NJ: Princeton University Press.

Düppe, T. 2012. "Gerard Debreu's Secrecy: His Life in Order and Silence." *History of Political Economy* 44 (3): 413–449.

Edgerton, R. 1982. "Available Energy and Environmental Economics." Lexington, MA: Lexington Books.

Farmer, J. D., and Geanakoplos, J. 2009. "The Virtues and Vices of Equilibrium and the Future of Financial Economics." *Complexity* 14 (3): 11–38.

Ferroni, F., and R. J. Hopkirk. 2016. "Energy Return on Energy Invested (ERoEI) for Photovoltaic Solar Systems in Regions of Moderate Insolation." *Energy Policy* 94:336–344.

Feynman, R. 1948. "Space-Time Approach to Non-Relativistic Quantum Mechanics." *Review of Modern Physics* 20:367–387.

Forbes. 2022. *"The World's Real-Time Billionaires."* Continuously updated webpage. https://www.forbes.com/real-time-billionaires/#7d3336cf3d78. Accessed December 22, 2022.

Frederick, S., G. Loewenstein, and T. O'Donoghue. 2004. "Time Discounting and Time Preference: A Critical Review." In *Advances in Behavioral Economics,* edited by C. Camerer, G. Lowenstein, and M. Rabin. Princeton, NJ: Princeton University Press.

Friedman, M. 1953. *Essays in Positive Economics.* Chicago: University of Chicago Press.

Galbraith, J. 1998. *Created Unequal: The Crisis in American Pay*. New York: Free Press.

Galbraith, J. 2008. *The Predator State: How Conservatives Abandoned the Free Market and Why Liberals Should Too*. New York: Free Press.

Galbraith, J. 2014. *The End of Normal: The Great Crisis and the Future of Growth*. New York: Simon & Schuster.

Galbraith, J. 2016. *Inequality: What Everyone Needs to Know*. New York: Oxford University Press.

Galbraith, J. K. 1952. *American Capitalism: The Concept of Countervailing Power*. Boston: Houghton Mifflin.

Galbraith, J. K. 1958. *The Affluent Society*. Boston: Houghton Mifflin.

Galbraith, J. K. 1967, *The New Industrial State*. Boston: Houghton Mifflin.

Gechert, S., T. Havranek, Z. Irsova, and D. Kolcunova. 2021. "Measuring Capital-Labor Substitution: The Importance of Method Choices and Publication Bias." *Review of Economic Dynamics* 45 (July): 55–82.

Georgescu-Roegen, N. 1971. *The Entropy Law and the Economic Process*. Cambridge, MA: Harvard University Press.

Gisolfi, C., and F. Mora. 2000. *The Hot Brain: Survival, Temperature, and the Human Body*. Cambridge, MA: MIT Press.

Gordon, R. 2016. *The Rise and Fall of American Growth: The US Standard of Living since the Civil War*. Princeton, NJ: Princeton University Press.

Hall, C. 2004. "The Myth of Sustainable Development: Personal Reflection on Energy, Its Relation to Neoclassical Economics, and Stanley Jevons." *Journal of Energy Resource Technology* 126 (2): 85–89.

Hall, C. A., and K. A. Klitgaard. 2011. *Energy and the Wealth of Nations*. New York: Springer.

Hall, C. A. S., C. J. Cleveland, and R. Kaufmann. 1986. *Energy and Resource Quality: The Ecology of the Economic Process*. New York: John Wiley & Sons.

Hirsch, A. 2018. "If You Talk about Russian Propaganda, Remember: Britain Has Myths Too." *The Guardian*, March 21.

Inhaber, H. 1997. *Why Energy Conservation Fails*. Westport, CT: Quorum Books.

Jablonka, E., and M. J. Lamb. 2006. *Evolution in Four Dimensions: Genetic, Epigenetic, Behavioral, and Symbolic Variation in the History of Life*. Cambridge, MA: MIT Press.

Janszen, E. 2008. "The Next Bubble: Priming the Markets for Tomorrow's Big Crash." *Harper's Magazine*, February, 39–45.

Jaynes, E. T. 1957. "Information Theory and Statistical Mechanics." *Physical Review* 106:620–630.

Jenkins, R. 2001. *Churchill*. London: Macmillan.

Jevons, W. S. (1865) 1965. *The Coal Question: An Inquiry Concerning the Progress of the Nation, and the Probable Exhaustion of Our Coal-Mines*. London: Macmillan.

Jevons, W. S. 1871. *The Theory of Political Economy*. London: Macmillan.

Kac, M. 1951. "On Some Connections between Probability Theory and Differential and Integral Equations." In *Proceedings of the Second Berkeley Symposium on*

Mathematical Statistics and Probability, edited by J. Neyman, 189–215. Berkeley: University of California Press.

Kaldor, N. 1985. *Economics without Equilibrium*. Abingdon, UK: Routledge.

Kellogg, E. A. 2001. "Evolutionary History of the Grasses." *Plant Physiology* 125:1198–1205.

Kennedy, R. F. 1968. "Remarks at the University of Kansas." March 18. https://www .jfklibrary.org/learn/about-jfk/the-kennedy-family/robert-f-kennedy/robert-f -kennedy-speeches/remarks-at-the-university-of-kansas-march-18-1968.

Keynes, J. M. 1936. *The General Theory of Money, Interest and Employment*. London: Macmillan.

Kimmel, R. 2011. *The Second Law of Economics: Energy, Entropy and the Origins of Wealth*. The Frontiers Collection. New York: Springer.

Klug, W. S., and M. R. Cummings. 2003. *Concepts of Genetics*. 7th ed. London: Pearson Education.

Knight, F. H. 1921. *Risk, Uncertainty and Profit*. Boston: Houghton Mifflin.

Kuhn, T. 1996. *The Structure of Scientific Revolutions*. 3rd ed. Chicago: University of Chicago Press.

Lane, N. 2002. *Oxygen: The Molecule That Made the World*. Oxford: Oxford University Press.

Liu, L., X. Kong, and J. Chen. 2015. "How Project Duration, Upfront Costs and Uncertainty Interact and Impact on Software Development Productivity? A Simulation Approach." *International Journal of Agile Systems and Management* 8 (1): 39–52.

Longo, G. 2018. "Interfaces of Incompleteness." In *Systemics of Incompleteness and Quasi-Systems*, edited by G. Minati, M. R. Abram, and E. Pessa. New York: Springer.

Lorenz, E. N. 1963. "Deterministic Nonperiodic Flow." *Journal of Atmospheric Sciences* 20 (2): 130–141.

Lowenstein, R. 2000. *When Genius Failed: The Rise and Fall of Long-Term Capital Management*. New York: Random House.

Malthus, T. R. 1798 [1986]. "An Essay on the Principle of Population." In vol. 1 of *The Works of Thomas Robert Malthus*, edited by E. A. Wrigley and David Souden. London: Pickering & Chatto Publishers.

Mandelbrot, B. 1999. "A Multi-Fractal Walk down Wall Street." *Scientific American* 280 (2): 70–73.

Martens, P., and R. Martens. 2022. "Credit Default Swaps Blow Out on Credit Suisse as Its Stock Price Hits an All-Time Low of $2.82." Wall Street on Parade, December 1. https://wallstreetonparade.com/2022/12/credit-default-swaps -blow-out-on-credit-suisse-as-its-stock-price-hits-an-all-time-low-of-2-82/.

Marx, K. 1867 [2024]. *Das Kapital*. Translated by P. Reitter. Princeton, NJ: Princeton University Press.

Maxwell, J. 1871. *Theory of Heat*. London: Longmans, Green.

Meadows, D. H., Meadows, D. L., Randers, J., and Behrens, W. W., III. 1972. *The Limits to Growth*. Club of Rome. https://www.clubofrome.org/publication/the-limits-to-growth/.

Mehrling, P. 2005. *Fischer Black and the Revolutionary Idea of Finance*. New York: John Wiley & Sons.

Michels, R. 1915. *Political Parties: A Sociological Study of the Oligarchical Tendencies of Modern Democracy*. New York: Hearst's International Library.

Mill, J. S. 1871. *Principles of Political Economy*. London: Penguin Books.

Minsky, H. 2008. *Stabilizing an Unstable Economy*. New York: McGraw Hill.

Mirowski, P. 1989. *More Heat Than Light: Economics as Social Physics, Physics as Nature's Economics*. Cambridge: Cambridge University Press.

Móczár, J. 2020. "The Arrow-Debreu Model of General Equilibrium and Kornai's Critique in the Light of Neoclassical Economics." *Journal of Banking, Finance, and Sustainable Development* 1 (1): 42–68.

Montesquieu, Baron de. (1748) 1949. *The Spirit of Laws*. Translated by Thomas Nugent. New York: Colonial Press.

Newell, R., and W. Pizer. 2003. "Discounting the Distant Future: How Much Do Uncertain Rates Increase Valuations?" *Journal of Environmental Economics and Management* 46 (1): 52–71.

Nobel Foundation. 2018. "Economic Growth, Technological Change, and Climate Change." Scientific Background on the Sveriges Riksbank Prize in Economic Sciences in Memory of Alfred Nobel, Nobel Foundation, Stockholm, Sweden, October 8. https://www.nobelprize.org/uploads/2018/10/advanced-economicsciencesprize2018.pdf.

Nunez, C. 2022. "Grasslands Explained." *National Geographic*, May 20. https://education.nationalgeographic.org/resource/grasslands-explained.

Odum, H. T. 1971. *Environment, Power and Society*. New York: John Wiley & Sons.

Øksendal, B. 1998. *Stochastic Differential Equations: An Introduction with Applications*. 5th ed. Berlin: Springer.

Ormerod, P. 2005. *Why Most Things Fail: Evolution, Extinction and Economics*. London: Faber and Faber.

Orwell, G. 1937. *The Road to Wigan Pier*. New York: Harmondsworth.

Pasinetti, L. L. 1981. *Structural Change and Economic Growth: A Theoretical Essay on the Dynamics of the Wealth of Nations*. Cambridge: Cambridge University Press.

Perry, C. 2021. "One-Third of U.S. Families Are Net Worth Poor, Study Finds." *Very Well Family*, February 4. https://www.verywellfamily.com/one-third-us-families-net-worth-poor-5097260.

Pimentel, D., and Patzek, T. W. 2005. "Ethanol Production Using Corn, Switchgrass, and Wood; Biodiesel Production Using Soybean and Sunflower." *Natural Resources Research* 14 (1): 65–76.

Pinker, S. 1997. *How the Mind Works*. New York: W. W. Norton.

Rando, O., and K. Verstrepen. 2007. "Timescales of Genetic and Epigenetic Inheritance." *Cell* 128:655–668.

Raugei, M., S. Sgouridis, D. Murphy, V. Fthenakis, R. Frischknecht, C. Breyer, U. Bardi et al. 2017. "Energy Return on Energy Invested (EROEI) for Photovoltaic Solar Systems in Regions of Moderate Insolation: A Comprehensive Response." *Energy Policy* 102:377–384.

Ray, J. 2022. "Declaration of John J. Ray in Support of Chapter 11 Petitions and First Day Pleadings." Case 22-11068-JTD, *United States Bankruptcy Court for the District of Delaware*, November 17. https://pacer-documents.s3.amazonaws.com/33/188450/042020648197.pdf.

Rees, W. 1992. "Ecological Footprints and Appropriated Carrying Capacity: What Urban Economics Leaves Out." *Environment and Urbanisation 4 (2): 121–130.*

Ricklefs, R. 2001. *The Economy of Nature.* 5th ed. New York: W. H. Freeman.

Robbins, L. 1935. *An Essay on the Nature and Significance of Economic Science.* London: Macmillan.

Romer, P. M. 1986. "Increasing Returns and Long-Run Growth." *Journal of Political Economy* 94 (5): 1002–1037.

Rubí, J. M. 2008. "The Long Arm of the Second Law." *Scientific American* 299 (5): 62–67.

Saith, A. 2022. *Cambridge Economics in the Post-Keynesian Era: The Eclipse of Heterodox Traditions.* Cham, Switzerland: Palgrave MacMillan.

Samuelson, P. A. 1970. "Maximum Principles in Analytical Economics." Nobel Memorial Lecture, Massachusetts Institute of Technology, Cambridge, MA, December 11. https://www.nobelprize.org/uploads/2018/06/samuelson-lecture.pdf.

Samuelson, P. A. 1972. *The Collected Scientific Papers.* Vol. 3. Cambridge, MA: MIT Press.

Samuelson, P., and Nordhaus, W. 1998. *Economics.* 16th ed. New York: McGraw Hill.

Scarf, H. 1960. "Some Examples of Global Instability of the Competitive Equilibrium." *International Economic Review* 1 (3): 157–172.

Schmidt-Nielsen, K. 1997. *Animal Physiology.* 5th ed. Cambridge: Cambridge University Press.

Schneider, E. D., and D. Sagan. 2005. *Into the Cool: Energy Flow, Thermodynamics, and Life.* Chicago: University of Chicago Press.

Schrodinger, E. 1944. *What Is Life?* Cambridge: Cambridge University Press.

Schumpeter, J. 1942. *Capitalism, Socialism and Democracy.* Cambridge, MA: Harvard University Press.

Shannon, C. 1948. "A Mathematical Theory of Communication." *Bell System Technical Journal* 27:379–423, 623–656.

Shiozawa, Y. 2016. "The Revival of the Classical Theory of Values." In *The Rejuvenation of Political Economy*, edited by N. Yokokawa, K. Yagi, H. Uemura, and R. Westra, 151–172. New York: Routledge.

Shubik, M. 1961. Review of *Theory of Value: An Axiomatic Analysis of Economic Equilibrium*, by G. Debreu. *Canadian Journal of Economics and Political Science* 27 (1): 133.

Shubin, N. 2008. *Your Inner Fish*. New York: Pantheon Books.

Smil, V. 2003. *Energy at the Crossroads: Global Perspectives and Uncertainties.* Cambridge, MA: MIT Press.

Solow, R. M. 1966. Review of *Capital and Growth*, by J. Hicks. *American Economic Review* 56 (5): 1257–1260.

Sraffa, P. 1960. *Production of Commodities by Means of Commodities*. Abingdon: Routledge.

Stearns, S. 1992. *The Evolution of Life Histories*. Oxford: Oxford University Press.

Stiglitz, J. E. 2002. *Globalization and Its Discontents*. New York: W. W. Norton.

Thaler, R. 1981. "Some Empirical Evidence on Dynamic Inconsistency." *Economics Letters* 8 (3): 201–207.

Treynor, J. 1996. "Remembering Fischer Black." *Journal of Portfolio Management* 23 (December): 92–95.

Trivers, R. 1985. *Social Evolution*. Menlo Park, CA: Benjamin/Cummings.

Vilks, A. 2021. "On an 'Important Principle' of Arrow and Debreu." *B. E. Journal of Theoretical Economics* 22 (2): 621–627. https://doi.org/10.1515/bejte-2021 -0074.

Wackernagel, M., and W. Rees. 1995. *Our Ecological Footprint: Reducing Human Impact on the Earth*. Gabriola Island, CA: New Society Publishers.

Walras, L. 1873. *Elements of Pure Economics*. Translated by William Jaffe. Homewood, IL: Richard D. Irwin.

Weintraub, E. R. 2002. *How Economics Became a Mathematical Science*. Durham, NC: Duke University Press.

Whitfield, J. 2006. *In the Beat of a Heart: Life, Energy, and the Unity of Nature.* Washington, DC: Joseph Henry Press.

Willey, J. M., L. M. Sherwood, and C. J. Woolverton. 2011. *Prescott's Microbiology*. New York: McGraw-Hill Higher Education.

Wrangham, R. 2009. *Catching Fire: How Cooking Made Us Human*. New York: Basic Books.

Wray, L. R. 2006. *Understanding Modern Money*. Cheltenham, UK: Edward Elgar.

Xue, Y., Y. He, and X. Shao. 2012. "Butterfly Effect: The US Real Estate Market Downturn and the Asian Recession." *Finance Research Letters* 9 (2): 92–102. https://doi.org/10.1016/j.frl.2012.02.003.

Index

Page numbers in italics refer to figures and tables.